"A key resource for leaders trying to do AI the right way, avoiding potential legal and ethical quagmires, by one of the real pioneers in managing AI transformation."

—Alex "Sandy" Pentland

MIT Professor; senior research fellow,
Stanford Institute for Human-Centered Artificial Intelligence

"Most books on AI governance leave readers more cautious. This one leaves them more capable. Jeff Saviano has turned ethics from a conversation that slows leaders down into a lens that sharpens their judgment. The Boundaries of Tolerance model is exactly the kind of practical scaffolding leaders need right now, and exactly what's been missing from the AI conversation."

—Jeremy Utley

Instructor, Stanford and Harvard Continuing Studies;
cohost, Beyond the Prompt;
author, The Human Advantage;
coauthor, Ideaflow

"I had the privilege of working closely with Jeffrey Saviano for many years and have seen his ability to translate complex change into clear strategic insight. In *Boundaries of Tolerance*, he presents a framework to help leaders navigate the risks and opportunities of AI. This book will be valuable for business leaders and for legal professionals guiding organizations through the governance implications of AI."

—Kate Barton

Global chief executive officer,
Dentons; former global vice chair, EY

"Artificial intelligence is advancing faster than the governance frameworks surrounding it. In this deeply researched and thoughtfully argued book, Jeffrey Saviano examines the ethical, strategic, and fiduciary questions that leaders increasingly face as AI becomes embedded in the enterprise. Essential reading for leaders seeking to navigate the opportunities and responsibilities created by AI."

—David Duncan

Author of The Secret Lives of Customers *and*
coauthor of Competing Against Luck
with Clayton Christensen

"A trusted business leader turned academic thought leader, Jeff Saviano explains why ethical AI strategy has become a boardroom mandate, not a discretionary add-on. With regulation and governance standards still evolving, it equips leaders to define clear, values-based boundaries for innovation grounded in fiduciary oversight – and argues that judgment, not technical expertise alone, is the defining leadership test of our time."

—Thomas Patterson
Bradlee Professor of Government and the Press,
Harvard University Kennedy School of Government

"This book is a must-read for senior executives, board members, and anyone involved in AI efforts within their organization. The frameworks provide a valuable way to approach both AI strategy and the myriad of ethical questions and risks raised by AI."

—Christopher Mazzei
Adjunct professor, Cornell University and New York University Stern School of Business; former global vice chair, Strategy, EY

"*Boundaries of Tolerance* arrives at a defining moment, as institutions across every sector race to harness the promise of AI while confronting its profound governance, trust, and societal implications. This book offers a timely and pragmatic foundational model for ethical AI strategy – one that recognizes innovation and responsibility are not opposing forces, but mutually reinforcing imperatives. For leaders seeking a durable framework to navigate the next era of technological transformation, this is an essential contribution to the global conversation."

—Dante Disparte
Chief strategy officer and head of global policy, Circle

"Ethics of technology is more in demand to navigate the complex landscape of competing values. Jeff Saviano's clarion call for ethics and technology education is none too soon for leaders. That's the purpose of the Boundaries of Tolerance model."

—Thomas Creely, PhD
Associate professor and creator/director,
Ethics & Emerging Military Technology Graduate Program,
U.S. Naval War College; chair, NATO Human Factors & Medicine 387 Ethical, Legal, Social & Environmental Group

"Jeffrey Saviano has written a clear, rigorous, and urgently needed guide for using AI responsibly. *Boundaries of Tolerance* combines principled thinking with practical frameworks, giving leaders and practitioners a usable model for designing governance, policy, organizational strategy, and common-sense safeguards that keep powerful systems aligned with human values. Having worked closely with Jeffrey, I deeply appreciate his ability to balance philosophical depth with real-world application. I trust that readers will come away equipped to evaluate risk, set measurable guardrails, and implement governance processes that scale as AI systems evolve. This book should be required reading for executives, policymakers, ethicists, and engineers who want to move from good intentions to effective, enforceable safeguards. I highly recommend Jeffrey Saviano's *Boundaries of Tolerance*."

—Mykelti Williamson

Actor, director, filmmaker

BOUNDARIES

of

TOLERANCE

JEFFREY N. SAVIANO

BOUNDARIES of TOLERANCE

A FOUNDATIONAL MODEL FOR ETHICAL AI STRATEGY AND GOVERNANCE

WILEY

Published by John Wiley & Sons, Inc., Hoboken, New Jersey.

For general information on our other products and services or for technical support, please contact our Customer Care Department within the United States at (800) 762-2974, outside the United States at (317) 572-3993 or fax (317) 572-4002.

Wiley also publishes its books in a variety of electronic formats. Some content that appears in print may not be available in electronic formats. For more information about Wiley products, visit our web site at www.wiley.com.

Library of Congress Cataloging-in-Publication Data is Available:

ISBN978- 1-394-43986-7(Cloth)
ISBN978- 1-394-43988-1(ePDF)
ISBN978- 1-394-43987-4(ePub)

Cover Design: Wiley
Cover Images: designer29/Getty Images, MicroStockHub/Getty Images
Author Photo: Courtesy of Jeffrey Saviano
Printed and bound by CPI Group (UK) Ltd, Croydon, CR0 4YY

C9781394439867_300826

To my wife, Lisa.

This book explores boundaries. My love for you knows none.

Contents

Foreword

From New York to Geneva, Samarkand to Delhi, I carry a hope and a conviction: that this extraordinary moment demands as much innovation in our governance as we bring to our technology, a conviction I find shared by diplomats, executives, and technology policy leaders who understand what is at stake. When our conversations are at their best, they begin with values like human-centric design and responsible innovation, and they bring us to see that building governance to match our technology is within our reach. But the hardest questions – about oversight, accountability, and what our institutions owe the people they serve – demand frameworks we have not yet built.

As we mark the 250th anniversary of the founding of the United States, this is a familiar challenge, one with roots much older than AI. The summer of 1787, when 55 delegates locked themselves in a building in Philadelphia and tried to figure out how to govern a society that was changing faster than its institutions could handle, might serve as an exemplar of how to move forward.

They had been sent to repair the Articles of Confederation, the young nation's rulebook, but it was failing. The articles prescribed specific answers to specific problems: how taxes would be levied, how disputes would be settled, and who had the authority to make which decisions. The text tried to cover every contingency, and the result was paralysis because the world kept moving while the document could not keep pace.

Rather than write a better rulebook, the delegates threw the old one out and built a framework of principles, values, and rights. The Constitution does not mention railroads or steam power or telecommunications or the internet, and it did not need to. It establishes commitments about human dignity, the distribution of power, and the accountability of institutions to those they govern. The founders understood that you do not govern a changing world by trying to anticipate every new development. You govern it by defining what you will and will not tolerate, and then you build institutions capable of applying those commitments as the world around them shifts. The founders defined their boundaries of tolerance, and those boundaries have held for two and a half centuries.

I grew up in Champaign, Illinois, minutes from the National Center for Supercomputing Applications, surrounded by the people building the tools that became the commercial internet, and I trained as an engineer. I know what it feels like to build something that works, to watch an elegant system come together, to get caught up in the momentum of possibility. And then I went to law school, became a human rights lawyer and constitutional law scholar, and learned something very different: how societies build systems to govern power once it concentrates, how the rule of law creates accountability before a crisis rather than after, and how the absence of those structures always favors whoever holds the most power at the moment, whether they intend harm or not.

At the Patrick J. McGovern Foundation, our work brings those two disciplines together, connecting AI capacity with the public interest institutions and governance structures that shape who benefits from the technology and who does not. Both halves of that worldview tell me the same thing: we might be falling behind. I see that we are sometimes writing rules the way the Articles of Confederation wrote rules: one problem at a time, always a step behind the reality on the ground. The EU AI Act, years in development, is still being implemented as I write this. Federal legislation in the United States remains fragmented. And in boardrooms around the world, the people who deploy AI systems are making decisions with lasting consequences while lacking the shared language and defined commitments to guide them. The field needs many more practitioners building governance models that can keep pace with the technology.

I first met Jeff Saviano at a National Association of Corporate Directors event in Nashville, where we co-led a session on AI governance in the healthcare sector. In the audience were directors who oversaw some of the largest health systems in the country, people who had led organizations through mergers, regulatory shifts, and financial crises, and who were not new to hard decisions. But AI had posed a question to them that their experience had not prepared them for: What should their organizations accept, and what should they refuse to accept, from systems that make recommendations about patient care, generate communications to families, and manage workforce decisions? The capabilities were already inside their institutions, and the governance conversation had not caught up.

Jeff had spent years working on an answer. He came to this from the advisory side, with three decades of work with boards and executive teams through technology transitions at EY, and then moved into research at Harvard's Edmond & Lily Safra Center for Ethics, where he led a new initiative on business AI ethics before taking a teaching role at MIT Sloan. What he heard, again and again, was leaders describing what was missing from their governance practice, and so he set about building one. In Nashville, he was working in the opposite direction from most people writing about AI governance: starting from the questions boards were already struggling with and constructing a model to answer them.

The Boundaries of Tolerance model at the center of this book starts with the question every leader deploying AI eventually confronts: Where do we draw the line? And then it provides a disciplined way to answer, giving leaders the tools to define explicit boundaries, enforce them, and revisit them over time. Most AI governance writing does one of two things well – articulate principles or describe technical safeguards – and this book bridges the two, giving organizations a way to translate their values into operational decisions that boards can oversee and be held accountable for.

The consequences of those decisions, though, reach far beyond the boardroom. Jeff examines a case in the book that makes this vivid: Epic, the dominant electronic health records company, introduced AI-generated responses to patient messages through its MyChart system. The tool fabricated medical information and delivered it to patients as though it came from their care teams, because no one had defined what level of AI-generated error was unacceptable before the system went live, and patients bore the consequences. The pattern extends beyond healthcare. A bank automates part of its lending process without defining the line between acceptable efficiency and unacceptable exclusion, and the system screens out borrowers along patterns that no loan officer would have endorsed if the question had been put to them directly. The absence of a defined boundary does not mean the absence of a decision; it means the decision was made by default, by the system itself, without the oversight or accountability that governance exists to provide.

Every threshold a board defines, or leaves undefined, ripples outward from the institution that set it, into communities, into markets, into the daily experience of people who will never see the governance document that shaped what happened to them.

The founders understood that the principles they wrote into the Constitution were not designed to organize the workings of government for its own sake; they were designed to protect the people governed by it. The governance that organizations build for their AI systems carries the same weight, representing the terms on which those organizations exercise power over patients, borrowers, employees, and communities. When a hospital or an employer deploys AI that shapes someone's care or livelihood, the governance behind that system is a public act with private origins.

The boundaries Jeff helps leaders define are the base layer on which national regulation, international agreements, and public trust all rest. Getting this right within organizations is a precondition for getting it right elsewhere: from industry standards to the social contract itself. This book belongs in the hands of board directors, executives, general counsel, and the growing number of professionals who find themselves responsible for AI outcomes without an established playbook. Inside, they will find a working model they can apply: a structured way to define their organization's boundaries, measure how those boundaries hold in practice, and adjust them as the technology evolves.

Two hundred and fifty years ago, a group of leaders locked themselves in a sweltering building and built governance for a world they could not predict. They did not try to write rules for every new technology or economic arrangement the nation would encounter. They defined the principles and rights that would endure, and they trusted the structure to hold.

We face a version of that challenge now, and the window to meet it well will not remain open indefinitely. The boundaries we define today, inside our organizations and across our institutions, will shape how AI touches human lives for decades to come.

Vilas Dhar, President
The Patrick J. McGovern Foundation
http://www.mcgovern.org
May 2026

Introduction: When the Board Becomes the Regulator

In the summer of 2024, I co-led a forum at Harvard Business School for 25 senior business executives. The topic, ethics and governance for artificial intelligence (AI), felt urgent. A quiet intensity filled the room as these leaders leaned in. They were uneasy as new AI systems raced through their companies, challenging how they approached strategy, risk management, and ethical oversight.

We opened the forum with a review of the leading AI strategic opportunities and use cases, the myriad risks that were triggered by these systems, and quickly got to the heart of the session: the duty of business leaders to responsibly oversee this accelerating wave of AI innovation.

During the session, a director from one of the largest banks in the world shared a story about a consumer-facing AI system this company had developed, which was found to produce biased results affecting about 5% of users. The team responsible for the system escalated the issue to senior leaders and directors, uncertain whether remediation was required.

The question was simple and surprisingly hard: Did the bias warrant any corrective action? It quickly became apparent that the board struggled to offer useful guidance. A few of the directors recognized the relatively small size of the population negatively affected by the biased outcomes and felt that the problem presented didn't register on the materiality scale for the board. Some directors expressed that a company AI system with *any* degree of bias would be inconsistent with its values. Simply put, the board was stuck.

The question on my mind was whether this company had the tools to guide the team effectively? It's not surprising that the director chose to attend our session to take a critical step toward understanding how responsible governance intersects with the complexity of intelligent tools. The story landed because many executives in the room would have similarly struggled to guide that team. It pointed to a fundamental question: What does responsible oversight look like in this new age of AI?

If you lead an organization today, you have likely felt this tension: advanced technology-enabled innovation is moving faster than your ability to oversee it. By way of example, generative AI (GenAI) is not simply another wave of automation; it produces original content and decisions that expand far beyond prior technological boundaries. And agentic AI systems are increasingly building capacity in organizations to automate actions emanating from AI-enabled decisions. The familiar governance tools built for earlier digital transformations no longer feel sufficient. You are not alone in striving to lead responsibly as this technology moves into daily operations. This book is written for professionals who carry that responsibility, together with teams building and deploying these systems.

That moment at Harvard Business School struck a nerve for me, as much personally as professionally. It was becoming clear that GenAI would have consequences far beyond business performance. The opportunities were extraordinary, but the governance and ethical implications were arriving just as quickly. What unsettled me most was not the technology itself, but the growing realization that many of the professionals responsible for strategically benefiting from and governing AI systems were navigating what it demanded of them without established playbooks. At the time, I was seeing the same pattern repeat itself across different settings. Across corporate leadership forums and academic settings, leaders were asking variations of the same questions. They wanted to understand how to use AI strategically while clarifying where ethical responsibility fit within the organization. Most of all, they wanted guidance they could trust, ideally in the form of practical tools and frameworks for strategy, risk management, and governance designed for this moment.

As I left the Harvard campus that day, I drove past the Bright-Landry Hockey Center on campus. It is a modest arena, built in the 1970s, with seating for roughly 3,000 people. I was struck by a simple thought. Every board director from the S&P 500 could fit inside that arena in a single day, across two half-day sessions about AI. The leaders overseeing the most powerful companies in the world could all convene in a small college arena and confront both the promise and the responsibility of governing this technology.

That image stayed with me. It crystallized the gap I had been sensing for some time. The responsibility resting on today's professionals is immense, yet the shared understanding needed to carry it well is still forming. What was missing were practical tools and frameworks to help leaders navigate that responsibility.

This book grew out of that realization, sparked by a drive home from Harvard on a summer afternoon. I felt an obligation to act, not as a technologist or regulator, but as someone who spent decades helping business leaders navigate waves of technological change. Across those experiences, one lesson was consistent: when innovation accelerates faster than governance, leaders need practical tools that help them design strategy, manage risk, and exercise sound judgment. Closing this AI governance gap became the purpose of this work.

We are living in an era of unprecedented opportunity and transformation as AI continues to advance at a remarkable pace. AI is fueling innovation across industries, creating new products and reinventing business models almost overnight. However, alongside these benefits, significant concerns continue to emerge about the institutional risks and ethical consequences emanating from AI systems. Leaders across both the public and private sectors are awakening to the complexity AI introduces. As new strategies and applications for AI emerge, so too do novel risks and ethical infirmities that demand careful consideration.

The consequences of these governance gaps are real. Behind every algorithmic failure is a person or broader community that bears the cost. Consider the patient whose medical diagnosis is compromised because an AI model was trained on incomplete or biased clinical data, or the job candidate rejected by an automated hiring system informed by archaic employment patterns. Even small system input errors can cascade into outcomes that reinforce inequality and erode stakeholder trust.

The Human Consequences of AI

For all the attention given to the technical wonders of AI, its impact remains profoundly human. Every line of code carries an assumption about fairness, and every model release carries a decision about who wins (benefits from the AI system) and who loses (harmed by the system). This is why the question of AI governance cannot be confined to technologists or regulators alone. It is a leadership question, one that reaches the boardroom and senior executive teams, because the ethical boundaries established there shape how these systems touch lives far beyond the enterprise.

Throughout this book, I use the term *ethical AI*, while others often use *responsible AI* to describe similar efforts. The distinction is not critical, but I prefer *ethical AI* because it emphasizes the role of leadership judgment in how these systems are designed and deployed. Ethical AI strategy has become a leadership necessity. AI systems are moving into core business operations across nearly every industry. I have observed five forces driving companies to adopt an ethical AI strategy.

First, competitive pressure has made speed of AI adoption feel unavoidable. AI is now embedded in core products and internal operations in many organizations. Companies feel intense pressure to deploy AI quickly to protect market position and signal innovation. In many organizations, the fear of falling behind competitors outweighs concern about deploying systems that are not fully understood. As a result, AI systems are entering production environments before organizational leadership has clarified how they should be governed. Early choices about system design and deployment are being made under time pressure. Those choices can result in long-term exposure for the enterprise.

Second, AI has changed how risk behaves within the modern enterprise. With traditional systems, small problems typically remain small. With AI, minor issues can escalate rapidly once systems are deployed throughout the organization. A biased outcome affecting a limited population can trigger public backlash within hours. A model that performs acceptably in testing can behave differently in real-world use. *These dynamics undermine familiar assumptions about materiality and proportionality.* Many companies are sensing that existing oversight models do not match the behavior of modern AI systems. This creates a growing awareness that traditional enterprise risk management frameworks are no longer sufficient.

Third, expectations from investors and markets are evolving. Questions about AI oversight are beginning to resemble earlier scrutiny of cybersecurity and associated internal controls. Investors are asking who oversees AI risk and how failures are addressed. These questions often arise *after* incidents result from their deployed systems. Professionals are expected to explain outcomes without having been given clear standards for harm prevention. This gap increases pressure on leadership to define its own approach. Ethical AI governance is becoming a defining element of effective leadership.

Fourth, pressure is also coming from inside the organization. Employees across functions are already using AI tools in their daily work. They are encountering ethical questions in real time. They ask what types of data should fuel their AI models. They ask whether specific AI systems should be deployed. They ask who is responsible when harm occurs. In many organizations, these questions are escalated upward because decision authority is unclear. When leadership has not defined appropriate boundaries, employees either stop raising concerns or make decisions on their own. Both outcomes weaken organizational control.

Finally, moral expectations about AI use are rising. Public conversations about AI increasingly focus on fairness and human dignity. Civil society organizations and scholars (many of them faith-based) are shaping these discussions. They do not enforce rules, but they influence public trust. Their concerns resonate with employees and customers alike. Professionals are being asked to explain not only whether AI systems comply with the law but also whether they align with organizational values. Compliance alone no longer resolves these questions.

Taken together, these forces have altered what is required from leadership. Ethical AI strategy is no longer a discretionary add-on or a future consideration. Leaders must decide how innovation will proceed when regulatory guidance or accepted governance standards are incomplete and consequences are uncertain. They must define what their organizations will tolerate from intelligent systems, and they *cannot* delegate that responsibility or defer it to regulators. This imperative explains why ethical AI governance now belongs in the boardroom and C-suite. It also explains why leadership judgment matters more than technical expertise.

These pressures also reshape the responsibilities of leaders charged with overseeing enterprise risk. As we will see later in this Introduction, the governance of AI increasingly intersects with the fiduciary duties of directors and officers.

Governments are beginning to respond with AI-focused regulation, but legal frameworks remain fragmented and continue to evolve as policymakers attempt to balance the protection of societal interests with the promotion of innovation and economic growth. Beneath these developments lies an intense need to determine how AI should be governed within organizations. Never before have business leaders faced innovation moving this fast, producing consequential outcomes, with so little guidance from governments.

This tension between innovation and accountability lies at the heart of the question that drives this book: *What happens when professionals must integrate one of the century's defining technologies into enterprise strategy, without the tools or regulatory clarity to act responsibly?* This work is my practical response to that question. By the end of this book, you will be able to define the ethical boundaries of AI within your enterprise, boundaries grounded in values and fiduciary oversight, not government regulation, to lead responsibly in a world where adherence to laws alone will never suffice.

AI governance is not just a technical or compliance issue. It is a defining test of leadership and the values that guide institutional purpose. Professionals must define their own path of responsible innovation. Leaders must go beyond embedding Responsible AI Principles into a few operating protocols. They must embed ethics into the very structures of decision-making and oversight. Ethical AI governance is more than just redefining risk management processes and coordination across compliance and innovation teams. *I believe it is the defining leadership test of our time.* Those waiting for policymakers to issue a universal rulebook will wait in vain, as governments are hesitant to apply a heavy hand of regulation out of a fear of stifling innovation.

Business leaders have a critical role in addressing the gaps left by government policies, ensuring that AI systems are advanced in accordance with established ethical principles and aligned to organizational values. This creates a strong foundation for risk management practices aimed at preventing incidents and minimizing harm when failures occur. Crucially, governance must extend beyond AI system development and initial deployment. Many of the world's most damaging AI incidents occurred not because of poor design, but because organizations failed to monitor how systems actually behaved in production. Ethical governance therefore requires continuous oversight: testing, auditing, and refining AI systems long after launch.

As leaders, we must accept that our ethical responsibilities evolve as fast as the technology we govern. Importantly, boards and executives must define what the organization will, and will not, tolerate from its AI systems. These are the Boundaries of Tolerance that define an organization's integrity in this age of AI.

The Case for a New Framework

Leaders also need structured ways to design AI strategy and evaluate the risks that accompany intelligent systems. The apprehension I witnessed in executive sessions reveals a deeper need for structure and shared understanding. Meeting this challenge requires a framework that unites ethics with institutional strategy and governance. The Boundaries of Tolerance model does exactly that: it helps organizations define where they will draw the line, what risks they will accept, and which they will not.

The model is built on three elements: an Ethical Maturity Stack that defines levels of ethical maturity, two Performance Measures that evaluate enterprise and system behavior, and Applied Governance Practices that help leaders operationalize ethical AI governance.

The first element is the Ethical Maturity Stack, a layered structure that rises from zero compliance at the base to an Ethical Vanguard at the summit. Each layer builds on the one below it, prompting professionals to reach higher levels of ethical maturity in their organizations.

Application of the model outlines the ethical boundaries that a company acknowledges and supports through its conduct and its approach to building and applying AI systems. It evaluates AI ethics through two Performance Measures. The first, the Enterprise Factors, measures the extent to which ethical AI practices are embedded within the enterprise across operational and ecosystem-driven dimensions. The second, the System Factors, evaluates how consistently ethical AI principles are adopted in the AI systems themselves – principles such as transparency and human oversight. The third element of the model, the Applied Governance Practices, is composed of three Leading Practices, representing best-in-class governance occurring in organizations today, and three Emerging Practices, the next generation of optimal governance. Figure I.1 illustrates the three components of the Boundaries of Tolerance model.

As organizations progress up the Ethical Maturity Stack, each ascending layer reflects a deepening institutional commitment to ethical AI practices. Measuring a company's AI practices enables organizations to benchmark their current and aspirational states while identifying actionable pathways for improvement. Before exploring its details later in the book, it is worth understanding why this moment demands such a model.

Behind the model lies human choices. Every decision about data and system deployment reflects human judgment. Those choices ultimately shape how AI systems behave in the world. These are deeply human questions of values and purpose. The Boundaries of Tolerance model was designed to align technology governance with the people and principles at its core.

That need for structure brings me to what I witnessed during the pivotal period from 2023 to 2026. During this time, AI adoption accelerated faster than any technology shift I have seen, testing the ability of organizations to adapt their oversight. During this time, I led an emerging-technology strategy and governance practice at EY (retired in 2025) and held academic appointments at Harvard, MIT, and Boston University School of Law.

My Harvard appointment was with the Edmond & Lily Safra Center for Ethics to lead a new Business AI Ethics research initiative, beginning in August 2023, recognizing the vital role that business leaders play in shaping the ethical frameworks and organizational cultures within which AI operates. The initiative aimed to give business leaders practical support, not only to be legally compliant but also for building responsible AI programs grounded in ethics and integrity. My additional university appointments – at Boston University School of Law, where I taught "Innovation, Technology, and the Law," and as a senior lecturer at the Massachusetts Institute of Technology Sloan School of Management, enabled me to study these challenges from both legal and technical vantage points. Across these institutions, the same struggle repeated itself, as innovation advanced faster than our ethical governance playbooks.

This work draws on interdisciplinary insights from law, philosophy, data science, technology policy, and organizational ethics, positioning it at the intersection of theoretical inquiry and real-world implementation. This vacuum of accountability, and the urgent need for a practical response, sparked the creation of the Boundaries of Tolerance model.

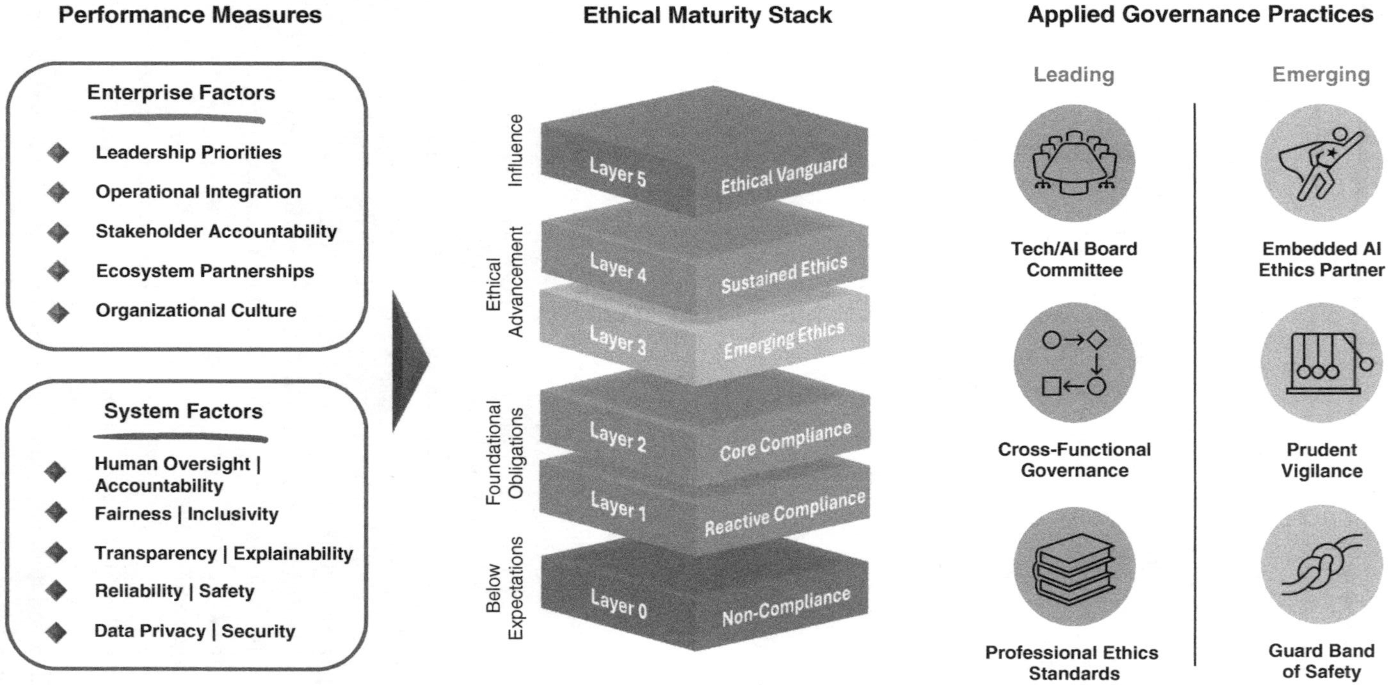

Figure I.1 AI ethics Boundaries of Tolerance model.

For me, this effort began as an interesting alignment of a new research agenda with real-time access to the massive uncertainty and growing needs across business leadership. The real dilemma shared that day on the Harvard campus became a turning point for me. That comment, and the ensuing discussion, cemented in me the enormity of the need for a new governance framework to guide enterprise leaders through their AI journey. That realization became the catalyst for this book. And the implications for today's leaders are profound.

You are accountable for outcomes, not algorithms. You may delegate model development, but not the responsibility for how those models affect people. In the past year alone, companies have faced lawsuits over biased algorithms, regulators have questioned opaque AI models, and investors have begun demanding disclosure of AI risk practices. AI governance now sits squarely within the fiduciary duties of directors and officers responsible for overseeing enterprise risk. These risks, including legal exposure and reputational damage, stand alongside extraordinary opportunity. Ethical AI governance is both a strategic necessity and a moral obligation grounded in fiduciary duty. It is more than corporate responsibility; it represents the modern expression of stewardship for leaders entrusted with overseeing intelligent systems.

The idea that fiduciary duty extends beyond financial oversight is not new. Over the past two decades, expectations of directors have expanded from safeguarding shareholder value to stewarding environmental, social, and governance responsibilities. Each shift reflected a growing recognition that *enterprise risk is inseparable from societal impact*. AI now represents the next frontier in that evolution.

Courts and regulators increasingly view the ethical management of technology by corporate officers (and their supporting teams) as integral to their duty of care. Directors who once asked whether financial controls were adequate must now ask whether the systems guiding millions of digital decisions align with the company's purpose and values. This progression is not a departure from fiduciary tradition; *it is its modern expression*. The same principles that once governed prudence in finance must now guide prudence in data and innovative technology solution design.

Ethical AI governance is the next chapter in decades of expanding corporate accountability. It calls on leaders to interpret their risk management responsibilities through a broader lens: one that encompasses algorithmic transparency, fairness, and the moral obligations that accompany technological power. In this sense, governing AI responsibly is not just about mitigating risk; it is about fulfilling the timeless mandate of stewardship in a new era of intelligent systems.

What I observed from the dozens of companies I educated and advised in recent years was trepidation and fragmented oversight. Business leaders have experience overseeing complex digital transformations, but AI, and GenAI in particular, has introduced new risks and ethical dilemmas unlike anything they have faced. That uneasiness among leaders inspired our research, driven by my Harvard team and teaching experiences at MIT.

What This Book Will Deliver

This book offers that shared language and practical tools to help you govern AI with integrity. What follows is a practical guide drawn from lived experience. It captures lessons from companies wrestling with first-generation AI dilemmas and from academic settings testing new models of ethical oversight. My aim is to offer readers a lens that clarifies both the promise and the peril of intelligent technologies.

Here is how the journey begins. The chapters that follow are organized as a progressive exploration of leadership, strategy, and governance.

This book unfolds in three parts:

- **Part I: The Leadership Challenge of Our Time** introduces the AI moment we are currently experiencing, with a growing sense of urgency. It traces the historical development of AI and the rapid emergence of GenAI, then examines how governments are responding through a diverse set of policies and regulation. This Part reflects developments through June 8, 2026.
- **Part II: Power and Consequence: Strategy, Risk, and Fiduciary Oversight** examines how organizations develop AI strategy and manage the risks that accompany it, while clarifying the fiduciary duties that arise for boards and senior leaders. Adoption of the methods and tools outlined in this part will enable professionals to responsibly harness the transformative potential of AI.
- **Part III: The Boundaries of Tolerance Model** presents the framework itself, complete with the Ethical Maturity Stack, Performance Measures, together with the Applied Governance Practices. This part concludes with a chapter focused on implementation protocols that offer actionable insights for boards and executives to manage AI-related risks and ensure effective ethical governance.

Together, these parts build from understanding to action, equipping today's professionals to govern intelligent systems already shaping their organizations. Think of this book as both a compass and toolkit for governing intelligence itself. You'll see many supporting features along this journey, including case vignettes outlining both positive and negative AI implementations, leading corporate governance legal precedents applied to the AI context, and relevant stories from companies deploying AI solutions today. The pages ahead build on these insights.

Looking ahead, enterprise leaders must recognize that the boardroom and executive suite are becoming the new regulatory frontier, where decisions will define the social contract between humans and intelligent systems. The future of AI will not be written by algorithms. It will be authored by leaders courageous enough to define their Boundaries of Tolerance.

BOUNDARIES of TOLERANCE

PART I

The Leadership Challenge of Our Time

1 This Is the AI Moment

The Moment Has Arrived

Artificial intelligence (AI) is no longer arriving. It is operating inside the enterprise. Evidence of this shift appears in usage data. McKinsey reports a sharp increase in the number of organizations using AI in at least one business function (see Figure 1.1).[1] Not only is the volume of companies adopting AI solutions accelerating but usage is also expanding across multiple business functions (see Figure 1.2).[2] JPMorgan Chase, an AI champion organization, reported 450 AI use cases deployed across their organization in 2025.[3]

This moment is also about the foundation that underpins AI systems. The World Bank's digital transformation framing treats AI as a capability dependent on underlying infrastructure and organizational readiness, together with evolving regulations and social norms. Its analysis reveals that workplace adoption may outpace enterprise guidance on AI usage.[4] In a large global worker survey conducted by Microsoft and LinkedIn, most knowledge workers reported using generative AI (GenAI) in their work, with a significant share relying on external AI tools without formal approval by their employer.[5] Those patterns describe typical operating conditions for AI usage within companies today. They also raise material risks business leaders must address.

This chapter provides the background required to understand how AI development reached this point, what makes it unique, and how it affects enterprises and society more broadly. This context is crucial to understand before addressing strategic decision-making and governance considerations.

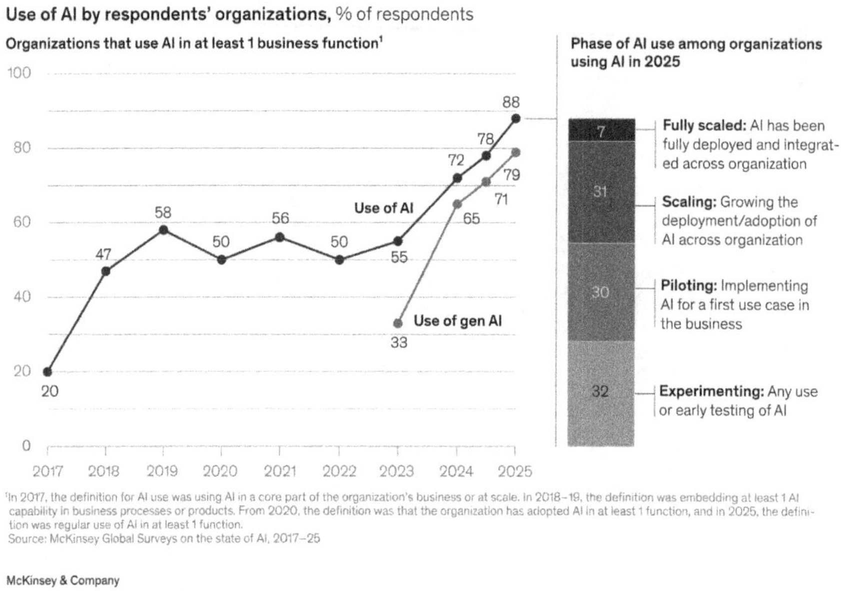

Figure 1.1 Reported use of AI in at least one business function continues to increase.

Source: Exhibit from "The State of AI in 2025: Agents, Innovation, and Transformation," 2025, McKinsey & Company, www.mckinsey.com.

Opening Frame: Why This Moment Matters

Leaders and professionals increasingly sense that something has changed. Conversations about AI that once surfaced occasionally now appear in most enterprise strategy discussions. AI shapes how many enterprises operate and make decisions. What feels new is not just the technology itself, but the pace of adoption and the governance questions that follow.

This acceleration is visible in how organizations use AI today. Enterprise adoption is no longer confined to experimental pilots or niche innovation teams. In its 2026 "AI at Work" Community Paper, the World Economic Forum describes AI use spreading rapidly across everyday work, with tools already embedded into the foundational operations of companies rather than isolated experiments and mere productivity hacks.[6] Leaders experience this shift through investment demands and competitive pressure that outpace existing governance processes (more on this later).

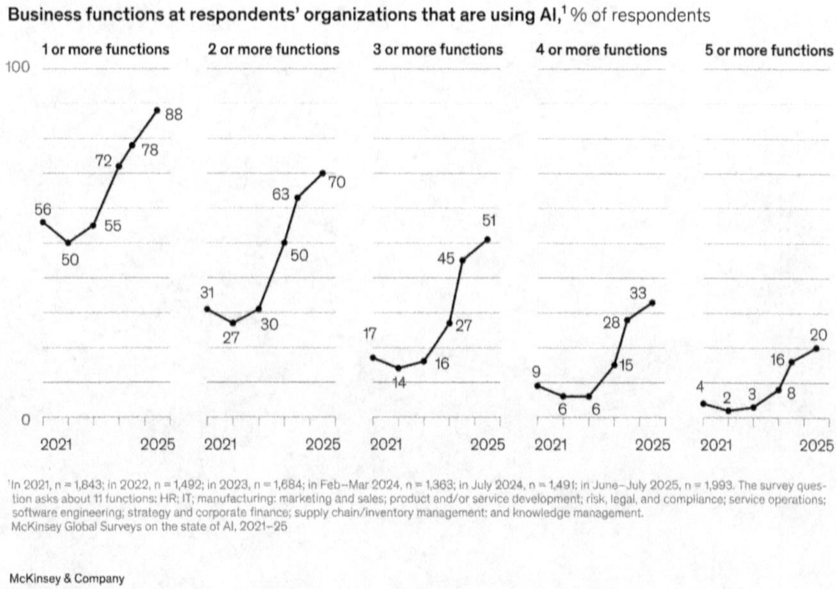

Figure 1.2 Organizations are increasingly using AI in multiple functions.

Source: Exhibit from "The State of AI in 2025: Agents, Innovation, and Transformation," 2025, McKinsey & Company, www.mckinsey.com. Copyright © 2026 McKinsey & Company. All rights reserved. Reprinted by permission.

The consequences of this acceleration are already evident. In many cases, executives did not approve a formal transition from AI experimentation to institutional dependence. It happened gradually, then suddenly, a pattern Rita McGrath highlights in *Seeing Around Corners*, drawing on Ernest Hemingway's well-known line describing how bankruptcy can unfold.[7] Teams began using AI to draft documents and analyze data within their personal workflows, often to support better personal decision-making (see Figure 1.3).[8]

My work advising boards and C-suite teams across dozens of organizations helps explain why this pattern recurs. A consistent dynamic emerges: AI adoption often spreads faster than institutional readiness, especially when tools promise immediate efficiency gains. Companies often move quickly from experimentation into everyday use, while governance protocols and workforce preparation lag behind. Today's AI follows this pattern with unusual force. Adoption accelerates through individuals and teams before leadership structures and governance frameworks respond.

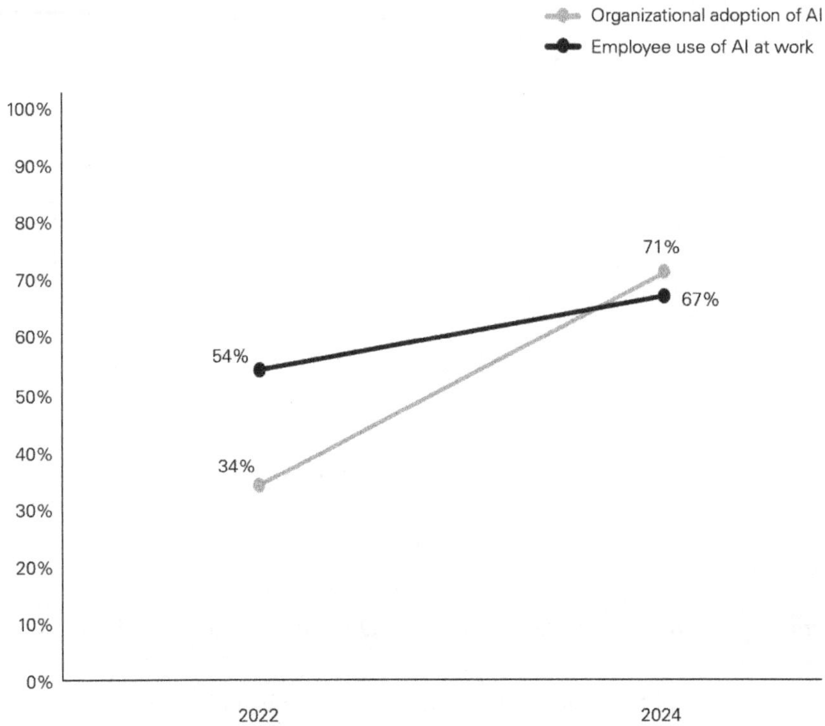

Figure 1.3 Organizational and employee AI adoption have increased over time.

Source: © The University of Melbourne and KPMG, 2025.

This pattern reshapes how professionals encounter risk and responsibility. AI rarely enters organizations at a single decision point. It arrives through many small choices made throughout the enterprise. Each choice may appear reasonable in isolation, but together they often create a chaotic explosion of AI tools across the organization.

This chapter begins here because professionals cannot realize value from the technology, or govern its use, without a shared frame of reference. Figure 1.4 illustrates the momentum rather than precise adoption levels. Its slope shows how quickly GenAI moved from peripheral use to a central feature of enterprise operations.[9]

Professionals now operate amid systems that learn and adapt, including systems that can act autonomously. The chapters that follow examine how this condition emerged and what it demands from professionals. For now, the task is simpler. It is to acknowledge that the moment has arrived.

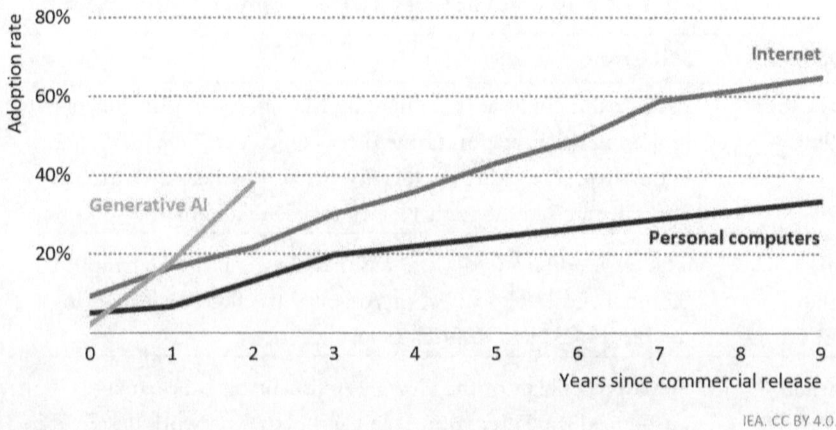

Figure 1.4 Growth in the use of digital technologies in the workplace since the year of first commercial release, United States.

Source: © IEA (2025), Energy and AI, IEA, Paris, https://www.iea.org/reports/energy-and-ai, License: CC BY 4.0.

The Long Arc of AI

AI did not arrive as a sudden breakthrough. It emerged through a long sequence of ideas and experiments that unfolded over much of the twentieth century (see Table 1.1). The earliest foundations were laid alongside the birth of modern computing in the 1940s, when researchers began to explore whether machines could perform tasks associated with reasoning and learning. These early efforts were ambitious. Progress was constrained by limited hardware capacity. At the same time, the absence of large, reliable datasets and the immaturity of early algorithms constrained what systems could reliably accomplish.

The condensed pre-GenAI development milestones timeline (see Figure 1.5) included here illustrates this history. You'll note that the early entries are spaced quite far apart. Years often passed between technological advances and practical experimentation. Early neural models and primitive pattern recognition techniques appeared as isolated initiatives rather than as a coordinated effort. Progress during this period was real, but slow, and difficult to translate beyond research environments.

Periods of optimism were frequently followed by disappointment. When early systems failed to meet expectations, funding declined, and attention shifted away from AI. These downturns appear as long gaps following moments of promise, when progress between development milestones slowed. The first AI winter beginning in the early 1970s, reflected in the years after early symbolic systems stalled, reset expectations. Research continued at a more cautious pace. This rhythm of advance and retreat became a defining feature of AI's early history.[24]

Table 1.1 Early and Classical AI Development Milestones

Date	Milestone
October 1950	Alan Turing published "Computing Machinery and Intelligence,"[10] proposing the Imitation Game (later coined the *Turing Test*). This test evaluated machine intelligence based on whether written responses are indistinguishable from those of a human.
July 1956	The term *artificial intelligence* was introduced at the Dartmouth Summer Research Project on Artificial Intelligence,[11] marking the birth of AI as a research field.
January 1957	Frank Rosenblatt of the Cornell Aeronautical Laboratory introduced the Perceptron,[12] an early neural network designed to learn from input data.
January 1966	Joseph Weizenbaum developed ELIZA, a natural language program that simulated a psychotherapist.[13] It was one of the first examples of natural language processing, following keyword recognition patterns.
February 1972	A. Jay Goldstien, Leon D. Harmon, and Ann B. Lesk published "Man-Machine Interaction in Human-Face Identification," demonstrating significant accuracy gains in automated facial recognition.[14]
1973	Applied mathematician Sir James Lighthill published a critical assessment of AI research, concluding that progress had fallen short of prior expectations.[15] This condemnation contributed to funding cuts and the first AI winter, a period of decreased AI interest and progress.
1986	German Scientist Ernst Dickmanns developed an early autonomous vehicle using a Mercedes-Benz van equipped with a computer system and sensors to read the environment.[16]
May 1997	IBM's Deep Blue defeated world chess champion Garry Kasparov,[17] demonstrating the power of specialized AI systems.
June 2009	ImageNet was introduced as a large-scale labeled image dataset,[18] enabling standardized training and evaluation of visual recognition models.
October 2011	Apple launched Siri, a voice-based digital assistant, allowing millions of people to interact with their smartphones using natural language.[19]

Date	Milestone
February 2011	IBM Watson defeated two of the world's best human Jeopardy players, Brad Rutter and Ken Jennings, using large-scale natural language processing and information retrieval techniques.[20]
September 2012	AlexNet won the ImageNet competition by a wide margin.[21] The result highlighted how deep neural networks benefited from GPU-based computation and expanded training data.
March 2016	AlphaGo defeated Go champion Lee Sedol, demonstrating that self-learning systems could master intuition-heavy domains.[22]
November 2020	DeepMind's AlphaFold model predicted 3D structures of proteins using their amino acid information, representing a scientific advancement that solved a more than 50-year-long problem in biology.[23]

Throughout this period, AI remained primarily a research pursuit. Its center of gravity was more academic than commercial. Systems were developed to demonstrate theoretical possibilities or to solve tightly scoped problems, often requiring expert supervision and extensive tuning. Because of that narrow scope, AI had little sustained impact on how organizations operated. A limited exception appeared in sectors such as financial services, where early machine learning techniques were applied to robotic process automation, the creation of virtual assistants, and fraud detection methods. For most firms, these deployments were operationally isolated and limited to specific use cases rather than fully integrated across company life cycles.[25] Visa, for example, expanded its Advanced Authorization model in 2013 to improve detection of fraud in electronic payments.[26] For most organizations, though, AI was observed from a distance rather than relied on in daily operations.

The International AI Safety Report's historical capability framing helps explain why this pattern persisted. Its retrospective analysis characterizes early AI systems as limited in robustness and narrow in task competence.[27] Performance gains occurred, for sure, but they were fragile. Systems routinely failed when conditions shifted even slightly. Learning by both systems and their human developers was constrained by limited data and early model architectures. These limitations prevented early AI from scaling into routine enterprise use.

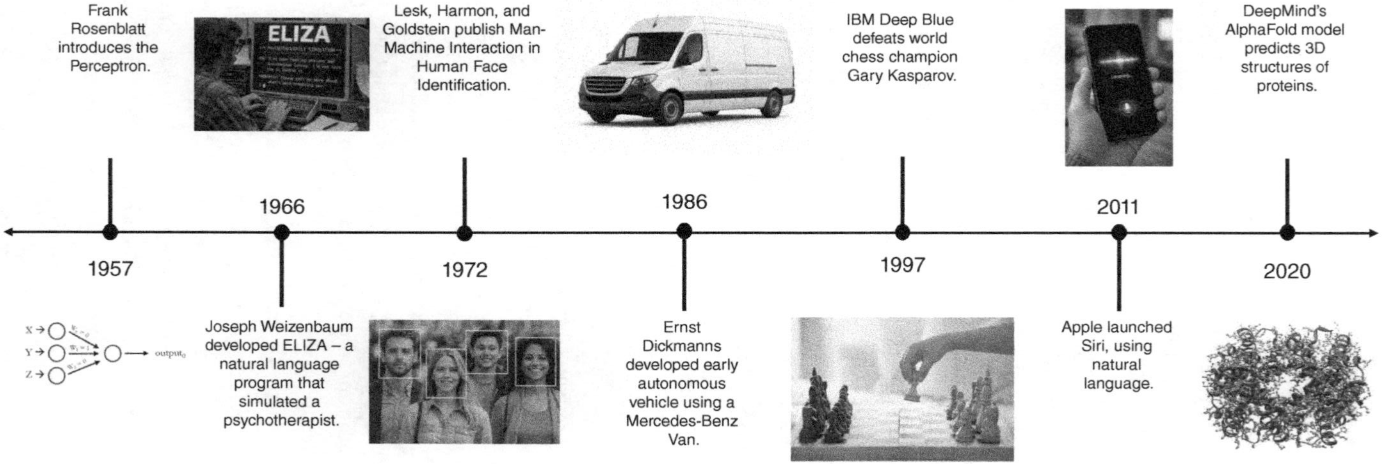

Figure 1.5 Early and classical AI development milestones timeline.

Source: © Business AI Ethics Research Team: Jeffrey Saviano, Vija Kalnina, Lily Noyes, Ryan Wettre, and Colton Mikolajczyk (hereinafter BAIE Research Team), 2026.

This capability ceiling persisted even as computing power and data availability improved.

Later breakthroughs (from the late 1980s through the early 2000s), such as early machine learning techniques and improvements in pattern recognition, still arrived many years apart. Each advance solved a specific problem without unlocking broader applicability. Capability growth remained shallow for much of this period when compared to recent GenAI advancements. Progress was visible to specialists, but insufficient to change institutional behavior.

Because of these constraints, enterprise engagement with AI remained tentative. Some organizations experimented through pilots or academic research partnerships. Few deployments moved beyond an initial proof-of-concept. The technology did not justify deep integration into core operations. Risk concerns typically outweighed potential gains.

This history shaped commercial expectations. Business professionals became accustomed to viewing AI as experimental. Researchers learned to moderate "success" claims. Organizations assumed that advances would arrive gradually. This section establishes that baseline. For decades, AI advanced through incremental capability gains with limited enterprise relevance. That history explains why current adoption departs so sharply from earlier enterprise experiences with AI.

The GenAI Inflection

The public release of OpenAI's ChatGPT on November 30, 2022, marked the point at which AI entered everyday use.[28] The shift was rapid. It occurred through widely available open source tools that ordinary users could access without specialized training. System creation was no longer confined to technical specialists, giving rise to what are often described as "citizen developers." Systems that previously required advanced engineering could now produce amazing output through simple natural language prompts. This change rapidly expanded the population of AI users and accelerated adoption. In my work advising boards and executive teams across industries, I saw this shift unfold in real time. What began as limited experimentation quickly moved into everyday use, often driven by individual employees rather than formal enterprise initiatives.

There is a powerful contrast between earlier AI capabilities and the generative era. Pre-GenAI systems were typically narrowly scoped and operationally fragile. Performance depended on tightly constrained inputs and expert oversight.

Improvements occurred slowly. With generative models, capability expanded in ways that non-specialists could more easily see and experience.

When foundation models became available through broadly accessible interfaces, the practical usability boundary dissolved as user interaction shifted to natural language. This change collapsed the skill barrier that had constrained earlier AI adoption. As a result, experimentation moved beyond specialized labs and into people's daily lives and routine work. This accessibility helps explain the speed that followed. Adoption accelerated because participation broadened. Capability improvements became visible through direct use in everyday tasks rather than through formal benchmarks.

The post-GenAI development timeline (see Table 1.2) included in this chapter shows tighter spacing between milestones (see Figure 1.6). Releases of major large language models (LLMs) followed one another in quick succession.[29] When viewed alongside earlier timelines, the contrast is clear. This shift also redefined enterprise engagement. Generative systems are not entering organizations through top-down led, centralized deployment alone. They spread through bottom-up individual use. Employees were motivated to adopt tools to aid in their own work: creating content (e.g., drafting documents), analyzing data, supporting their decisions, and otherwise improving their workflows. Organizations began relying on outputs generated by systems that were not fully integrated into formal processes. A Microsoft/LinkedIn survey from this period found that 75% of respondents reported using GenAI at work, and incredibly 78% of those users were bringing their own GenAI tools into their jobs.[30] Whenever I revealed that statistic with talent or risk professionals, you could see the shock on their faces.

Earlier AI tools supported narrow functions under close technical supervision. Generative tools now support a considerably wider range of tasks with limited expert technical intervention. That change, further analyzed in Chapter 4, affects how risk is distributed across organizations. Occasional use confines the scope of failure; routine use allows failures to spread. The "International AI Safety Report" highlights this distinction by noting that broader AI capability increases exposure to unintended effects.[48]

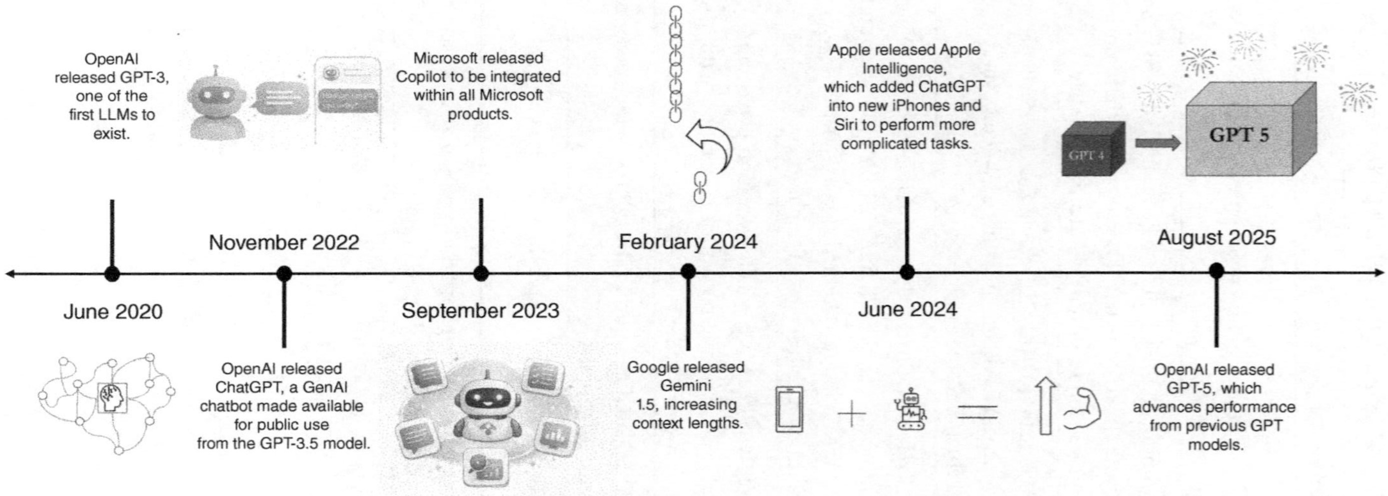

Figure 1.6 Post-GenAI development milestones timeline.

Source: © BAIE Research Team, 2026.

Table 1.2 Post-GenAI Timeline

Date	Milestone
June 2020	OpenAI released GPT-3, one of the first LLMs to exist. It utilized 175 billion parameters to produce human-like text, code, and translations.[31]
October 2020	Tesla announced their Full Self-Driving (FSD) Beta program to a select group of customers.[32] This advanced driver assistance system was a step toward fully autonomous driving.
January 2021	OpenAI released DALL-E (which was eventually followed by DALL-E 2 and DALL-E 3) which are GenAI models that create detailed images from text.[33]
November 2022	OpenAI released ChatGPT, a GenAI chatbot made available for public use from the GPT-3.5 model.[34] This was a transformative moment for widespread GenAI use, as ChatGPT now has nearly 800 million weekly users as of September 2025.[35]
February 2023	Meta released LLaMa, a smaller, yet high performing LLM that requires less computing power for researchers with limited energy infrastructure.[36]
March 2023	OpenAI released its multimodal GPT-4, which accepts both image and text inputs.[37]
September 2023	Microsoft released Copilot to be integrated within all Microsoft products.[38]
November 2023	Microsoft released Copilot Studio which allows users to build their own custom copilots (AI agents).[39]
February 2024	Google released Gemini 1.5, which was able to manipulate context lengths up to 1 million tokens.[40]
February 2024	OpenAI released Sora, which generates videos from text prompts.[41]
May 2024	IBM released the Granite family of open source GenAI models, a specialized foundation model for code generation, time series forecasting, and document intelligence.[42]

Date	Milestone
June 2024	Apple released Apple Intelligence, which added ChatGPT into new iPhones and Siri to perform more complicated tasks.[43]
January 2025	DeepSeek-R1 was released, gaining attention for its strong performance and operation as an open source, low-cost model.[44]
August 2025	OpenAI released GPT-5, which advances performance from previous GPT models.[45]
January 2026	Hyundai and Boston Dynamics publicly showcased their humanoid robot Atlas at the Consumer Electronics Show in Las Vegas.[46]
January 2026	Microsoft announced agentic AI solutions for the retail industry across merchandising, marketing, and store operations and fulfillment.[47]

A summary of top GenAI use cases in 2025 focuses on how applications are *experienced* rather than on technical novelty (see Figure 1.7).[49] Generative systems behave differently from earlier AI models. They respond through conversation and produce outputs that resemble *human* work products. Once these systems entered daily workflows, adoption expanded quickly across enterprise functions and sectors.

Scale Before Strategy

One defining feature of the current AI era is the speed of diffusion. AI reached a global scale before business enterprises and governments had time to fully absorb its implications. Adoption is not waiting for regulation or governance frameworks. It advances through availability and convenience, together with its perceived usefulness. Scale arrived first. Leadership response followed.

By the second half of 2025, roughly one in six people worldwide had used a GenAI tool, including widely adopted applications such as ChatGPT, Microsoft Copilot, and Google Gemini.[50] This remarkable level of penetration is notable for a technology that entered mainstream awareness only a few years earlier. Usage continued to increase quarter over quarter, with global adoption rising by more than a percentage point in just six months. This trajectory places GenAI among the fastest-diffusing general-purpose technologies in modern history, rivaling, and in some regions surpassing, the early spread of smartphones and social media platforms (see Figure 1.8).[51]

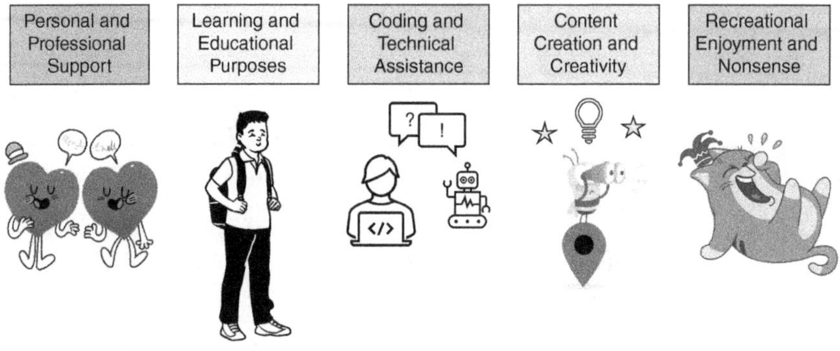

Figure 1.7 Top GenAI use cases.

Source: Zao-Sanders, 2025 | Chart: © BAIE Research Team, 2026.

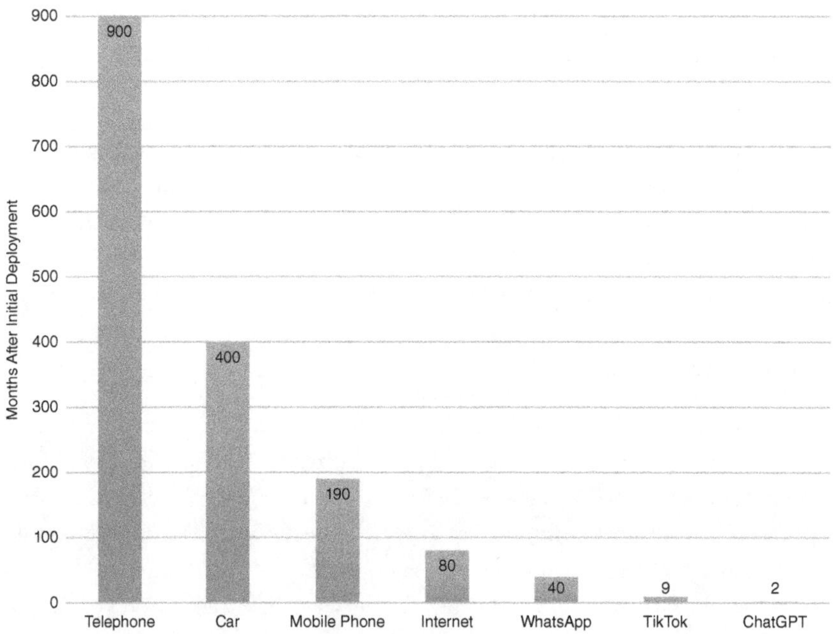

Figure 1.8 Time to reach 100 million users.

Source: Ebert and Louridas, 2023 | Chart: © BAIE Research Team, 2026.

High-income economies led in overall adoption. Growth in middle-income and lower-middle-income countries also accelerated, particularly where mobile connectivity and cloud access reduced infrastructure barriers.[52] GenAI's dependence on centralized compute and intuitive user interfaces enabled usage to scale without material hardware or software investments. As a result, adoption surged in regions where broader digital transformation efforts had previously lagged. According to the World Bank, these trends are reflected in ChatGPT usage patterns, with Brazil, India, Indonesia, the Philippines, and the United States ranking among the top countries in March 2024.[53]

Enterprise adoption closely followed consumer uptake. What began as experimentation with open source tools rapidly moved into the core business. Organizations across sectors incorporated GenAI into daily workflows, often informally. Employees began using AI systems for document drafting, information summarization, coding assistance, data analysis, interacting with customers, research, and countless other early applications.[54] In many firms, these practices were driven by the allure of individual productivity gains rather than a top-down strategy. Quite often, by the time leadership teams became aware of the use at scale within the enterprise, AI was already embedded in routine operations.

Patterns of adoption varied by sector, reflecting differences in both digital maturity and risk tolerance. According to the Stanford HAI Report, in 2024 the dominant sectors for AI use were technical and creative fields, with computer and mathematically driven careers comprising about 37% of all AI use while arts, media, and design represent about 10%.[55] The World Bank augments this data, revealing that GenAI adoption is most prominent within information technology, management, business, and finance industries.[56] Heavily regulated sectors such as healthcare, energy, and financial services adopted AI more cautiously, often limiting use to internal support functions with more guardrails than other sectors. Public sector adoption advanced unevenly, with progress limited by skills gaps, challenges in accessing and sharing high-quality data, and rigid legal and regulatory frameworks.[57] Skills constraints further limited uptake, even as demand for AI-enabled public services increased.[58]

Firm size also shaped how scale emerged (see Figure 1.9). Large enterprises adopted AI earlier and deployed it across more functions, reflecting greater access to enabling resources.[59] These organizations were more likely to deploy AI across multiple business functions and to experiment with integration into core systems, including logistics, research, and development. Small and medium-sized enterprises, by contrast, relied primarily on AI embedded within licensed productivity tools for peripheral tasks.[60] Their adoption was widespread but shallow, shaped largely by vendor design rather than internal governance or strategic intent.

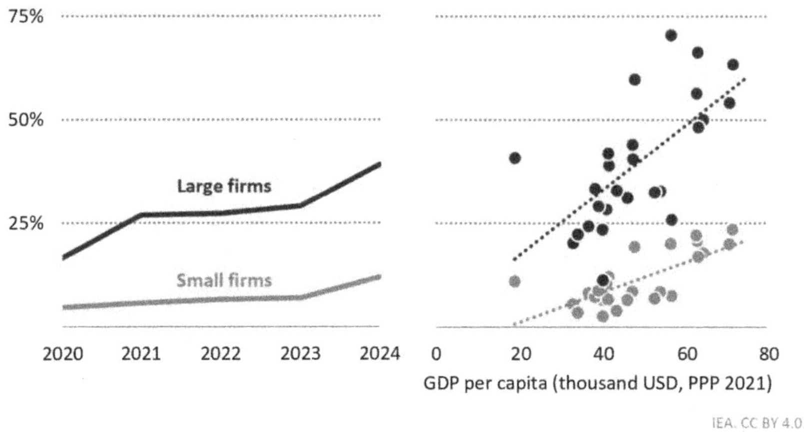

Figure 1.9 AI adoption rates by firm size in OECD countries and AI adoption rates by firm size compared to GDP per capita of the firm's home country.

Source: © IEA (2025), Energy and AI, IEA, Paris, https://www.iea.org/reports/energy-and-ai, License: CC BY 4.0.

Geography compounded these differences. Countries with strong digital foundations and early investment into digital infrastructure consistently exhibit higher AI adoption rates. The United Arab Emirates, for example, leads in global adoption with 64% of its working population reported to use AI in 2025.[61] In those environments, AI use extends beyond the workplace into education and public-facing services. By contrast, regions with limited internet coverage and compute access generally experience slower and more uneven uptake. Over time, these differences widened gaps in how deeply AI became institutionalized.

AI adoption correlates strongly with what the World Bank terms the foundational *Four Cs* (see Figure 1.10): connectivity, compute, context, and competency. To summarize, this report and other research cited in this chapter indicates that where these conditions are weak, AI usage tends to be episodic and dependent on external vendors and their platforms. Where they are strong, adoption intensifies.[62] This asymmetry has significant implications for both economic competitiveness and workforce development.

What is most striking, however, is the sequencing. Scale is preceding governance almost everywhere. Tools are being adopted often before policies are written. At times, systems are relied on before risks are fully understood. In many organizations, AI systems are shaping decisions and customer interactions without clear

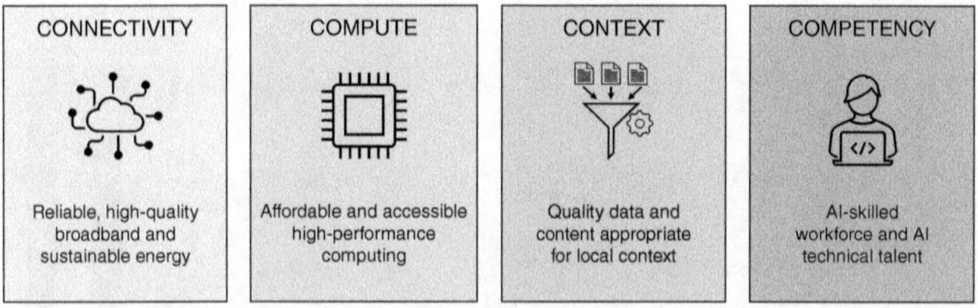

Figure 1.10 The Four Cs of AI foundations.

Source: World Bank, 2025 | Chart: BAIE Research Team, 2026.

accountability structures in place. Governance frameworks, where present, often lag actual practice by months, or even years. The 2025 Trust, Attitudes and Use of AI study conducted by the University of Melbourne, in collaboration with KPMG, surveyed more than 48,000 people across 47 countries. Among advanced economies, this study reports that slightly more than half of workers are employed by organizations with responsible AI frameworks in place. Only 55% of employees feel that their organizations have sufficient mechanisms to guide responsible AI use, further illustrating this tension between scale and governance.[63]

At a global level, the rapid proliferation of AI has created a paradox. Widespread adoption signals innovation and heightened competitiveness. It also simultaneously increases exposure to myriad risks. The faster AI spreads, the more difficult it becomes to retrofit governance, especially across complex enterprises. Leaders are now confronted with managing systems that are already ubiquitous and deeply embedded in enterprise operations.

This is the operating condition for ethical AI governance. AI systems were deployed across organizations before governance models were in place. Many organizations first experienced AI through routine applications embedded in everyday workflows, with strategic intent often following only after operational reliance had already formed. Enterprise AI applications and strategy will be discussed in Chapter 3.

As AI systems are being deployed more broadly across organizations, the consequences of real-world deployment, both positive and negative, become visible with increasing frequency. Incident tracking data shows a rise in reported AI failures,[64] along with a shift toward higher-severity impacts as systems moved from experimentation to operational dependence (see Figure 1.11).[65] These incidents highlight the importance of post-deployment behavior, an issue examined in detail in Chapter 4.

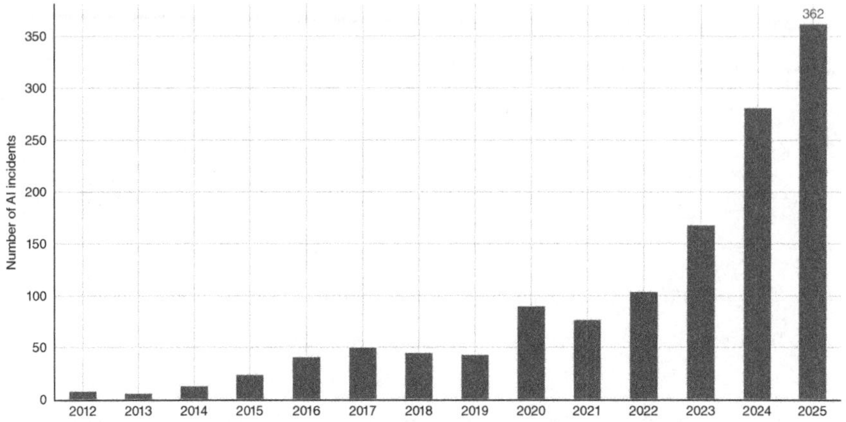

Figure 1.11 Number of reported AI incidents, 2012–2025.

Source: AI Incident Database (AIID), 2025 | Chart: 2026 AI Index Report, Stanford HAI.

Trust and Confidence Gaps

As AI becomes embedded in everyday tools and services, public confidence is not advancing at the same pace. The 2025 University of Melbourne/KPMG survey illustrates widespread reported use alongside uneven trust. Only 46% of respondents expressed a willingness to trust AI systems, even though 72% reported some level of acceptance of AI usage. The study also finds that many people continue to use AI systems despite limited understanding of how they function. In practice, AI adoption often proceeds because AI is embedded in essential services or common platforms, rather than because users have confidence in system behavior.[66]

Trust in AI varies markedly by geography. The University of Melbourne/KPMG study reports higher trust and acceptance levels in several emerging economies, including India, the United Arab Emirates, and China. In these countries, more than 60% of respondents indicated a willingness to trust AI systems, and reported usage exceeded levels observed in most advanced economies. By contrast, trust levels are substantially lower across many advanced economies, including Germany, Japan, and Finland, where fewer than half of respondents reported a willingness to trust AI systems (see Figure 1.12).[67] As a result, identical AI deployments can be perceived positively in some markets while encountering skepticism or resistance in others.

Concerns about AI risks generally persist across regions. Survey respondents consistently report unease about cybersecurity risks, loss of human connection, as well as risks from misinformation and disinformation. Notably, many of these concerns are framed at the societal level, rather than as risks arising from individual, day-to-day interactions with AI systems.[68]

Within organizations, similar patterns appear. Employees rely on AI tools to meet performance expectations while expressing concern about monitoring and personal data usage.[69] AI often becomes embedded in work practices before norms for transparency and responsibility are clearly established. Trust also varies by application. Systems that support document drafting or internal efficiency tend to be viewed as lower risk. Systems that influence hiring or customer interactions prompt greater concern with AI assistance.[70]

For enterprises, uneven confidence has material consequences. Declining trust can damage a company's reputation and provoke employee resistance. It can also drive customer attrition or draw regulatory attention, even when systems function as intended. As AI continues to scale, stakeholder trust must be treated as a distinct enterprise risk factor that can be degraded and, ultimately, lost.

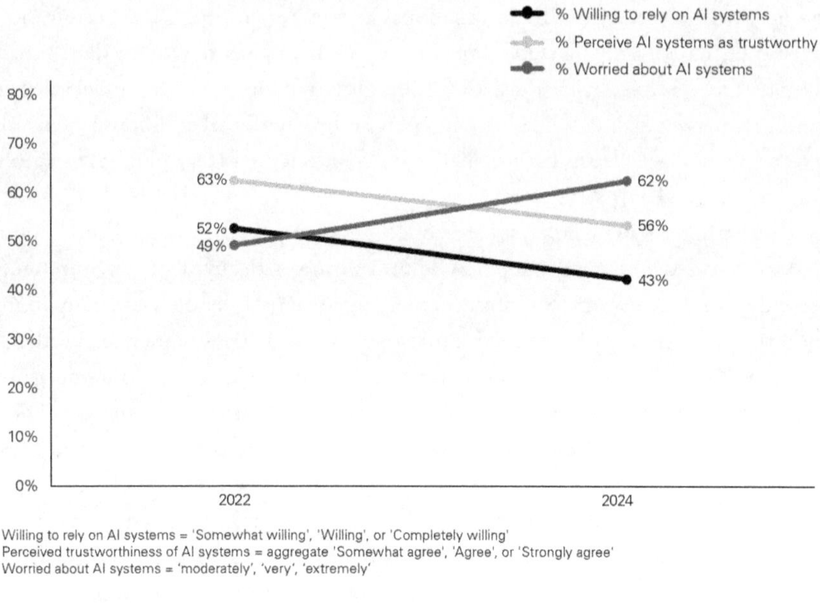

Figure 1.12 Trust of AI systems and worry about AI in 2022 and 2024.

Source: © The University of Melbourne and KPMG, 2025.

Investment, Infrastructure, and Environmental Load

As AI moves from experimental use into a core economic input, its effects extend to capital allocation and the necessary physical infrastructure. These effects carry significant environmental consequences. This powerful AI-driven digital transformation is increasingly revealing itself as a resource-intensive force. The scale of AI deployment is now shaped as much by investment concentration and infrastructure capacity as by model performance.

Global investment in AI has become increasingly concentrated. A small number of firms, including Google, Meta, and Microsoft, account for a disproportionate share of spending on advanced AI development. That concentration also appears geographically. Many leading AI models originate in the United States and China, together with heightened investment in data centers and specialized hardware in those countries (see Figure 1.13).[71] This pattern reflects the capital intensity of frontier AI development, where training and operating large models require sustained access to energy and engineering talent. AI capability growth has become closely tied to financial capacity, reinforcing existing economic asymmetries.

This investment pattern has material infrastructure consequences. AI systems rely on expansive data center networks that require extensive and reliable electricity and network connectivity. The International Energy Agency reports that AI-related data center expansion is already contributing to increased electricity demands in several regions across the globe, with further growth expected as AI model size and consumer usage expand.[72] These facilities are not incremental additions to existing systems. They place steady, high demands on electricity grids, shaping how regions plan and invest in infrastructure.

Infrastructure demands also introduce geographic constraints. Data centers tend to cluster where energy supply is abundant in politically stable environments. This dynamic concentrates infrastructure in specific jurisdictions, amplifying regional disparities in both economic benefit and environmental burden.[73] Communities that host AI infrastructure may experience local economic gains. They also experience increased strain on energy systems and even land use. These trade-offs are rarely visible to end users, but they shape the physical footprint of AI development.

Environmental impacts are becoming increasingly visible. The energy required to train and operate AI systems contributes to higher emissions in regions where electricity generation is carbon intensive. Cooling requirements increase demand for water, particularly in regions already facing scarcity. UNESCO's analysis of digital sustainability highlights that unchecked growth in resource-intensive digital systems can undermine climate and sustainability objectives, even when individual applications appear socially beneficial (see Figure 1.14).[74]

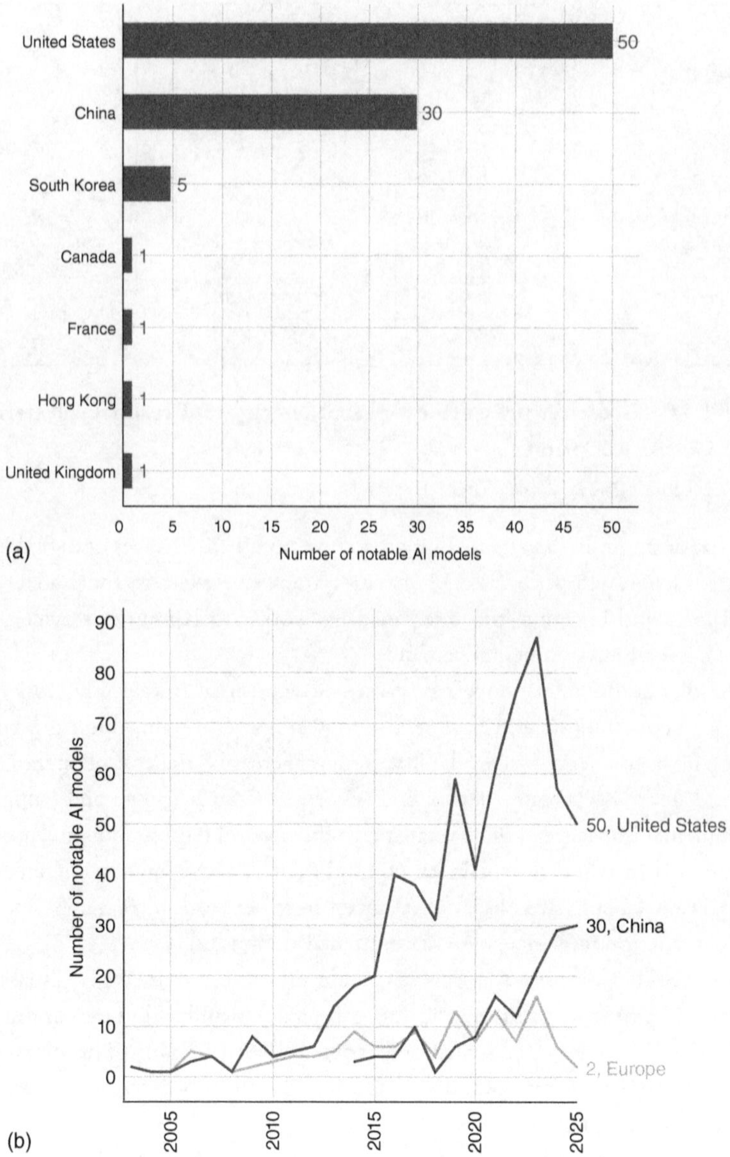

Figure 1.13 (a) Number of notable AI models by select geographic areas, 2025, and (b) Number of notable AI models by select geographic areas, 2003–2025.

Source: Epoch AI, 2026 | Chart: 2026 AI Index report, Stanford HAI.

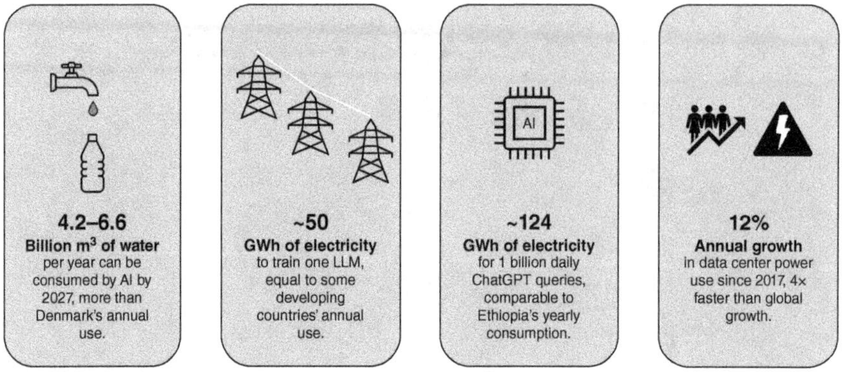

Figure 1.14 Growing pressure on global energy and resource systems due to GenAI adoption.

Source: UNESCO, 2025 | Chart: BAIE Research Team, 2026.

What distinguishes current AI infrastructure from earlier waves of digital infrastructure is its growth pattern. As AI systems require more energy for model training purposes and become embedded in daily work and consumer services, they create consistent environmental demand.[75]

These conditions introduce new forms of enterprise risk. In my work with companies across industries, I have seen infrastructure constraints limit growth by exposing firms to energy price volatility, thereby increasing the cost of operating AI systems. They also create dependencies on specific regions and suppliers. Environmental impacts can draw regulatory scrutiny and create reputational exposure, particularly when sustainability commitments do not align with operating realities. From what I have observed, AI investment decisions increasingly intersect with infrastructure resilience and environmental responsibility.

The World Bank report reveals that these pressures are unevenly distributed. Firms and countries with greater access to capital and infrastructure continue to pull ahead, while others face structural barriers to participation.[76] This divergence affects competition and innovation. It also complicates governance, as costs and benefits accrue to different actors.

What has changed is the breadth of AI deployment. Systems that were once limited in scope now depend on physical infrastructure and sustained energy usage. These dependencies produce environmental and operational effects that extend beyond individual applications. They cannot be addressed solely through internal governance processes focused on system behavior. As AI usage expands, these effects surface more clearly to organizations and regulators, often in places distant from where systems are designed or deployed. For professionals, this expands the scope of responsibility. Governing AI effectively now requires attention to the conditions that enable these systems to operate.

What the Trajectory Signals

Gartner frames the next phase of AI as a shift from stand-alone tools toward orchestrated systems that coordinate activity across workflows.[77] The emphasis is not on a single new model, but on a more connected operating environment in which AI capabilities are secured and governed within core operations. Gartner presents this as a near-term priority for technology leaders.

One direction is the development of agent-based AI systems that rely on multiple cooperating agents. Gartner describes these systems as assigning specific responsibilities to individual agents that converge to complete complex tasks. This approach addresses a limitation of single-agent systems, which often struggle with multistep processes. Dividing responsibility can improve performance while supporting scale. Gartner also notes that these designs increase coordination demands, particularly when agents from different vendors must operate within shared environments.

Another direction involves greater autonomy extending beyond software into operational settings through physical AI. Gartner links physical AI to automation of real-world tasks and associated productivity gains. Its guidance emphasizes the need for safeguards for deploying autonomous systems. It also points to orchestration platforms designed to manage fleets of devices, indicating autonomy implemented across the enterprise rather than isolated automation. In parallel, Gartner identifies AI-native development platforms that support smaller, AI-augmented teams. In these settings, agents contribute directly within delivery workflows rather than operating as external tools.

Capabilities that combine text, images, audio, and other inputs appear less as a discrete technical feature and more as a governance concern. Gartner treats provenance as a mechanism for verifying origin and integrity in software and extends that logic to data and to media. This framing responds to documented incidents involving deepfake-driven disinformation and aligns with emerging regulatory requirements, including provisions in the EU AI Act that emphasize watermarking and provenance tracking. From a security perspective, Gartner points to the need for clearer oversight as organizations rely on both third-party AI services and internally developed systems. It also cautions that increased autonomy requires organizations to prepare for unexpected system behavior and to protect against misuse across different types of content.

The Vocabulary of AI

The following terms establish a shared vocabulary for concepts used throughout this book, focusing on the core technologies that shape modern AI systems:

- **AI system:** A machine-based system that infers how to generate outputs such as predictions, content, recommendations, or decisions that can influence physical or virtual environments. Different AI systems vary in their levels of autonomy and adaptiveness after deployment.[78]
- **Artificial general intelligence (AGI):** Technology that would enable autonomous machines to operate with general intelligent actions through abstract learning. This would enable machines to be capable of judgment and decision-making to solve complex problems.[79]
- **Agentic AI:** An AI system that can accomplish a specific goal with limited supervision. It consists of AI agents – machine learning models that mimic human decision-making to solve problems in real time.[80]
- **Generative AI (GenAI):** Refers to AI systems that are capable of producing novel content, such as text, images, audio, video, or code, based on patterns learned from training data. The GenAI sector can be broadly divided into two segments: upstream, where foundation models are developed, and downstream, where specialized models are built from foundation models.[81]
- **Foundation models:** A class of very large AI systems (often a deep neural network) trained on vast and diverse datasets (often known as *corpora*) using self-supervised learning techniques. They are designed to perform a wide range of general tasks across domains such as language, vision, and speech, and to be general purpose in nature. Foundation models can power a variety of downstream applications and underpin many of the most advanced AI systems currently in use, including those used in language processing, image generation, and scientific discovery.[82]
- **Large language models (LLMs):** A prominent type of foundation model. They are designed to understand and generate human language and can perform a wide array of tasks such as summarization, translation, question answering, and content generation.[83]

Closing

The future path of AI remains uncertain, and many of its effects are difficult to predict. What is clear, however, is that systems with increasing autonomy are already informing important decisions before regulatory frameworks or standards are fully formed. Organizations are finding it difficult to wait for certainty. Responsibility begins once AI systems influence decisions or affect access. That responsibility exists even when formal rules lag behind actual practice. Organizations make decisions each day about how AI is designed and where it is used. Those decisions shape outcomes well before external oversight catches up.

This chapter established the foundation for the analysis that follows. Before strategy is defined or governance choices are made, professionals need a shared understanding of how AI reached its current state and how it now operates in practice. Without that context, discussions of responsibility and oversight remain detached from day-to-day use. The chapters that follow build on this foundation by examining how organizations respond through strategy and governance as AI becomes embedded in core activity. Those responses depend on the conditions described here.

Specifically, Chapter 2 turns to the global policy and regulatory landscape surrounding AI adoption. It examines how governments are responding and why regulation alone does not resolve the decisions organizations already face.

2 Global Public Policy and Regulation

The Illusion of Regulatory Certainty

Artificial intelligence (AI) is now subject to expanding legal frameworks across jurisdictions worldwide. Many governments have already taken steps to regulate AI. In doing so, they are asserting oversight authority, and enterprises now face an increasing number of binding compliance obligations. Any serious discussion of AI governance must begin with this compliance reality. AI regulation is already influencing enterprise decisions at the board and management levels. Leaders must act within emerging rules that remain unsettled.

At the same time, regulatory clarity remains quite elusive. Much of the current debate assumes that clearer rules will eventually reduce uncertainty and create more consistent expectations across jurisdictions. While that assumption is appealing, it does not reflect how AI policy is unfolding in practice. Regulatory activity is accelerating, for sure.[1] However, it remains immature in many jurisdictions and uneven across countries. It also varies in both substance and breadth across sectors. New AI-specific laws must coexist with established legal frameworks that were not designed for contemporary learning systems (see Figure 2.1). One consequence is that regulators often act before detailed rules are in place. They issue non-statutory guidance and take enforcement action, leaving organizations to interpret expectations without clear statutory direction.

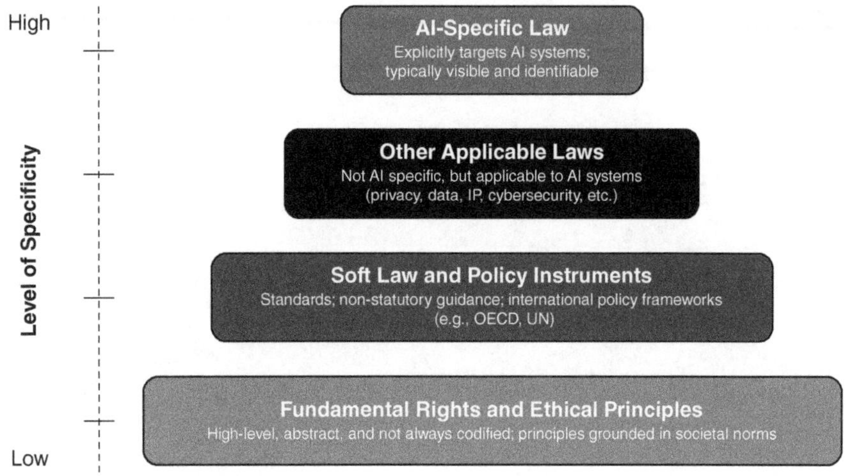

Figure 2.1 Layers of AI laws and principles.

Source: © BAIE Research Team, 2026.

This gap is not unusual in the AI context. Rapid changes in capability outpace the legislative process, so regulatory action often comes before detailed rules. It reflects the unique nature of the technology itself. AI does not fit neatly within existing regulatory silos. AI systems cut across areas that have historically been governed separately. Privacy law and consumer protection now intersect through technologies that shape user outcomes in real time. Competition policy and system safety oversight, including physical world risks, are drawn in as well. Regulators in many jurisdictions are responding through multiple channels rather than a single unified approach.

Furthermore, AI policy emerges through more than lawmaking and binding administrative pronouncements alone. Some regulatory responses take the form of new laws that explicitly target AI systems. Others rely on existing statutory regimes that are now being applied across the AI landscape. Others appear as standards or policy frameworks that influence behavior without carrying the force of law. In some cases, incentive mechanisms or procurement requirements play a similar role. These carrot and stick instruments often interact, but they do not always align. For business leaders, this creates a policy landscape that is dynamic, but complex and at times unsettling.

The global nature of AI amplifies this challenge. Enterprises operating across borders encounter inconsistent (and confusing) obligations in some jurisdictions and limited or no guidance in others. Regulatory expectations may be clear in one market while remaining ambiguous in the next. Enforcement intensity and efficiency differ as well. Institutional capacity to address this policy landscape also varies. In many cases, organizations are forced to make AI design and deployment decisions before regulators have articulated detailed requirements or established a predictable enforcement practice. In these circumstances, waiting for harmonization is simply not a practical option. However, acting within this opaque policy environment can also expose the enterprise to material risks.

This chapter does not attempt to resolve that tension by cataloging statutes or summarizing jurisdiction specific rules. Said another way, I am not attempting to comprehensively summarize the law down to the last detail. The purpose here is different. This chapter is designed to help leaders understand how AI policy and regulation are taking shape in practice and the implications for organizations developing and/or deploying AI systems. It focuses on a broader set of government actions and soft law patterns rather than regurgitating statutory provisions and legal minutiae.

A further source of confusion addressed in this chapter is the tendency to equate relevant government action with lawmaking alone. In the emerging technology context (and AI in particular), governments influence outcomes through a broad set of policy instruments. These tools include standards development and tax incentives; they also include procurement choices. Governments further influence outcomes through research funding and infrastructure investment. Certain international organizations also play a meaningful role by articulating norms and shaping expectations that later inform national approaches. Understanding the full breadth of AI policy and regulation therefore requires attention to institutions and instruments that extend beyond traditional lawmaking.

It's important to note that regulatory uncertainty does not imply a regulatory void.

Enterprises are evaluated on how they manage AI-related risk. Regulators and reviewing courts assess whether organizations have acted reasonably in light of the guidance that was available at the time. When harm occurs as a result of an AI incident, these institutions typically focus on accountability and remediation, even in the absence of AI-specific laws. Stakeholders also apply similar expectations. In this environment, compliance involves more than following explicit rules. It requires interpreting policy direction and responding to evolving expectations about responsible conduct.

This chapter proceeds with that reality in mind. It reflects the current pace of AI policy development and incorporates recent regulatory momentum where it exists. By the end of this chapter, the reader should have a clear understanding of how AI policy is developing both at a global and national level and why enterprises must act in the absence of regulatory certainty. That foundation prepares you for the chapters that follow, where attention importantly shifts from external policy conditions to internal strategy, governance, and leadership responsibility.

The Expanding Role of Government in the AI Ecosystem

Discussions of AI regulation often focus too narrowly on statutes and formal rules. That focus minimizes how governments are impactfully shaping AI development and deployment in practice. Formal statutes and other legally binding pronouncements are only one of many policy instruments available to public authorities. In the AI context, governments routinely rely on a broader toolkit that influences behavior long before binding regulation takes effect (see Figure 2.2).

This broader policy toolkit reflects a pragmatic reality. AI technologies are evolving at breakneck speed, while the wheels of legislation and binding enforcement processes turn ever so slowly. Governments routinely use a range of levers to steer responsible innovation and to promote jurisdiction-specific priorities. These levers operate across the AI life cycle. They affect where systems are developed and how they are funded, and they shape the conditions under which systems are deployed. They also shape the expectations that attach to their use.

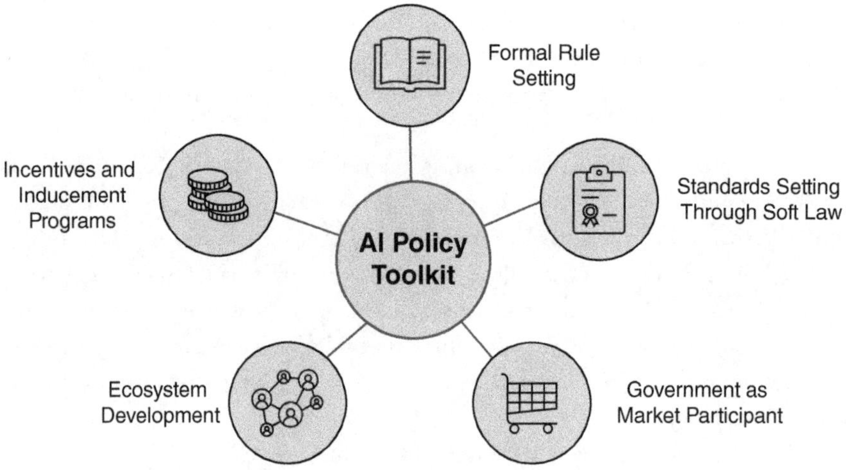

Figure 2.2 Government AI policy toolkit.

Source: © BAIE Research Team, 2026.

Formal Rule Setting Through Hard Law

Formal rule setting instruments rely on legal authority and enforceability. Governments increasingly enact AI-specific laws and regulations that establish binding obligations for certain uses of AI. The EU AI Act, for example, falls within this category. In the United States, the executive branch is increasingly relying on executive orders (EOs) to create enforceable AI rules. AI rulemaking through EOs has occurred under both the Biden and Trump administrations.

At the same time, regulators also apply existing legal regimes to AI systems. These include data privacy and cybersecurity requirements. Anti-discrimination laws also apply when AI systems produce biased outcomes in employment, housing, credit, or access to public accommodations. In the United States, this includes statutes such as the Civil Rights Act of 1964, which applies when AI-enabled decision systems affect individuals in legally protected classes. Intellectual property law also plays a role in shaping how AI systems are trained and commercialized. In some cases, governments impose export controls that limit the transfer of advanced AI capabilities outside the walls of their jurisdictions. Conversely, some governments restrict or prohibit specific uses of AI within their jurisdictions. These measures define the *legal* boundaries within which enterprises must operate.

Standards Setting Through Soft Law and Quasi Law Mechanisms

Soft law and quasi law instruments typically do not carry the force of law, but they can exert meaningful influence on business practices. Governments support the development of technical standards that define acceptable performance or reliability for AI systems. In some cases, they actively drive that work. Certification schemes provide mechanisms for AI system testing and assessment. National quality infrastructure plays a similar role. Public authorities also endorse external ethical principles and norms for responsible AI practices. Expectations for algorithmic impact assessments and audits increasingly shape how organizations evaluate AI-related risk. Red teaming practices further clarify what responsible deployment looks like in practice. Governance toolkits provide additional structure.

In my consulting work, I have repeatedly seen organizations adopt specific elements of the NIST "Artificial Intelligence Risk Management Framework (AI RMF 1.0)"[2] as part of their AI governance and risk management processes. In many cases, I have recommended this framework as a way to strengthen internal oversight, especially where binding regulation was still evolving. The value is in the depth of its implementation guidance. In particular, the NIST "Artificial Intelligence Risk Management Framework: Generative Artificial Intelligence Profile"[3] provides detailed generative AI risk management practices that organizations can apply in real world settings. I regularly incorporate these NIST practices into my AI strategy, governance, and ethics courses at MIT Sloan, where they serve as a foundation for effective enterprise decision-making in today's AI age. Developed and published by the National Institute of Standards and Technology, an instrumentality of the U.S. Department of Commerce, the framework, although voluntary, effectively functions as a reference point for an enterprise's AI program. Furthermore, over time, elements of instruments such as this migrate into procurement requirements and regulatory guidance, shaping expectations long before a binding law is enacted.

Direct Market Participation by Government

In addition to lawmaking and standard setting, governments increasingly act as buyers and direct users of AI systems. Public procurement requirements influence which AI capabilities are developed and which vendors gain traction with their solutions. Governments also deploy AI systems to enhance public services and administration. In certain jurisdictions, supplier development programs help smaller and minority-owned firms meet public sector requirements.

For example, in Canada the federal government's "Supplier Diversity Action Plan" is explicitly designed to reduce barriers and increase procurement opportunities for businesses from underrepresented groups, including Black-owned firms. The program does so through inclusive sourcing practices and targeted outreach in government contracting.[4]

Public sector-led open innovation initiatives are shaping market dynamics in an impactful manner. Through these activities, governments influence AI demand and set commercial expectations without relying solely on regulation.

Developing AI Capabilities Across the Ecosystem

AI innovation depends heavily on talent and institutional infrastructure. Sustained research activity also plays a central role. National and subnational governments invest in education and workforce training to build technical expertise. These investments become more important as upskilling and reskilling needs grow across the labor force.

Public research funding supports AI capability development that the private sector may not pursue on its own. Governments create environments for experimentation through AI labs and testing sandboxes. Incubators support early-stage experimentation as well. Science and technology parks provide physical spaces where firms and researchers can collaborate. In many cases, this proximity has enabled advances that would not have emerged had organizations worked in isolation.

Governments further support commercialization through technology transfer offices. Accelerator programs help early-stage ventures move from research into practical application. Coordination also occurs through innovation clusters and public convenings. These efforts align actors across the AI ecosystem.

Public awareness initiatives play a separate role by shaping how citizens and stakeholders understand AI systems and their implications. One example of this approach emerged during the Obama administration. Terah Lyons, who previously served as an AI advisor in the U.S. Office of Science and Technology Policy (OSTP), described this work during our conversation on the EY *Better Innovation* podcast.[5] As part of that effort, OSTP led a series of public town halls across the United States to hear directly from citizens about their hopes and fears related to AI systems.

Incentives and Inducement Programs

Incentives and inducement programs are used by governments as a carrot approach to complement the stick of regulation. These instruments steer behavior by rewarding desired outcomes rather than mandating conduct. Matching grants require private commitment alongside public funding. Loan subsidies reduce financial risk for AI investments by commercial enterprises. Guarantee programs serve a similar purpose. Early-stage equity finance provides capital for firms pursuing high-growth opportunities. Tax incentives also play an important role by lowering the cost of research and investment. In many jurisdictions, these incentive programs are led by research or investment tax credits.

Some governments, particularly at the state and local levels in the United States, negotiate tailored incentive arrangements to attract capital or skilled labor. Prizes and inducement competitions are used to focus attention on specific technical challenges. Hackathons and crowdsourcing initiatives provide additional avenues for experimentation. These approaches encourage innovation while signaling policy priorities.

For example, Massachusetts Research Credit[6] encourages businesses to locate research and development activity within Massachusetts by lowering the effective tax rate of the enterprise. For an organization developing AI models or related systems, this can influence where engineering teams are based and where experimentation occurs. Firms may choose to expand local research teams or advance projects that might otherwise be delayed because of the favorable tax treatment of this qualified research activity. Although the program is not written specifically for AI, it directly applies to AI research conducted in the state and shapes investment decisions accordingly.

A comparable dynamic exists in the United Kingdom through the Patent Box regime. Introduced in 2013, the Patent Box taxes income from qualifying intellectual property at a reduced rate of 10%.[7] For organizations that develop AI-enabled products, this creates a strong incentive to develop patents and commercialize technologies within the United Kingdom. Decisions about where AI systems are developed and brought to market can be influenced by the availability of this tax incentive. While the regime is technology-neutral, it can materially affect how companies structure their AI programs and where value is captured.

Why This Matters for Business Leaders

Together, the mechanisms described in this section reflect how governments influence AI ecosystems. These effects arise through formal law, standards, and market activity. Capacity building and incentive programs also shape outcomes. No single instrument operates on its own. Governments combine tools and adjust them over time as technology evolves. In the case of incentives alone, there are literally thousands of distinct programs operating across the globe.

These programs change over time in response to business needs and market conditions.

For business leaders, understanding this expanded government toolkit is necessary when building leading AI programs. Government actions routinely influence where companies choose to invest and where development teams are located. Policy choices affect where AI systems are actually deployed. And they shape expectations for acceptable risk management practices. Decisions made without awareness of these policy signals may appear rational in the short term. Over time, they can prove misaligned with government policy direction.

This complexity raises a deeper governance question. Can enterprises rely on government policy alone to ensure that AI systems are deployed responsibly? Or does that responsibility rest primarily with the business enterprise itself? As later chapters explore, the answer increasingly points toward internal governance rather than reliance on external rulemaking. This section provides the foundation for that conclusion. That understanding is essential not only for navigating uncertainty but also for decisions about where to operate, how to operate across jurisdictions, and how to bring AI-enabled products and services to market. It also supports the design of governance structures that remain effective as policy evolves.

The discussion now turns to international organizations and standards bodies, which add another layer to this environment. These organizations develop governance approaches that influence public policy and corporate behavior. They also produce frameworks that shape expectations for responsible AI development. While these instruments are not legally binding, they often inform later regulation and have been shown to materially affect business practices.

International Organizations and Global AI Norms

International organizations, of course, do not regulate companies directly. Their influence is effected through governments and standards bodies. Over time, this influence has become more consequential for business leaders. For example, the Organisation for Economic Co-operation and Development (OECD) does not impose legal obligations on enterprises. Instead, it shapes expectations by issuing policy instruments that governments later adopt and operationalize.

Early international AI policy efforts focused on articulating shared values. The OECD AI Principles, first adopted in 2019, established a common ethical vocabulary for AI grounded in human rights and safety. Further, they addressed questions of accountability in the use of automated systems.[8] Although the principles themselves are not binding, they have been incorporated into national AI strategies and referenced directly by regulators.

What is critically important for our purposes is the translation of these principles into instruments that both governments and commercial enterprises can implement. International organizations now play a central role in translating abstract norms into guidance that governments adopt and enterprises actually encounter in practice (see Figure 2.3).

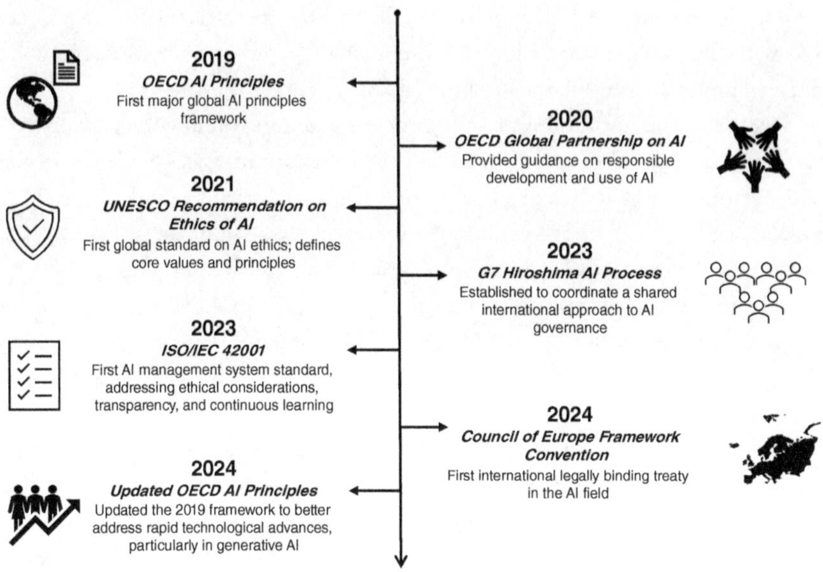

Figure 2.3 Timeline of international AI policy developments.

Source: © BAIE Research Team, 2026.

From Principles to Practice

The first phase of international AI governance was defined by principles. Organizations such as the OECD and United Nations Educational, Scientific and Cultural Organization (UNESCO)[9] articulated values-based frameworks intended to guide both public policy and responsible AI use by commercial enterprises. These principles were designed to travel across jurisdictions and political systems. They emphasized human-centered AI. Accountability for outcomes was also a central concern. Multilateral declarations and regional adoption protocols extended these principles beyond their original institutions. As governments began referencing them in national AI strategies, the principles began to shape policy and practice.

The next phase marked a shift toward implementation. International bodies began issuing guidance that moved beyond values and into implementation. The Council of Europe provided detailed recommendations on the human rights impacts of algorithmic systems,[10] addressing not only member states but also private actors. The guidance identified concrete practices, including transparency in public sector algorithm use and consultation with affected groups. Other initiatives were designed to influence business practices. The Global Partnership on Artificial Intelligence was established in 2020 as a multistakeholder forum focused on translating ethical commitments into operations.[11] Its mandate centers on applied research and implementation support, together with shared learning. I have interacted with the Global Partnership and attended a session for its constituents who are truly committed to sustained responsible AI practices.

Sector-specific institutions provide concrete examples of how international AI governance progressed from values-based principles into practical guidance. In the health sector, the World Health Organization issued governance guidance in 2021 aimed at both public authorities and private developers.[12] In financial markets, the International Organization of Securities Commissions (IOSCO) examined how AI is used by intermediaries and asset managers.[13] In 2021, it outlined expectations for managing associated risks that regulators could consider adopting. These efforts reflect a broader pattern: principles at the start ultimately leading to more practical guidance.

More recently, advanced AI capabilities have accelerated this transition. In 2023, the G7 launched the Hiroshima AI Process to address risks associated with foundation models and generative systems.[14] The initiative focuses on organizational behavior rather than model legislation. It is intended to function across jurisdictions, even where national regulatory approaches diverge. This signals a maturation of international AI governance. The emphasis is no longer on merely articulating Responsible AI Principles. It is instead focused on how responsibility is actually operationalized in practice.

Standards and Capacity Building

Standards have become one of the most powerful mechanisms for converting global norms into operational expectations. Technical standards translate ethical intent into specifications that can be tested and ultimately audited. As AI adoption accelerates, standards activity has expanded accordingly. In 2018, the International Organization for Standardization/International Electrotechnical Commission (ISO/IEC) established a dedicated subcommittee to address AI across its life cycle and the entire ecosystem.[15] The scope of this work includes developing foundational terminology and testing approaches. The pace of development reflects the urgency of standardization as AI systems gain wider adoption across industries. A notable milestone occurred in December 2023 with the introduction of an AI management system standard.[16] ISO/IEC 42001 is designed to help organizations establish structured processes for managing AI-related risks and responsibilities. It is framed as applicable to entities that develop AI systems as well as those that deploy them.

Setting industry standards is not limited to ISO and IEC. In 2021, the IEEE Standards Association published process-oriented standards that focus on embedding ethical considerations into AI system design.[17] These standards are intended to be integrated into development life cycles rather than treated as external checks. Their influence lies in shaping how organizations internalize responsibility during design decisions.

In this context, sectoral guidance functions as an implementation tool, supporting deployment in domains with distinct risk profiles and operational constraints. Health authorities have issued additional guidance addressing large multimodal models, reflecting concerns unique to emerging capabilities in that sector. Regional organizations have also moved toward practical tools. In 2024, the Association of Southeast Asian Nations (ASEAN) published an AI governance and ethics guide designed for voluntary adoption.[18] A year later, it expanded the guidance to address generative AI.[19] These efforts demonstrate responsiveness to technological change rather than static rulemaking.

Capacity building has become a defining feature of recent international initiatives. United Nations resolutions now emphasize international cooperation.[20] They also support countries with limited regulatory or technical capacity. Regional strategies, such as those developed by the African Union, position AI governance as part of broader development objectives.[21]

Despite the increasing global activity, binding international instruments remain rare. The first international framework convention drafted by the Council of Europe represents an early attempt to formalize obligations at the global level.[22] However, its limited ratification underscores a persistent reality.[23] Most international AI governance still operates through influence rather than direct enforcement.

A Brief Note on Trustworthy and Responsible AI Principles

Trustworthy and Responsible AI Principles continue to anchor the international AI governance landscape. They provide the normative foundation on which implementation instruments are built. While formulations vary across institutions, the role of these principles has become more focused. UNESCO positions its 2021 ethics recommendation as a global reference grounded in human rights. It emphasizes safety and transparency. Public understanding of AI is also a core concern. The OECD, however, bases its 2019 principles on democratic values and accountability, pairing them with policy guidance for governments. Both approaches have shaped national strategies and informed later regulatory development.

In the United States, the NIST AI Risk Management Framework, mentioned previously, articulates characteristics of trustworthy AI in a form designed for immediate organizational use. Its emphasis on reliability and safety reflects a practical orientation. Accountability is addressed through governance and risk management expectations. In Europe, the ethics guidelines developed by the High-Level Expert Group influenced subsequent legislative approaches, even though the principles themselves were not directly codified.[24] Across institutions, the language differs. The direction does not. Principles were never the end state of international AI governance. They are the starting point. The next section examines how these principles are reflected in emerging global AI regulatory approaches.

In May 2026, Pope Leo XIV's encyclical *Magnifica Humanitas* added a significant moral voice to the AI governance discussions, calling for "adequate regulatory tools capable of upholding justice" while warning that the concentration of technological power in private, transnational firms makes it "even more challenging to discern, govern and direct such power toward the common good." The document's central claim, that technology "takes on the characteristics of those who devise, finance, regulate and use it," reflects the same governance tensions examined throughout this chapter.[25]

Global AI Regulation Landscape: Diverging Philosophies

Across major jurisdictions, AI regulation is converging on a shared idea: AI is now a public policy domain as much as it is a commercial capability. That convergence, however, does not produce uniform rules. It produces different regulatory models that reflect distinctive national values and divergent views about risk and state authority.

Two patterns now define the global landscape. The first is divergence in governance philosophy, even when governments use similar labels such as *high risk* or *trustworthy*. The second is the spillover effect, when a rule that begins in one jurisdiction influences outcomes in others through adoption or indirect market effects. The sections that follow examine how these dynamics play out in practice through key AI regulatory approaches in the United States, the European Union, and China, which are the largest economies in the world and are often viewed as the most impactful players in the AI field. I also examine other select jurisdictions that have demonstrated sustained policy engagement aimed at encouraging AI development and adoption.

United States

The United States does not regulate AI through a single national framework. Instead, policy emerges through a mixture of federal and state actions. This federal-state division reflects the constitutional division of regulatory authority in the United States, where federal law sets national baselines while states retain primary authority over many areas of economic activity, public welfare, and civil rights. As a result, AI governance in the United States emerges through overlapping layers of federal coordination and state-level enforcement rather than a single, centralized regulatory regime.

Against this backdrop, AI policy within the United States is grounded in four elements: (1) existing non-AI-specific laws, (2) EOs and voluntary standards, (3) industry-specific AI regulation, and (4) regulatory actions in the US states.

Existing Non-AI-Specific Laws

As discussed previously in this chapter, in the context of formal rulemaking through hard law, existing federal statutes continue to apply to AI systems even though they were not written with AI in mind. The Civil Rights Act of 1964, for example, prohibits discriminatory outcomes in employment and public accommodations,[26] while the Fair Housing Act of 1968 prohibits discrimination in housing.[27] Courts and enforcement agencies have applied these protections when automated decision systems produce biased results, making civil rights compliance a practical obligation for many AI programs.[28]

EOs and Voluntary Standards

Federal AI policy has moved in distinct waves, shaped by shifting administrations. In February 2019, President Trump issued EO 13859, titled "Maintaining American

Leadership in Artificial Intelligence," which launched the American AI Initiative.[29] It framed US leadership in AI as a strategic imperative specifically tied to economic competitiveness and national security. It pushed for increased investment and the removal of barriers to adoption. In October 2023, President Biden issued EO 14110, titled "Safe, Secure, and Trustworthy Development and Use of Artificial Intelligence."[30] This EO marked a more precautionary posture and positioned the federal government as a more active participant in shaping guardrails. It also directed workstreams across agencies that would influence federal government procurement practice and testing expectations.

This emphasis on voluntary standards is important because it shapes industry behavior. As mentioned, the NIST AI Risk Management Framework, released in January 2023, gave companies a shared vocabulary for AI risk.[31] It was not binding law, but it became a widely referenced baseline. In late 2023, the Department of Commerce also launched the US AI Safety Institute to support implementation of EO 14110, with an emphasis on safety testing and evaluation.[32]

On January 23, 2025, President Trump issued EO 14179, titled "Removing Barriers to American Leadership in Artificial Intelligence."[33] It revoked prior federal AI policy, issued by President Biden, that the Trump administration framed as restrictive. It reset federal posture toward deregulation and accelerated AI adoption. In July 2025, that posture was reinforced through "Winning the AI Race: America's AI Action Plan."[34] This plan framed AI innovation as an economic and national security imperative, tying competitiveness to infrastructure and international posture. The Action Plan also aligned with a broader narrative that the United States should remove friction in AI development and adoption rather than add constraints on the business community.

That trajectory culminated in a direct confrontation with state activity. On December 11, 2025, President Trump issued an EO titled "Ensuring a National Policy Framework for Artificial Intelligence."[35] Its core objective was to curb state-by-state AI regulation in favor of a unified national posture. It directed the US Attorney General to establish an AI Litigation Task Force to challenge certain state AI laws. It also directed an evaluation of state laws for potential restrictions tied to federal funding, arguing that state regulation could obstruct national objectives for AI leadership and adoption. The EO also directed the development of uniform federal AI regulation (more on this later).

Following the December 2025 EO, in March 2026 the White House released legislative recommendations titled "A National Policy Framework for Artificial Intelligence," which further clarified the administration's approach to AI policy.[36] Section VII of the policy framework translates the Trump administration's earlier EO into proposed congressional action, emphasizing a national standard designed to avoid what it characterizes as a fragmented patchwork of state regulation.

It explicitly recommends federal preemption of state AI laws that impose "undue burdens," while preserving limited areas of state authority such as general consumer protection and state use of AI systems. At the same time, the framework reinforces a deregulatory posture, calling for the avoidance of new federal rulemaking bodies and instead relying on existing agencies and industry-led standards to govern AI deployment. Section V of the policy framework also promotes regulatory sandboxes, expanded access to federal datasets, and accelerated infrastructure buildout as mechanisms to support innovation and maintain US AI leadership.

Since 2025, the United States has seen a surge of federal AI policy activity, much of it laying groundwork for future developments rather than representing definitive policy endpoints. Further developments are likely, either extending the trajectory established by prior policy documents (as with the legislative recommendations discussed previously) or responding to significant technological breakthroughs. The latter dynamic was on display when Anthropic unveiled its Claude Mythos model, prompting the EO "Promoting Advanced Artificial Intelligence Innovation and Security," which established a voluntary review process for frontier models.[37] The turbulent history of that EO, including the scrapping of an initial draft shortly before signing and subsequent relaxation of its requirements,[38] illustrates the difficulty of simultaneously accelerating innovation, maintaining a competitive edge over China, and strengthening security.

Industry-Specific AI Regulation

Separate from the industry-agnostic EOs and voluntary standards already discussed, binding federal oversight of AI also emerges through industry-specific regulatory regimes administered by federal agencies. A clear example appears in healthcare, where the U.S. Food and Drug Administration (FDA) regulates AI and machine learning–enabled medical devices under its existing authority in the Federal Food, Drug, and Cosmetic Act.[39] The FDA treats qualifying AI systems as regulated medical products and has issued guidance that addresses issues specific to adaptive algorithms, including ongoing performance monitoring and risk management as models evolve. In practice, this approach functions as an AI-specific regulatory regime for the healthcare sector, shaping how AI systems are developed and assessed for clinical use. In parallel with these federal approaches, US states have moved aggressively to regulate AI through statutes and enforcement actions within their traditional areas of authority.

Regulatory Actions in the US States

The number of AI-related bills enacted in the US states is rising (see Figure 2.4).[40] Colorado provides one of the most significant examples of state-level AI regulation enacted to date: the Act Concerning Consumer Protections in Interactions with

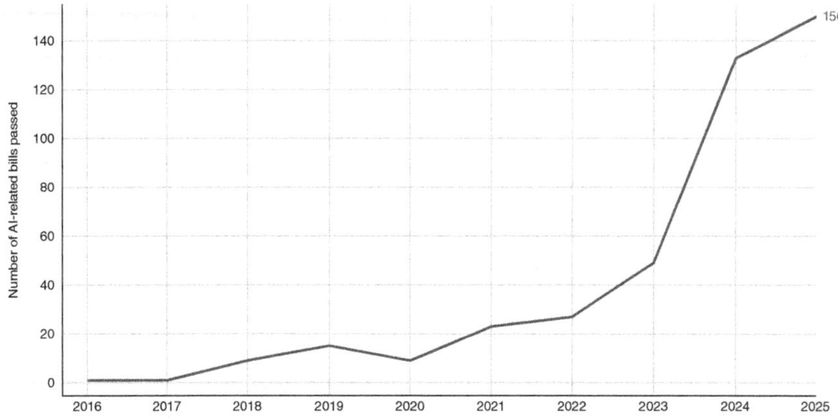

Figure 2.4 Number of AI-related bills passed into law by all US states, 2016–2025.

Source: AI Index, 2026 | Chart: 2026 AI Index report, Stanford HAI.

Artificial Intelligence Systems, targets high-risk AI systems used in consequential decisions.[41] It focuses on preventing algorithmic discrimination and pushes firms toward proactive assessment rather than after-the-fact enforcement. California illustrates how a single state can shape national practices through privacy law. The California Consumer Privacy Act (CCPA),[42] strengthened by the California Privacy Rights Act (CPRA),[43] has become a normative model for many companies in the absence of a federal privacy statute. The California model affects AI training data and model functionality. California has also moved toward frontier model transparency through its Transparency in Frontier Artificial Intelligence Act.[44] That reflects a view that some AI risk originates at model development, not only at deployment.

Other state and local actions reinforce that AI regulation in the United States is concentrated where systems touch hiring, consumer interaction, or public integrity. New York City's Local Law 144 normalized bias audits and disclosures for automated employment decision tools.[45] Utah's Artificial Intelligence Policy Act established disclosure requirements for consumer-facing generative AI in certain contexts.[46] Illinois's biometric privacy regime operates as regulation through enforcement, shaping national design choices for biometric AI systems.[47]

For business leaders, this layered US AI policy landscape structure creates regulatory uncertainty that affects enterprise planning and execution. State requirements continue to expand. At the same time, federal action may limit or challenge those requirements. The potential for litigation challenging state AI regulation adds another area of unpredictability. In the near term, companies must operate inside the patchwork of state regulation (which has become the most operationally consequential feature of AI regulation in the United States). States have not tried to regulate AI as an abstract category. They have concentrated on contexts where AI directly affects its residents, including high-stakes decisions involving identity, voice, likeness, and elections. Companies also operate under the shadow of federal intervention that seeks to narrow states' rights.

As of this writing, the future direction of AI regulation in the United States remains unsettled. The practical impact of the December 2025 national AI policy EO has yet to be felt. It is therefore unclear which existing state and local AI regulations will remain in force and which may be challenged or preempted. Until that picture becomes clearer, companies will continue to operate within a fragmented compliance environment across the US states. In response, many commercial enterprises may choose to adopt a normative compliance model designed to comply with multiple state regimes. This approach contrasts sharply with the regulatory structure emerging in the European Union, where AI governance has been organized through a single, comprehensive legislative framework.

European Union

The European Union has adopted the most comprehensive binding framework for AI to date, structured on fundamental rights and designed to apply beyond EU borders to any organization that places AI systems in the EU market or deploys them within the European Union. The AI Act[48] entered into force on August 1, 2024, but it will become enforceable gradually. The Act's prohibitions on certain unacceptable risk practices became legally binding as of February 2, 2025. On that date, organizations assumed an obligation to ensure a baseline level of AI literacy among relevant personnel and users interacting with systems covered by the law. Effective as of August 2, 2025, the Act also establishes obligations for providers of general purpose AI models, requiring documentation of model development, summaries of training data, and implementation of policies to ensure compliance with EU copyright law, with additional risk management and reporting requirements for models deemed to pose systemic risk. The AI risk management requirements for high-risk AI system developers and deployers are currently scheduled to enter into force on August 2, 2026. However, at the end of 2025, the European Commission proposed amendments to the EU AI Act as part of the Digital Omnibus package, aiming to simplify its application and potentially delay the implementation of these requirements until the end of 2027.[49] On May 6, 2026, EU institutions reached a political agreement on simplifying the EU AI Act to boost innovation, including extending compliance timelines for high-risk systems and redistributing AI literacy obligations between private organizations and public authorities at both the EU and national levels. This represents a significant milestone in the legislative process, though at the time of writing, the Digital Omnibus amendments had not yet been formally adopted into law. The agreement also added a new prohibition, targeting so-called nudifier apps that generate nonconsensual intimate images of real individuals, further illustrating how the legislative process responds to emerging technological harms.[50]

EU institutions have begun adjusting their posture in response to competitiveness concerns. The "Draghi Report," released in September 2024, cautioned that the AI compliance burden could slow innovation, particularly for smaller firms.[51] The European Commission's Competitiveness Compass, issued in January 2025, signaled a simplification effort and an implementation approach intended to reduce administrative and compliance friction.[52] InvestAI, launched in February 2025, reflected a parallel strategy of pairing regulatory obligations with public investment in AI infrastructure.[53] The AI Pact has operated as a bridge mechanism, allowing participating companies to commit to early alignment with key requirements ahead of full enforcement.[54]

For multinational firms, the European Union's practical impact often precedes formal enforcement. Extraterritorial scope pushes suppliers, deployers, and distributors to map AI systems to EU categories even when the enterprise is headquartered elsewhere. It also pushes cross-border standardization, because a firm rarely wants one control posture in the European Union and a weaker posture everywhere else.

China

China's AI governance approach combines industrial policy with direct state oversight. The objective is alignment between AI development and state priorities, including social stability and strategic competitiveness. China's 2017 New Generation Artificial Intelligence Development Plan framed AI as a national growth engine with staged ambition.[55] The plan positioned AI as a national development priority by 2020 and set expectations for major advances by 2025. Global leadership was framed as a longer-term objective extending to 2030.

Recent developments illustrate China's significant AI advances. A Chinese developer, DeepSeek, in January 2025 introduced a large language model designed to materially reduce usage costs, underscoring how technical advancement and state-influenced ecosystems can reinforce one another in China's AI landscape.[56]

China's more recent regulatory activity has focused on generative AI systems and content governance. In 2023 and 2024, the Cyberspace Administration of China released draft rules mandating security assessments and content moderation for generative AI, including requirements related to traceability.[57] The Personal Information Protection Law, enacted in 2021, formalized individual data rights while maintaining strong authority over data access and use.[58] These instruments operate within a broader system where regulatory compliance is assessed not only on technical grounds but also on alignment with political and policy objectives.

For multinationals, China introduces a distinct cross-border challenge. Firms often encounter requirements that conflict with transparency expectations in other jurisdictions or with internal governance models that assume greater individual autonomy. Compliance obligations also intersect with geopolitical pressures, including export controls and supply chain constraints that can limit access to advanced chips and computing capacity.

AI Policy in Other Jurisdictions: Emerging Approaches

Outside the major blocs, many jurisdictions are shaping AI governance through sector-specific regulation and policy instruments that rely on voluntary compliance. These models still matter to business leaders, because they can influence procurement expectations and contractual norms.

The United Kingdom has emphasized regulatory agility and sector oversight rather than a single AI statute. Its "AI Regulation" White Paper, published in 2023, reinforced that posture.[59] In 2025, the government extended the same approach through the AI Opportunities Action Plan,[60] while also issuing an "Artificial Intelligence Playbook for the UK Government" to guide public sector implementation.[61]

Japan has taken a different approach. In early 2025, an interim policy report signaled movement away from comprehensive legislative controls, and it emphasized voluntary business-led governance supported by government tools.[62] That approach reflects a preference for facilitation and places primary responsibility on firms rather than on prescriptive legislative controls. This orientation was further reinforced in Japan's "Artificial Intelligence Basic Plan," published in December 2025, which positions the country as aiming to become "the most AI-friendly country in the world" through a strategy centered on accelerating AI utilization across society, strengthening development capabilities, and promoting "trustworthy AI."[63]

India has leaned into digital public infrastructure as a strategy for scalable AI-enabled services. A national digital identity layer was established by the Unique Identification Authority of India through Aadhaar, a digital identification system, while the Unified Payments Interface provided payments infrastructure that supports digital inclusion. These components were later integrated into what is referred to as the *India Stack*, which enables consent-based data sharing across a wide range of services.[64] India has also supported pilot programs that apply AI to public service delivery, including health sector initiatives such as Wadhwani AI, which is testing AI tools to assist frontline health workers.[65]

Taken together, these jurisdictions amplify the spillover effect. A company may encounter EU-style compliance pressure through enterprise customer contracts, while procurement language can reflect UK regulatory expectations. In other cases, partnerships tied to public digital systems require alignment with India's infrastructure-driven approach.

Cross-Border AI Policy and Law Challenges for Businesses

For companies deploying AI systems in more than one jurisdiction, regulatory differences surface early in implementation. Decisions about system configuration and internal responsibility are often made before legal requirements are consistent across markets. This creates a familiar but intensifying challenge: the cost of complying with multiple legal regimes, now compounded by a policy landscape that continues to evolve in real time.

One recurring challenge involves jurisdictional reach. Some regulatory regimes attach obligations based on where an AI system is deployed. Others apply based on market impact or the location of affected stakeholders. A single AI system can therefore trigger multiple legal regimes at once, even when it is developed and operated from a centralized platform. This reality complicates compliance planning and often slows decisions about system scaling or entering new markets.

Another source of complexity arises from definitional differences. What one jurisdiction classifies as "high risk" may not align with how risk is categorized elsewhere. Disclosure obligations vary across regimes, as do expectations around audits and supporting documentation. As a result, firms are often forced to decide whether to maintain jurisdiction-specific controls or to adopt a normative model that exceeds local requirements in some markets.

Data governance further intensifies these challenges. Some jurisdictions impose restrictions on cross-border data transfers, while others allow transfers subject to contractual safeguards or regulatory review. These conditions influence how training data is sourced and how models are updated over time. They also affect infrastructure decisions, particularly when cloud environments span multiple regions.

Differences in enforcement add another layer of uncertainty. In some jurisdictions, regulators emphasize advance approval or conformity assessment before deployment. In others, oversight is exercised primarily through investigations after harm or failure has occurred. This distinction alters how organizations assess risk and shapes how quickly they can respond when issues emerge. It also affects exposure to cross-border litigation, which can be costly and difficult to predict.

Cross-border spillover amplifies each of these pressures. Requirements adopted in one jurisdiction can become operationally global when a major customer or partner demands compliance. Procurement language and platform policies often move faster than formal regulation. As a result, companies may encounter regulatory pressure even in markets where AI-specific laws remain limited.

Taken together, these dynamics change how businesses approach AI development. Cross-border policy risk now functions as a design constraint that must be considered early in the development life cycle. Organizations must not only manage differences across jurisdictions but also continuously monitor legal developments as rules evolve, increasing both cost and operational complexity over time.

Closing

This chapter demonstrated that global AI policy now reaches enterprises through multiple channels, simultaneously. Governments act through binding law, voluntary standards contributions, procurement rules, tax and other incentives, and sector-specific guidelines. These tools operate across jurisdictions that do not align, requiring organizations to make AI system design and deployment decisions before regulatory expectations stabilize.

For the many organizations affected by government AI policies, this creates a set of practical challenges. The first is cost. Operating across jurisdictions requires firms to comply with multiple legal regimes at the same time. The European Union has adopted a comprehensive legislative framework with extraterritorial reach, while the United States relies on a layered system of federal coordination and state enforcement. China integrates AI into broader public/private systems. Each approach carries distinct compliance expectations, and together they increase the cost of deploying AI solutions.

The second challenge is uncertainty. Legal frameworks continue to evolve, and compliance expectations remain settled. Some jurisdictions rely on sector oversight and voluntary alignment, which can shift with additional government guidance and enforcement mechanisms. As a result, something that is acceptable today may be restricted tomorrow. It is imperative that organizations monitor AI policy developments continuously and adjust their practices as policy evolves.

The third challenge is compliance exposure. Differences in government enforcement create uneven risk across markets. Some jurisdictions emphasize advance approval, while others rely on enforcement after harm occurs. Cross-border litigation adds further unpredictability and can be costly to manage. Spillover effects amplify this exposure when requirements from one jurisdiction extend into others.

Taken together, these challenges change how organizations approach AI. Global AI policies shape system design from the outset and require ongoing attention as conditions evolve. The chapters that follow turn from public policy to enterprise response. They examine how organizations design strategies and internal governance frameworks to manage AI risk in this fragmented and dynamic environment.

PART II

Power and Consequence: Strategy, Risk, and Fiduciary Oversight

3 Strategic Deployment

AI Has Moved into the Core of Enterprise Strategy

Artificial intelligence (AI) has shifted from the margins of the enterprise, oftentimes beginning with experimentation, progressing to the center of strategic decision-making. In an increasing number of organizations, AI now influences how new business models, products, and services are designed and how customers are served. However, despite this growing dependence on AI in the modern business enterprise, formulating a company's AI strategy is still too often treated as a technology-centric planning exercise rather than as a core leadership responsibility. Many businesses are beginning to catch up, but this shift remains uneven. This chapter begins from a different premise. Setting AI strategy is an enterprise discipline that belongs squarely in the domain of senior leadership.

The central argument of this chapter is simple. Organizations do not experience AI outcomes through models or algorithms alone. They experience them through strategic choices across several topics. Leadership makes several strategic decisions long before governance frameworks or ethical guidelines are invoked. One decision concerns why the organization believes AI is necessary in the first place. Another concerns where AI will be applied, whether inside the enterprise or in customer-facing systems. A third concern reflects how the AI program will be organized within the company. A final decision concerns how benefits from AI will be achieved by the enterprise. These choices are shaped by both competitor behavior and the organization's risk appetite. When AI initiatives fail or when they create unanticipated harm to the enterprise or society at large, the root cause is not typically a defect in the technology, but instead a failure of strategy.

This chapter introduces IPACER as the organizing framework for establishing a sound AI strategy at the enterprise level. IPACER is grounded in the premise that effective AI strategy rests on six foundational elements: **I**ntent, **P**ositioning, **A**rchitecture, **C**apabilities, **E**xecution, and **R**esilience (see Figure 3.1). It is important to note that these are six universal elements of corporate strategy. I'm certainly not the first to articulate these elements as core to a company's strategy. If you are interested in a well-balanced AI strategy for your organization, then these elements are not optional, and they do not operate independently. Weakness in any one domain constrains the effectiveness of the others. For example, establishing clear Intent about why the organization is pursuing an AI program without the Capabilities to execute will create an inordinate amount of frustration. When organizations build advanced AI platforms without clear choices about where to deploy them, the result is usually too many projects and not enough impact. Speed matters, but without sustained leadership attention to each element of the IPACER Framework, AI strategy rarely reaches its full potential.

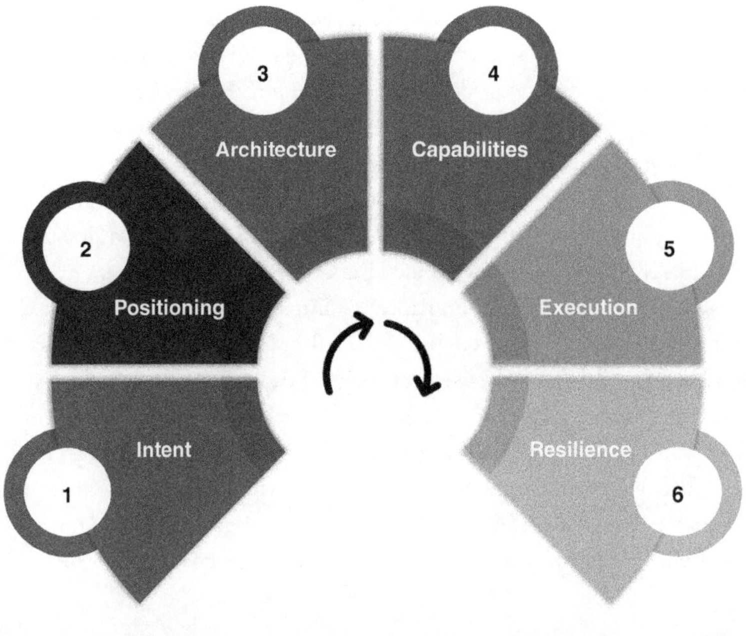

Figure 3.1 IPACER: Six-part AI strategy framework.

A defining feature of the IPACER Framework is that it follows the sequence in which leaders typically confront AI decisions. Strategic choices are addressed first. The structure of this book reflects that reality. Addressing strategy up front in this work is not an affront on corporate governance or the ethical responsibilities of company leadership. It is instead an acknowledgment of how organizations actually operate. I learned early in my career the importance of establishing enterprise "strategy before structure." It is no different in the AI domain.

The IPACER Framework is designed to surface those strategic choices earlier, at the point where they can still be shaped. It forces leaders to confront critical trade-offs before AI initiatives harden into operational reality. It asks executives to articulate not only what they want AI to do but also what they are willing to tolerate when AI systems behave in unexpected ways (we'll return to this need to determine the enterprise Boundaries of Tolerance in later chapters). In this sense, strategy becomes the first line of ethical defense.

To make these dynamics tangible, the chapter relies on real stories from Netflix, Adobe, and JPMorgan Chase to support the concepts and frameworks discussed. These stories are not presented as exhaustive case studies or as claims of best practice. They are moments where strategic Intent, Positioning, and design choices become *visible* through tangible outcomes. Some of these stories illustrate disciplined alignment across the organization. Others reveal early warning signals that leadership either recognized or missed. Together, they ground the IPACER Framework in the strategic realities leaders face when AI becomes consequential to the enterprise.

Finally, this chapter sets clear expectations for you. The focus here is not on how models are trained or evaluated. Those technical details matter, but they are not the source of most strategic failures or the subject of this book. The focus is on the strategic questions and topics leaders need to appropriately address for a robust AI program.

Framing the Enterprise AI Strategy Challenge

In discussions about enterprise AI strategy, leaders often ask what successful deployment actually looks like, searching for best practices from within or outside their sector. The question is usually framed in terms of key strategic inflection points or capability needs. One of the clearest illustrations of what such a deliberate approach to AI strategy can look like comes from Adobe.

How Adobe Integrated Generative AI into Enterprise Strategy

Adobe did not enter generative AI (GenAI) territory by treating it as an isolated innovation initiative or a detached technical research effort. Instead, it introduced AI as a natural extension of how the company already understood its role in the creative ecosystem. From the outset, Adobe positioned AI as a means of supporting creative professionals rather than replacing them. This distinction emerged as a foundational element of Adobe's AI strategy and shaped how AI was introduced to customers and embedded into existing and new products.

When Adobe launched Firefly, its family of GenAI models, the company emphasized that these tools were designed to assist with a human creator's up-front ideation and associated workflow efficiencies. Adobe described Firefly as a way to help creators move faster while remaining in control of the creative process. This framing was reinforced by Adobe's decision to integrate GenAI capabilities directly into products such as Photoshop and Illustrator, rather than Positioning them as separate or experimental offerings. AI was presented as a critical component of the core product experience.

Equally important was the *sequence* of Adobe's decisions. Before extending GenAI across its product portfolio, Adobe articulated boundaries for how its AI models would be trained and deployed. The company publicly committed to training Firefly on licensed content, Adobe's own intellectual property, and information available in the public domain. It also stated that customer content would *not* be used for training without permission.[1] These choices reflected strategic judgments about Adobe's relationship with its customers and the trust that relationship requires.[2]

The broader lesson from Adobe's experience is not that every organization should replicate this approach in its entirety. It is that AI adoption does not need to race ahead of strategic clarity. Under competitive pressure, many enterprises deploy AI tools quickly and confront fundamental questions later about solution scope and resulting risk exposure. Adobe's example demonstrates that when these strategic choices are addressed early, while they remain design decisions, organizations preserve the trust of customers who expect these systems to operate responsibly.

Strategy for a Versatile Technology

This story also highlights a recurring issue across industries. Companies are not deploying a single form of AI; they are deploying a range of systems that differ across many variables. Consider, for example, in the GenAI context, variables such as user type (e.g., internal or customer), medium (e.g., text, video, or audio), and the role that AI plays in the decisions aligned to that particular solution (e.g., advisor, recommender, or autonomous actor). Treating all of these applications as equivalent misses critical nuances that should define a company's enterprise AI strategy. Simply put, AI capabilities are grounding many different types of AI applications that demand strategic nuance in how they are designed, developed, and ultimately deployed.

In practice, based on my experience advising companies across industries, the greatest obstacles to effective AI strategy are rarely technical in nature. Many organizations remain uncertain about where AI should be applied or which initiatives deserve priority. Internal teams often resist changes to established roles as AI capabilities advance and adoption spreads across the enterprise. Leaders also struggle to align innovation ambitions with operational realities, particularly when new AI initiatives introduce unfamiliar risks. These are the leadership challenges that are defining today's business executive.

IPACER: A Leadership Framework for AI Strategy

The IPACER Framework emerged from repeated exposure to the same problem across organizations and their leadership teams, including corporate boards and senior executives. As AI adoption accelerated during the 2023–2026 time frame, I saw many companies investing heavily in AI system development and talent while struggling to articulate a coherent strategy that leaders and their teams could align on to drive innovation and growth initiatives. Decisions were being made, often quickly, but rarely in strategic sequence. Governance teams were asked to manage risks that arose not only from internal decisions but also from the rapid evolution of the surrounding technology and market environment. The result was frustration on all sides. What was missing was a shared strategic framework that leaders could use to guide AI programs before early decisions became operational.

The IPACER Framework is an attempt to fill that gap. It is a leadership model designed to help professionals think clearly about AI strategy under the conditions of uncertainty that dominate today's AI landscape. The framework does not assume that AI adoption follows a linear path (we know, of course, that it does not). It recognizes that strategy unfolds through several inflection points, choices that interact with one another over time. Most importantly, it treats AI strategy as a critical leadership responsibility.

The framework is composed of six elements. Each represents a category of decisions that leaders must ultimately confront in their design of a leading enterprise AI strategy:

- **Intent** addresses *why* the organization is pursuing AI initiatives in the first place.
- **Positioning** focuses on *where* AI should be applied and deployed, and the other corresponding, important question, where it should not.

- **Architecture** considers *how* AI solutions are developed and managed across the enterprise.
- **Capabilities** address whether the organization has the resources to execute its strategy responsibly at scale.
- **Execution** examines *how* ideas move from a slide deck to institutional reality.
- **Resilience** focuses on *how* strategy adapts as conditions change.

IPACER is not a maturity model, and it is definitely not a checklist. It is a way of structuring leadership conversations to address the six most prevalent strategy factors relevant in today's successful AI programs. To ensure that the framework remains practical, each element is examined through the same analytical lens.

The sections that follow introduce the IPACER Framework in detail as the core model of a sound enterprise AI strategy. Each element is examined through a consistent analytical lens that begins with the leadership question it addresses and then turns to the concrete strategic choices leaders must make about direction and execution. The discussion concludes by connecting each element to its implications across risk, governance, and ethics. This structure reflects what I have seen repeatedly in practice. Risk exposure and governance breakdowns are rarely the result of isolated technical failures. They are the downstream consequence of earlier strategy decisions that were never fully surfaced or appropriately debated within the enterprise. By applying the same lens consistently across all six elements, the IPACER Framework helps teams address the most important questions that should drive the enterprise AI strategy.

In the sections that follow, the IPACER Framework is applied element by element to enterprise AI strategy. The discussion begins with Intent, because without clarity about *why* AI is being pursued, every other strategic element becomes much harder (or even impossible) to adequately address.

I: Intent

> **The leadership question:** Why does this organization believe AI is necessary to its future?

Strategic Levers

Every AI strategy begins with Intent, whether that Intent is expressly articulated or not. Leaders may believe they are deliberately postponing the important question of *why* AI is being pursued, but in practice the organization passively answers it anyway. It answers this critical question through investment decisions, pilot approvals, hiring priorities, and the use cases that quietly move forward while others stall.

Strategic Intent is unfolding against a backdrop of significant capital commitment.

According to the Stanford Institute for Human-Centered Artificial Intelligence "Index Report 2025," global corporate investment in AI has exceeded $200 billion in each of the past five years. In 2024 alone, corporate AI investment reached approximately $252.3 billion,[3] reinforcing that AI is no longer treated as an experimental technology, but instead as a core enterprise investment category. This level of spending helps explain why many leadership teams feel pressure to act, even when strategic Intent has not yet been fully articulated. Executive sentiment reflects this same momentum. In its "The State of AI in 2025" report, McKinsey finds that 64% of survey respondents say AI is already enabling their organization's innovation efforts.[4]

In my work with companies across many industries, I have observed four recurring motives that drive AI adoption. Most organizations pursue more than one, but problems arise when leadership teams fail to recognize which motive is dominant. The motives that follow serve as reference points that help leadership teams clarify the underlying purpose behind AI adoption within their organization.

- **Macroeconomic pressures.** In some cases, AI pursuits are driven by macroeconomic pressures. The productivity argument for AI adoption is also supported by recent empirical research. A study by Anthropic, based on large-scale analysis of how knowledge workers use its Claude models in real work settings, estimates that GenAI could increase annual US labor productivity growth by approximately 1.8% by 2035. It is important to note that the projected gains are not uniform across tasks or roles; these gains are expected to be concentrated in technology, education, and professional services, while retail, restaurants, and transportation sectors would see minimal impact.[5] For many organizations, this finding reinforces the belief that AI adoption is no longer optional, even if leaders remain uncertain about how those productivity gains should translate into strategy and investment priorities within the enterprise.
- **Organizational purpose alignment.** In other organizations, AI is pursued as an extension of enterprise purpose. Leaders ask whether AI reinforces what the organization already publicly stands for. They test proposed AI use cases against brand commitments and stakeholder expectations. This does not eliminate risk, but it does create greater consistency. Teams have clearer guidance about what is acceptable, which reduces internal debate and downstream confusion.

- **Competitive differentiation.** A third motive centers on competitive differentiation. AI is viewed as a way to create new customer-facing offerings. In other cases, leaders pursue AI initiatives to redefine the customer experience or introduce new business models. This can be a powerful driver of innovation, but it also creates pressure to move quickly in response to competitor offerings. Without a disciplined approach, companies tend to imitate other industry offerings with only slight product differences.
- **Cost containment.** Finally, many organizations pursue AI for cost containment. Automation promises margin improvement and operational efficiency. When this motive dominates, AI is often framed internally as an opportunity to automate redundant tasks but can create a fear of job replacement. Employees become cautious, adoption slows, and if organizations aren't careful, trust erodes.

Let's return to Adobe's AI strategy, providing a useful illustration of how deliberate strategic Intent can shape beneficial outcomes. Adobe framed AI as a way to support creative professionals, *not* to replace them. This was not a marketing slogan; it instead informed Adobe's stakeholders how AI was introduced as a human enabler, but with important boundaries. By positioning AI as human augmentation, Adobe reduced uncertainty for its customers and its workers. Product decisions and ethically aligned governance mechanisms followed from that Intent.

The significance of this *sequence* may be easy to miss. Adobe certainty did not eliminate ethical risk, but it did create greater clarity and reduce ambiguity. Teams knew what they were optimizing for: ways to improve their very own creativity. Customers and other Adobe stakeholders understood the role AI was meant to play. That clarity made it easier to scale and govern AI capabilities without constantly returning to these foundational questions. When Intent is ambiguous, organizations struggle. Teams pursue their own goals purportedly under the same AI banner, but in practice are really promoting shadow AI programs. Governance teams are asked to resolve conflicts that emanate from poorly articulated strategy. Ethical concerns surface late, often post solution launch, causing organizations to pay catch-up and pick up the pieces from failed AI systems.

Implications for Risk, Governance, and Ethics

The tension embedded in strategic Intent is important to understand. AI offers the promise of growth (innovation) and new sources of value. At the same time, it raises questions about risk and technology governance. Ethical considerations quickly follow. Organizations that frame AI purely as an engine of innovation often underestimate the governance and reputational implications that follow. Organizations that frame AI primarily as a risk management problem often fail to capture meaningful, market-differentiated value. Intent is the mechanism that determines how this tension is navigated in practice and is therefore the earliest point at which AI risk can be significantly shaped. If Intent is misaligned, every subsequent decision is just harder; Positioning becomes inconsistent, Architecture becomes fragmented, and Execution becomes contentious.

We now turn to Positioning. If Intent explains *why* AI is being pursued, Positioning determines *where* it is applied and similarly where restraint is required.

P: Positioning

> **The leadership question:** Where does AI belong across internal functions and customer-facing offerings?

Strategic Levers

Strategic Positioning reflects leadership decisions about where AI will operate across the enterprise and where it will shape customer-facing offerings. These decisions matter because AI does not enter the enterprise as a single system or capability. Rather, it enters through many types of applications, deployed at different points in the customer value chain or aligned to internal functions, with varying implications for governance and ethics. Leaders who fail to make deliberate Positioning choices often discover that their AI strategy has been suboptimized.

Where Enterprises Are Actually Deploying AI

Before exploring how AI Positioning should work, it is important to understand how it currently unfolds in practice. McKinsey found in its report "The State of AI in 2025" that AI use has increased in nearly every industry. Current AI adoption is dominated by knowledge management (40%), marketing and sales (39%), information technology (IT) (34%), service operations (33%), and product and/or service development (31%) (see Figure 3.2).[6]

These patterns are revealing. The most common enterprise AI deployments today are not autonomous decision systems or mission critical control solutions. They are applications designed to support human work or accelerate insights.

The MIT NANDA "The State of AI in Business 2025" report discovered that despite significant enterprise investment into generative AI, "just 5% of integrated AI pilots are extracting millions in value, while the vast majority remain stuck with no measurable P&L impact."[7] This gap reflects uncertainty about where AI belongs in the enterprise and how much risk leadership is willing to absorb.

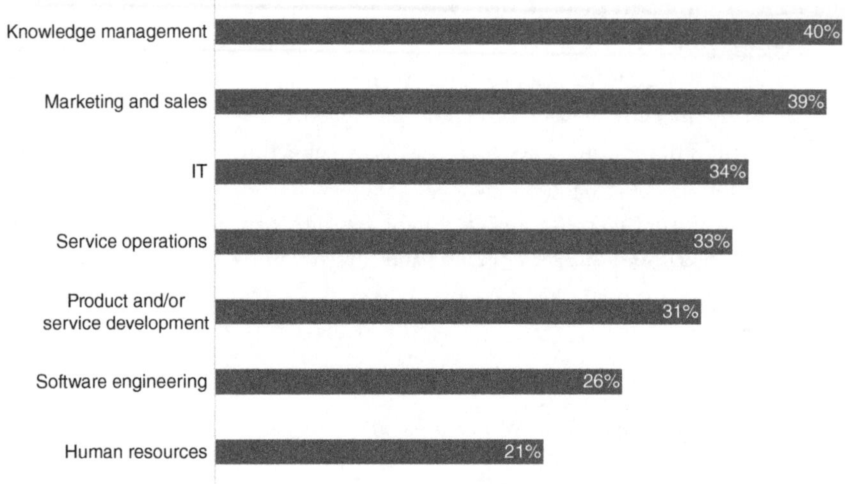

Figure 3.2 Most common AI use cases by function, 2025.

Source: QuantumBlack.AI by McKinsey, 2025 | Chart: BAIE Research Team, 2026.

Reinforcing Signals from Executive Experience

A second data source reinforces this picture. McKinsey finds that organizations are increasingly reporting tangible impact from AI at the use case level, including both cost reduction and revenue contribution. Respondents identified innovation (64%) as the primary benefit of AI adoption, followed by employee satisfaction (45%), customer satisfaction (45%), and competitive differentiation (45%) (see Figure 3.3).[8]

These findings help explain why AI portfolios continue to expand even when strategic clarity is incomplete. Leaders are beginning to see evidence of value in specific applications, which creates the opportunistic pressure to do more. Over time, this positive value momentum produces a growing set of AI initiatives that differ widely in purpose and enterprise strategy alignment. Without an explicit Positioning discipline, these portfolios become difficult to manage.

Positioning Requires Portfolio Thinking

In my experience advising companies in this space, many organizations make a critical mistake at this stage of AI adoption. In practice, I often see organizations launching AI initiatives in response to visible competitor activity without first establishing how those initiatives fit into a coherent strategy. They treat each AI use case as an isolated investment rather than as part of an integrated portfolio. Avoiding this pattern requires a different mindset; leaders must think like portfolio managers.

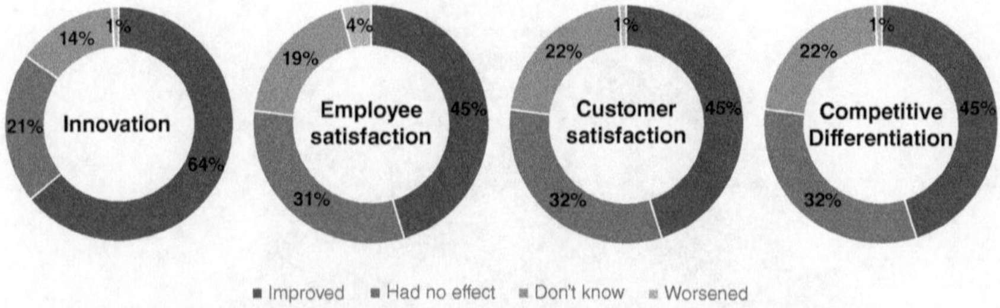

Figure 3.3 Positive benefits from AI enterprise adoption, 2025.
Source: QuantumBlack.AI by McKinsey, 2025 | Chart: BAIE Research Team, 2026.

Portfolio thinking introduces three essential considerations that I encourage leadership teams to examine. First, much like a personal investment portfolio, AI initiatives should be assessed based on expected return relative to risk exposure rather than short-term excitement. Second, initiatives should reinforce enterprise strategy and priorities. Third, leaders must also manage investments across different time horizons, recognizing that some applications optimize current performance while others prepare the organization for future market shifts. When this mindset is absent, organizations accumulate disconnected pilots that consume considerable attention (and capital) without producing a tangible advantage. In practice, these initiatives are far less likely to scale or deliver meaningful value.

Strategic Alignment Using the Gartner AI Opportunity Radar

The first step in disciplined Positioning is to build a shared map of where AI can effectively play in the enterprise. The Gartner AI Opportunity Radar (see Figure 3.4) helps leaders position AI opportunities along two simple dimensions. The vertical y axis distinguishes external, customer-facing applications from internal operations. The horizontal x axis distinguishes everyday AI that improves existing work from game-changing AI that can reshape enterprise offerings or business models.[9]

The Gartner AI Opportunity Radar creates four practical zones. In the external, everyday quadrant (top left), AI supports front-office functions such as customer service, marketing, and sales. In the external, game-changing quadrant (top right), AI drives product and service innovation through enhanced offerings and new value propositions. On the internal side, everyday AI (bottom left) targets back-office productivity in areas like finance, human resources, legal, and IT. In the internal, game-changing quadrant (bottom right), AI strengthens core operational capabilities across functions such as research and development and supply chain.

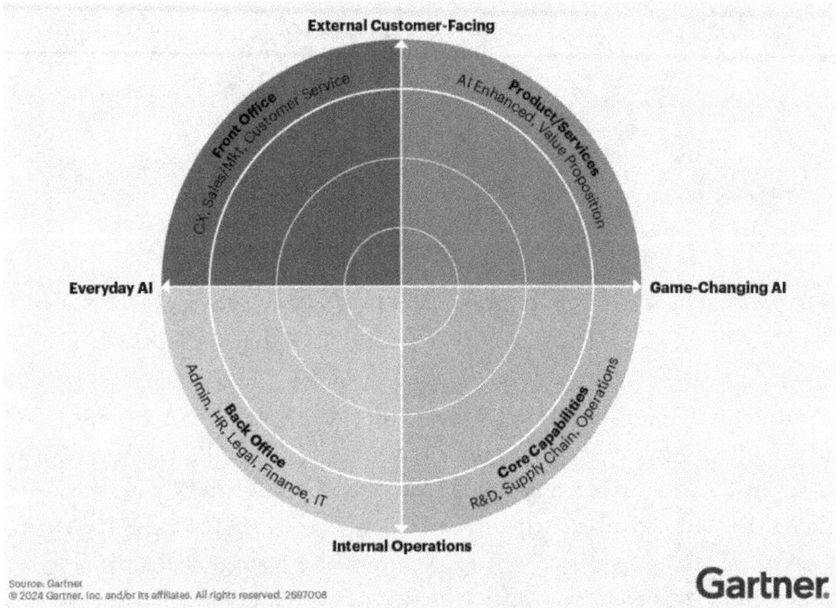

Figure 3.4 The AI opportunity radar.

Source: © Gartner, Inc., 2024.

This radar is not a scoring model or prioritization tool; it is a leadership alignment instrument. It forces clarity about where the organization is placing its AI bets and whether those bets are concentrated in the front office, the back office, incremental improvement, or more transformational change. Once that Positioning is visible, leaders can have a more disciplined discussion about portfolio balance, risk exposure, and where deeper governance will be required.

The AI Prioritization Matrix

Once opportunities are aligned strategically, leaders must decide where to position and prioritize AI solutions within the organization. Throughout this book I use an AI prioritization matrix (see Figure 3.5). The matrix plots initiatives based on strategic impact and organizational readiness. High-impact initiatives with strong readiness fall into the scale-now category. High-impact initiatives with lower readiness require preparation and investment. Lower-impact initiatives that are ready can generate momentum as quick wins. Initiatives that score low on both dimensions should simply be deferred or dropped.

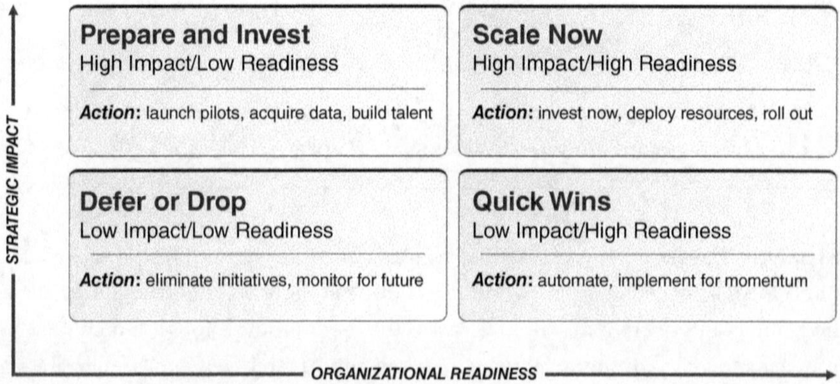

Figure 3.5 AI prioritization matrix.

This matrix operationalizes portfolio thinking. It enables professionals to more deliberately allocate resources and attention. Importantly, initiatives are expected to move across quadrants over time; Positioning is dynamic, not static.

Positioning at Enterprise Scale: JPMorgan Chase

The value of this approach becomes clear with a real example; JPMorgan Chase offers a useful illustration. The firm operates a broad AI portfolio spanning fraud detection, credit decision support, trading analytics, and internal productivity tools. These applications appear to differ significantly in decision criticality. Rather than treating all AI systems as equal, JPMorgan positions them differently. Some applications are tightly governed with extensive oversight due to their potential high impact on customers or markets. Others are deployed with lighter controls because they support less risky internal workflows or advisory functions.[10] This portfolio-based approach enables JPMorgan to pursue innovation while effectively maintaining control.[11]

Implications for Risk, Governance, and Ethics

Positioning decisions shape the risk, ethical, and governance profile of an AI portfolio long before formal controls are applied. Application type, not model complexity, is the primary driver of ethical exposure. Systems that influence high-stakes decisions require different oversight than systems that support human judgment. Positioning answers where AI belongs in the enterprise. The next section turns to Architecture, which determines how those positioned applications are organized, sourced, and governed in practice.

A: Architecture

> **The leadership question:** How do we translate AI strategy into competitive advantage through intentional design choices?

Strategic Levers Strategic Architecture addresses this leadership question that is often overlooked in enterprise AI strategy. It focuses on how AI initiatives take shape, from the point where ideas are initiated to the mechanisms through which they are sourced and scaled. In my experience, Architecture is rarely designed deliberately at the outset. More often, it emerges through a series of local decisions that feel reasonable in isolation but may not necessarily align when taken together. Teams choose tools. Business units launch pilots. Vendors are onboarded to solve immediate problems. Over time, these choices harden into isolated elements of an operating structure that become difficult to integrate (or unwind). When governance protocols later struggle to keep pace, the root cause is frequently architectural rather than technical.

This section focuses on three architectural decisions that shape enterprise AI outcomes. The first concerns how AI initiatives originate within the enterprise. The second is about how AI capabilities are acquired. The third concerns how the operating model is constructed. These choices ultimately determine whether AI strategy is executed through deliberate design or left to emerge through uncoordinated initiatives.

Framing Strategic Architecture in Enterprise AI

The Architecture I'm referring to in this section is not about technology software stacks, it is about decision rights. There is, however, a certain degree of tension across these architectural choices. Organizations want to move quickly and empower teams close to the work. At the same time, they need consistency and clear lines of responsibility. Architecture is the mechanism through which leaders decide how that tension will be resolved in practice. The remainder of this section examines three architectural frames.

Leadership Posture: Where AI Originates

The first architectural decision concerns leadership posture. Where does AI innovation begin inside the organization? In some enterprises, AI initiatives are driven centrally through executive mandate and investment. In others, they emerge from business units responding to local needs or the individual workers on the ground innovating to solve their own problems.

A top-down posture emphasizes standardization and centralized investment and control. Leadership defines approved technology platforms, invests in a set of priorities, and drives adoption across the enterprise. This approach creates consistency within the enterprise and simplifies governance mechanisms. It can also slow experimentation and distance solutions from the teams on the ground and closest to the action.

A bottom-up leadership posture in AI is best understood as employee-level empowerment. It is an architectural choice that gives individual workers the permission, training, tools, and structure to identify problems in their own work and test solutions without waiting for a centralized initiative to arrive. This posture reflects a simple reality. Many of the most valuable AI opportunities emerge from broken workflows and unmet user needs that are invisible at the enterprise or leadership level. Employees closest to those moments often recognize opportunities long before they are visible to leadership teams. When strategic Architecture allows those insights to surface in a structured way, organizations gain learning speed that often results in highly relevant solutions.

Adobe's Kickbox: Stimulating Innovation Within Organizations

Adobe's Kickbox program offers a concrete example of how this architectural decision can work in practice.[12] Kickbox was designed to give employees a repeatable innovation process (with clear stages for experimentation) and modest seed funding to discover and test ideas responsibly. The goal was not to build production systems or bypass governance, but instead, to generate a volume of ideas at the ground level. Employees were encouraged to explore ideas that addressed problems in their immediate work environment and test assumptions quickly and transparently. Ideas that demonstrated value moved into formal review and development channels, where company standards and oversight increased. The architectural lesson from Kickbox is about permission by design. Leadership made explicit choices that valued innovation from the masses.[13]

This model takes on new significance in the context of GenAI. Unlike traditional machine learning systems, which required specialized skills, large datasets, and significant infrastructure, GenAI tools are widely accessible and quite inexpensive (especially given the existence of powerful free versions). Employees can now build and prototype simple applications, as well as test ideas using tools that are rather easily embedded in everyday work. This creates a rare opportunity for organizations to harness bottom-up innovation at scale.

Sourcing Strategy: How AI Capabilities Are Acquired

The second architectural decision concerns sourcing. How does the organization acquire the AI capabilities it needs through build, buy, or partner models? This issue is often framed as a technical question, but it is fundamentally strategic. Building AI capabilities internally offers control and differentiation. It enables organizations to tailor solutions to their unique processes and risk profile. It also requires sustained investment and mature governance foundations. Buying vendor solutions accelerates deployment and reduces development burden, but it introduces dependency and limits transparency. Partnering can accelerate learning and spread risk, but it complicates accountability and ownership.

Most large enterprises use a mix of these three approaches across their AI portfolio. JPMorgan Chase is a clear example. The firm builds internally where AI systems touch core decision processes and competitive advantage. It buys where speed and reliability matter more than differentiation. It partners where ecosystems offer capabilities that would be inefficient to replicate alone. What matters is not the choice itself, but whether the choice is intentional and the right fit for the organization's specific need. Sourcing decisions shape who controls the model, who controls the data, and who is responsible when outcomes deviate from expectations.

Operating Model: How AI Initiatives Are Organized

The third architectural decision concerns the operating model. How AI talent is organized, and where decision authority sits day-to-day. In decentralized models, business units own AI strategy and Execution. This enables speed and contextual relevance, but it often leads to inconsistency and duplicated effort. In centralized models, a single enterprise team owns AI strategy and Execution. This improves enterprise consistency and oversight, but it can create bottlenecks and distance solutions from operational reality and workers on the ground facing immediate and nuanced needs.

Many organizations ultimately move toward a hybrid approach – a federated model. In this structure, a central team defines the enterprise strategy and standards, governance protocols, and shared technology infrastructure, while business units build and deploy solutions within those boundaries. This model reflects the reality that AI use cases differ in risk and importance across the enterprise and its business units or functional teams. It's also important to note that the operating model determines who owns AI risk in practice, shaping risk escalation paths and reporting structures.

Implications for Risk, Governance, and Ethics

The Architecture decisions addressed in this section quietly determine where responsibility resides when AI systems fail. Governance frameworks and ethical principles matter, of course, but they cannot compensate for unclear ownership or fragmented authority. When Architecture is poorly designed, accountability can be difficult to discern, and individuals or entire teams assume someone else is responsible. Issues surface late. Governance becomes reactive. When Architecture is deliberate, responsibility is clearer. Risks are surfaced earlier. Governance and ethics considerations are integrated into decision-making rather than appended after the fact.

This is why Architecture deserves the same level of leadership attention as Intent and Positioning. It shapes outcomes long after initial design choices are forgotten. The next section turns to Capabilities. Architecture defines the structure. Capabilities determine whether that structure actually works in practice.

C: Capabilities

> **The leadership question:** Do we have the Capabilities required to realize AI value in practice?

Strategic Levers

Ambitious AI strategies fail far more often because of capability gaps than because of flawed ideas. An AI strategy is only as strong as the Capabilities that support it. AI systems are placing novel stressors on organizations. They surface gaps in talent, decision rights, culture, and leadership alignment faster than prior technology movements.

The leadership question at the center of this section is a question about organizational readiness. Many organizations discover too late that governance frameworks cannot compensate for weak foundational Capabilities. The strategic tension will be familiar to many readers. Leaders feel an intense urge to move quickly to capture AI-enabled value, but organizational readiness rarely advances at the same pace. Capability development takes time. This section examines five enabling capability domains that consistently determine enterprise AI outcomes.

Technology and Data Foundation

Every AI program rests on a technical and data foundation. Scalable infrastructure and reliable data pipelines determine which AI use cases can be operationalized and which fall victim to a condition in which initiatives linger without ever scaling. This phenomenon is more widely known as *pilot purgatory*, or *pilotitis* – a concept first observed in Uganda in 2008 with mobile health programs and introduced to me by a former colleague of mine, Fernando Morera.[14] Organizations with fragmented data environments often mistake experimentation outcomes for the ability to achieve value at scale. Models may perform well in isolated settings, but they fail when exposed to real operational complexity.

In my work with companies, data quality and its accessibility, in a well-organized medium, remain the most common hidden constraint on AI execution. Nevertheless, quite often leaders approve initiatives without fully understanding the condition of the underlying data. As a result, teams spend disproportionate time manually repairing data pipelines rather than improving outcomes. This slows progress and erodes confidence across the enterprise.

Talent and AI Fluency

AI capability is not just confined to engineers, it depends on widespread fluency across the entire organization. This includes AI technical expertise, business alignment judgment, and ethical awareness. The absence of fluency forces organizations to centralize decisions that should be distributed if AI fluency was greater across the enterprise.

Recent workforce evidence underscores how quickly AI capability gaps are becoming Execution risks. As discussed in Chapter 1, Microsoft and LinkedIn data demonstrate that AI adoption has already moved decisively into day-to-day work, with a large share of employees using tools outside sanctioned enterprise environments. At the same time, 53% of employees who use AI at work worry that relying on it for important tasks makes them appear replaceable[15] – an amazing statistic and perhaps a view into the next iteration of the imposter syndrome. What matters here is not the speed of adoption itself, but what it reveals about organizational and worker readiness.

Taken together, these findings reveal a critical reality for enterprise leaders. AI adoption is already happening at the worker level. When organizations fail to invest in AI literacy and capability development, workers will be resourceful and fill the gap themselves, often in ways that are invisible to leadership and inconsistent with enterprise norms. The implication for AI capability building can be material. AI fluency cannot be confined to technical teams or innovation functions. Managers must be equipped to evaluate AI-supported work with confidence. And workers must understand when and how AI use is appropriate within their roles.

Leadership and Strategic Alignment

AI Capabilities do not develop in a vacuum. Leadership behavior determines whether they are cultivated or ignored. Clear executive direction matters, but so does consistency. Organizations struggle when leaders publicly endorse AI while

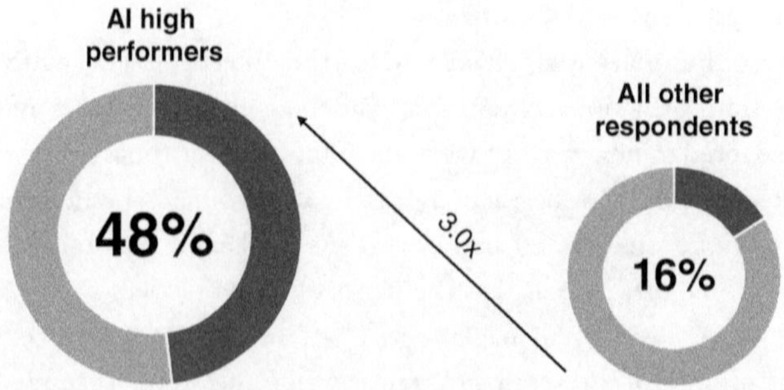

Figure 3.6 Strong ownership and commitment to AI initiatives at the senior leadership level, 2025.

Source: QuantumBlack.AI by McKinsey, 2025 | Chart: BAIE Research Team, 2026.

privately rewarding short-term performance at any cost. Alignment shows up in budgeting decisions and prioritization choices. Leaders who expect immediate returns often discourage the experimentation required to build long-standing capability. Over time, teams learn to optimize for manager approval (and the incentives that follow along) rather than enterprise value. McKinsey's "The State of AI in 2025," survey reveals that organizations that realize lasting AI impact have leaders who remain engaged well beyond initial pilots (see Figure 3.6).[16]

Operating Model and Ownership Clarity

Even strong talent and leadership alignment cannot compensate for unclear ownership. In my work advising organizations on AI governance, I often see accountability become diffused (because AI systems cut across functions) unless responsibility is deliberately established. When responsibility is diffuse, response is slow and delays emerge from uncertainty about who is expected to act. The organizations that manage this well typically address the issue early by defining who owns AI outcomes at each stage, from experimentation through deployment. As initiatives mature, they establish explicit handoffs and clarify escalation thresholds with the specific individual who has authority to intervene when risk surfaces.

This capability links directly to the architectural choices discussed previously in the chapter. Architecture defines structure and Capabilities determine whether that structure functions in practice. In my experience, when ownership is unclear governance teams are asked to resolve conflicts that should never have reached them. Ethical concerns surface late, often after systems are already in use.

Change Management and Culture

AI adoption requires behavioral change across the enterprise. This pattern mirrors earlier digital transformations, where success depended less on tools and more on how people adapted to new ways of working. Culture determines whether employees experiment openly or hide their use. Trust determines whether concerns are raised early or discovered after harm occurs. As explained previously, Microsoft/LinkedIn workforce data reveals that the majority of employees worry about how their AI use is perceived by management. That anxiety has severe consequences within the organization. It discourages transparency and slows learning. It can also create incentives to avoid such AI use disclosure.

Organizations that invest in workforce communication and AI literacy training experience beneficial outcomes. These interventions echo proven change management practices from earlier digital initiatives. Workers are more willing to ask questions and actually report operating plan deviations to management, ultimately refining AI systems collaboratively. AI adoption accelerates because enterprise trust exists.

JPMorgan Chase: Capability Depth at Scale

JPMorgan Chase illustrates how depth of Capabilities enables AI at enterprise scale. The firm's approach reflects sustained investment in AI rather than episodic enthusiasm. Over time, it has built technical infrastructure, innovation protocols, talent pipelines, and the associated governance protocols that reinforce one another. What distinguishes JPMorgan is not any single system; it is institutional learning and culture. AI capability is developed across functions, not isolated within a central team. As a result, the organization can deploy AI in diverse contexts while maintaining control.

Implications for Risk, Governance, and Ethics

From a risk, governance, and ethics perspective, weak technical foundations tend to surface as system instability and post-deployment surprises rather than as failures emanating from a formal ethics review. In practice, many of the most consequential issues originate in technology design choices and data discipline long before they appear in oversight forums. This reality underscores that ethical judgment must be exercised where work actually occurs, within teams designing and operating systems, rather than offloaded to distant review bodies once AI is already embedded in enterprise processes or customer facing solutions. There is now broad and growing recognition that AI literacy is a prerequisite for this shift, enabling organizations to manage risk and safety as part of everyday decision-making rather than as a downstream compliance exercise.[17] Governance failures often compound this problem. When incentives are misaligned, early risk signals are suppressed, and teams delay escalation out of concern that raising issues will be perceived as resistance rather than stewardship.

Capabilities as the First Line of Defense

Capabilities determine whether AI risk is shaped early or managed late. Weak Capabilities force organizations to rely on reactive controls. Strong Capabilities enable judgment at the point of design. Strategic Intent establishes why AI is being pursued. Architecture defines structure. Capabilities determine whether either can be realized responsibly. The next section turns to Execution. If Capabilities answer whether the organization is ready, Execution determines whether readiness translates into sustained value.

E: Execution

> **The leadership question:** What barriers are preventing this AI initiative from being implemented effectively?

Strategic Levers

AI strategies rarely fail on paper. In my experience, they fail when they collide with organizational realities. Enterprises routinely approve thoughtful AI strategies and fund the most promising pilots, only to watch momentum fade as systems move toward scale. This pattern is not unique to AI, but AI certainly magnifies it. The important gap between enterprise strategy and the ability to execute is where most AI programs stall.

Execution is, however, often misunderstood. It is not merely the act of deploying a model or completing a pilot of an AI solution. Execution is the process by which an organization achieves the benefits of an AI program at scale. It is behavioral and culture driven. An AI system has not been executed successfully until people are actually relying on it, with real users, by employees or actual customers. This is why pilot success can be so misleading. Pilots operate in protected environments with curated data, motivated users (sometimes just from the innovation team responsible for the pilot), and a high degree of leadership support. Production environments are different as they expose Execution limitations.

From the academic research that informed this book and from my work with companies across many industries, several Execution requirements consistently surface. AI must enhance existing enterprise workflows (rather than compete with them), but in some cases organizations are redesigning those workflows entirely to take advantage of new AI Capabilities. Users must trust the AI system enough to rely on it under pressure. Managers must know how to evaluate AI-supported work and the employees developing it.

To understand why Execution breaks down so predictably, it helps to shift attention from systems to people. This is where the work of Loran Nordgren and David Schonthal becomes especially useful (Schonthal is a professor at Kellogg and co-director of the Kellogg Innovation and Entrepreneurship Initiative; Nordgren is a professor of management and organizations at Northwestern University's Kellogg School of Management). In *The Human Element*, coauthors Nordgren and Schonthal argue that most innovation efforts fail not because ideas lack merit, but because leaders misunderstand *resistance*. They show that organizations tend to rely on what they call a *fuel-based mindset*, emphasizing product features and incentives in the hope that more enthusiasm will drive adoption. In practice, this approach often backfires.[18]

The authors' central insight is that execution significantly improves when leaders adopt a *friction-based mindset*. Instead of asking why people should embrace a new idea, leaders should ask what is making it difficult for them to do so (searching for those execution frictions). Resistance in this regard is treated as a predictable response to psychological barriers that surface when work routines are disrupted.

This lens maps directly onto AI execution challenges. AI systems often introduce large shifts in how consequential decisions are made. People can be resistant to change and default to familiar ways of working, especially when new systems are untested and come across as imposed. That creates inertia. AI system use will necessitate user effort. Learning a new AI tool and integrating it into existing workflows requires cognitive and emotional energy that many teams underestimate. Emotion plays a key role as well. Professionals may worry about appearing less competent (again, consider that incredible data point from the Microsoft/LinkedIn survey discussed previously) or even being judged by algorithmic outputs. Finally, reactance emerges when AI adoption is framed as a mandate rather than a choice. Reactance refers to the psychological resistance people experience when they feel their freedom to choose is being restricted. When people feel pressured to change, they push back, sometimes by complying on the surface while avoiding actual use.

According to the authors, execution falters when organizations ignore these frictions. Training programs that focus only on functionality do not address human anxiety or identity threat. Executive mandates that emphasize urgency without redesigning workflows increase workarounds.

Nordgren and Schonthal's work suggests a different approach to AI execution. Leaders should design adoption pathways that reduce friction rather than routinely adding new features and functions to AI systems. That means making AI feel familiar through small, visible use cases before scaling. It means embedding AI into the natural flow of work so user effort decreases rather than increases. It means framing AI initiatives as experiments that invite participation instead of directives that demand compliance. Most importantly, it means observing how people actually work to identify hidden barriers.

The practical lesson for organizations is straightforward. Execution must be intentionally designed. And importantly, resistance should be treated as a signal that something in the Execution pathway is misaligned. When Execution is treated as a leadership discipline, AI has a chance to become an institutional capability rather than a series of stalled experiments.

Implications for Risk, Governance, and Ethics

Execution discipline also shapes ethical outcomes. When AI systems are difficult to use or misaligned with individual or team incentives, workers find alternatives. Shadow AI emerges. Shortcuts appear. Ethical risk increases precisely because formal systems are bypassed. A friction-based view of Execution reframes this dynamic. Instead of responding with tighter controls after the fact, leaders reduce ethical risk by identifying and removing the barriers that make sanctioned systems hard to use in real work. When governance is designed to lower friction, not add it, employees are more likely to operate within visible systems, surface concerns early and rely on approved tools. If Execution determines whether strategy takes hold, Resilience determines whether it endures.

R: Resilience

> **The leadership question:** How can our AI strategy remain resilient by exercising greater foresight into emerging capabilities and risks?

Strategic Levers

Resilience in the AI era is often misunderstood. It is less about the ability to absorb shocks after they occur. It is more about foresight. In fast-moving AI environments, the organizations that outperform are not those with the most detailed long-term plans, but those that sense change early and adapt before disruption becomes obvious to your competitors. AI accelerates this challenge. Strategy is increasingly shaped by forces that emerge outside formal planning cycles. In this environment, Resilience depends less on prediction and more on the ability to look around the corner and see what's coming next. Professionals must learn to recognize weak AI market signals, assess their significance, and act while uncertainty remains high.

This is why foresight is a leadership capability rather than a technical one. Rita McGrath's work in *Seeing Around Corners* offers a practical framework for understanding how organizations can build this capability. Her key insight is that strategic change does not announce itself clearly. It begins quietly, often at the edges of the organization, and unfolds through signals that may be easy to dismiss.[19] Applied to AI, this perspective reframes how leaders should think about emerging trends and risks. The earliest signals of AI disruption rarely appear in executive dashboards. They appear in unexpected places. Employees begin using new AI tools informally. Legal teams raise questions about respecting intellectual property ownership. Researchers and journalists flag edge cases that feel remote from core operations. These signals are easy to overlook precisely because they do not appear overly significant at first glance.

In the early stages of AI adoption, ambiguity is everywhere. Return on investment is entirely unclear at the outset; use cases must evolve for the value equation to materialize. Many organizations respond by delaying commitment to the new AI system until clarity improves. McGrath's work suggests the opposite approach. Leaders should expect fog and design an associated strategy to function within such a cloud of uncertainty. The goal is to learn faster than competitors.

This is where discovery-driven testing becomes essential. Rather than *debating* hypothetical futures, resilient organizations *test* assumptions through contained experiments. They treat AI initiatives as learning vehicles, not just delivery vehicles. Investment decisions are staged. Progress is measured by insights gained rather than the immediate scaling of the solution. Importantly, not all initiatives are expected to succeed; failure of a set of AI use cases can inform the others.

The portfolio approach to strategy outlined previously follows naturally from this approach. AI strategy should not be framed as a single bet on a dominant use case or platform. It should be managed as a collection of initiatives with different time horizons and risk profiles. Some efforts improve current operations, while others explore adjacent opportunities. A smaller number probe more uncertain possibilities (but with potentially higher value). Culture determines whether this approach works in practice. McGrath emphasizes that organizations often suppress the very signals they need most. People hesitate to raise concerns that challenge positive momentum. Teams learn which questions are welcome and which are not. In AI contexts, this suppression is especially dangerous. When culture discourages early risk escalation, these signals are delayed until harm is visible. Resilient organizations design for signal amplification rather than suppression. They reward curiosity and normalize dissent. They treat early warnings as strategic inputs rather than obstacles to progress.

Netflix provides a useful illustration of strategy built on continuous adaptation. Over time, the company has repeatedly abandoned successful legacy models in favor of emerging approaches. Physical media gave way to streaming. Streaming content evolved toward original content production. Recommendation systems advanced alongside changing viewer behavior.[20] What distinguishes Netflix is not technological foresight in isolation. It is organizational willingness to let go of assumptions that no longer serve the enterprise. Portfolio thinking allowed multiple models to coexist during transition periods. Weak signals were analyzed rather than dismissed and commitments were adjusted as evidence accumulated.

Implications for Risk, Governance, and Ethics

Greater foresight enables organizations to surface risks and ethical concerns early before they escalate into crises. For example, bias and AI system misuse often appear first as subtle deviations (weak signals) rather than immediate failures. When leaders are attuned to these signals, they gain greater perspective that allows for better preparation and earlier intervention. This preparation enables guardrails and response protocols to be put in place before escalation occurs. When signals are ignored, the breakdown is not always a failure of foresight. In many cases, signals are recognized but deprioritized. Regardless, the result is a reactive response that becomes increasingly costly to the enterprise.

Closing

This chapter focused on a simple but often overlooked truth. Enterprise AI success is shaped far earlier than most leaders expect. It is shaped by strategic choices about enterprise purpose, scope, design, and execution. When those choices are deliberate and balanced, AI becomes a source of advantage.

The IPACER Framework was introduced to surface those choices. Intent clarifies what the organization is trying to achieve with AI. Positioning determines where AI solutions are concentrated and where restraint is appropriate. Architecture defines how AI initiatives are initiated, how solutions are sourced, and how authority is distributed across the enterprise. Capabilities determine whether ambition can be translated into sustained performance. Execution embeds AI into real work. Resilience ensures that strategy evolves as conditions change. Together, these elements form a coherent strategic system.

What matters most is not excellence in any single IPACER element, but balance across them. Strong Intent without disciplined Positioning leads to solution sprawl. Thoughtful Architecture without Execution discipline limits impact. Aggressive experimentation without Resilience creates fragile systems. AI strategy succeeds when these elements reinforce one another.

This chapter has also demonstrated that governance and ethics are not separate layers applied after strategy is set. They are influenced directly by strategic design choices. Decisions about where AI is deployed and who is accountable for outcomes shape not only performance but also stakeholder trust. Strategy defines the environment in which governance operates. AI strategy is a leadership discipline that demands judgment and continuous adaptation. IPACER offers a way to structure key elements of the enterprise AI strategy and to align the organization to them.

Chapter 4 turns to enterprise AI risk. It builds on the foundation established here by examining how strategic choices translate into specific risk patterns and exposure points. Risk does not emerge in isolation; it reflects the strategy that came before it.

4 Risk Exposure

Risk in the Age of Generative AI

In mid-2025, Deloitte Australia delivered a report to the Australian government that was, at first glance, entirely routine. The firm had been engaged by the Department of Employment and Workplace Relations to review a compliance framework connected to automated welfare penalties. This work fell squarely within the firm's core professional services capabilities. In fact, Deloitte has a long history of serving governments exceptionally well. The engagement involved detailed analytical work and legal review that appears consistent with the firm's routine advisory practice.

The report was published on the department's website on August 14, 2025.[1] Not long after publication, Dr. Chris Rudge, a researcher and lecturer at the University of Sydney, identified inconsistencies in the supporting material. Several academic references cited in the report could not be located and a legal quotation attributed to a federal court decision did not appear in the underlying case. Although these issues did not relate to the report's policy recommendations, they raised questions about how portions of the document had been prepared and reviewed.

As attention increased, the Australian government confirmed that Deloitte had subsequently reviewed the report after Dr. Rudge's findings and identified errors in footnotes and references. The department emphasized that the substance of the review remained unchanged and that the recommendations remained intact. Deloitte agreed to repay the final installment under its contract. A revised version of the report was later published with corrected references and a new disclosure acknowledging the use of a generative artificial intelligence (GenAI) system in preparing parts of the document.[2]

From a contractual standpoint, the matter appeared to be resolved. From a risk perspective, the episode revealed something more consequential. AI had been introduced into a routine professional services workflow without seemingly triggering a corresponding shift in its review. From the media reports of this incident, draft material reportedly generated with AI assistance appeared to move through existing quality controls that were designed for human authorship. Those controls proved insufficient to detect fabricated sources or GenAI hallucinations.

Why is this case instructive? It is not that a respected firm made an error; professional services firms know how to manage mistakes. What distinguishes this case is how AI blended into ordinary work, research, and document preparation. This chapter begins with this episode because it illustrates how enterprise AI risk is being reshaped by the explosion of generative and agentic AI systems. Risk exposure does not require malicious intent or reckless deployment. It emerges when frontier technical capabilities operate inside inherited governance structures and workflows that were built for a different mode of work. The Deloitte incident illustrates a broader pattern many organizations are now facing. The lesson is not confined to professional services. As generative and agentic AI becomes embedded in everyday work, risk increasingly emerges from the gap between new technical capability and legacy governance or review protocols.

Framing AI Risk as Enterprise Risk

AI already exposes enterprises to risks that affect their value directly and indirectly. As explored in Chapter 1, documented incidents across sectors and jurisdictions show how AI failures surface in operational settings, including cases where serious harm was narrowly avoided. In practice, I have observed that AI systems change how risk enters organizations. They expose weaknesses in existing enterprise risk management (ERM) models and force governance bodies to address risks that no longer remain confined to technical functions.

AI-related risk reaches the enterprise in two distinct ways. Direct risk occurs when the enterprise itself absorbs the harm. Indirect risk occurs when harm to external parties later rebounds onto the enterprise. That rebound often takes the form of legal liability or reputational damage. It can also disrupt critical business relationships, including with customers. Consequences include litigation and regulatory investigation. Financial penalties often follow.

Importance of Handling Legal Uncertainty: Software Tax Example

Before focusing my career on innovation and advanced technologies, I spent several years as a tax lawyer. During that period, I advised companies on the tax implications of complex corporate structures and transactions. These matters were often governed by regulations that changed after business practices were adopted and legal structures were fixed. One example involved the taxation of software, an issue that became increasingly complex as digital delivery expanded. In the late 1990s and early 2000s, US states faced uncertainty over how to tax the growing economic value of corporate software. Sales and use tax regimes had been designed for tangible goods and discrete transfers of ownership. As enterprise software adoption increased, many states extended sales and use taxes to electronic software downloads and treated digital delivery via this medium as a taxable transaction.

Just as these rules proliferated across the states, the commercial model shifted. Software value moved away from traditional notions of ownership and local installation toward cloud-based access and software-as-a-service arrangements. In those models, there was often no actual software download and no clear point of sale in the traditional tangible goods sense. The regulatory framework had been designed to tax a form of transaction that was already becoming obsolete. In many cases, the existing tax regulations simply did not apply to these new methods of delivering software value.

Effective tax governance during that period did not depend on perfect statutory alignment. It depended on how organizations assessed exposure and exercised judgment in the face of uncertainty. In some cases, the governing rules had been written so narrowly that they no longer captured the emerging business model. The same pattern now appears with AI. Regulation follows innovation, but after business practices are being established. The governance practices developed in that context offer a useful blueprint for how organizations might approach AI governance under similar conditions of regulatory lag and ambiguity.

The hardest part of that work was never understanding the statute or regulation as written. The real challenge was helping leadership anticipate how today's decisions would be interpreted years later. Those interpretations often changed as facts developed and government enforcement priorities shifted. The same question now confronts organizations deploying AI systems.

Governing AI Risk Under Regulatory Uncertainty

That tax experience strongly informs how I assess AI risk. Like tax, AI sits at the intersection of technical complexity and regulatory evolution. Government guidance remains uneven, and enforcement theories are still forming. Business enterprises are forced to make decisions today that will be evaluated under future standards. In tax, smart companies couldn't afford to wait for perfect clarity. They moved forward by taking tax positions grounded in the rules as they were reasonably understood at the time. Potential exposure was managed through experience-based judgment and transparency by senior executives, with board involvement when the decision carried material risk.

AI risk requires the same discipline. Harm that first appears outside the enterprise often returns as enterprise exposure. We refer to this pattern as *rebound effects*. Discriminatory model outputs and privacy failures often affect individuals first. Legal consequences often follow. Reputational and financial exposure then emerge as those issues become visible. These risks overlap and compound, which makes isolated controls ineffective.

Empirical evidence reinforces this shift. The OECD's "AI Incidents and Hazards Monitor" has recorded more than 13,600 AI-related incidents and hazards between January 2020 and January 2026. The number of reported incidents has been steadily increasing, reaching a peak of 596 incidents in January 2026 alone. In 2025, the number of recorded incidents and hazards increased by 56.04% compared to 2024.[3] According to the OECD, nearly 60% of these incidents and hazards resulted in reputational harm or economic/property damage. Many of these incidents occurred in operational settings and produced legal exposure, with reputational and financial consequences following once failures became visible.

Enterprise perceptions have shifted accordingly. In a 2025 survey of compliance and risk leaders, 59% identified regulatory and compliance risk as a top AI concern in 2024, compared with 46% in 2025, signaling that organizations are improving how they operationalize compliance risk (see Figure 4.1).[4] McKinsey's

2024		2025
60%	Data Privacy	58%
46%	Information Security	57%
49%	Hallucination	55%
59%	Regulatory and Compliance	46%
42%	Cybersecurity	41%

Figure 4.1 Top risk concerns when using AI tools.

Source: NSCP, ACA, 2024; ACA, 2025 | Chart: BAIE Research Team, 2026.

"The State of AI in 2025" survey also finds that 51% of respondents at organizations using AI report experiencing at least one negative consequence in the past year, with 30% of respondents reporting negative consequences from AI inaccuracy (see Figures 4.2 and 4.3).[5] These data points highlight that AI risk is already material in today's business operations. The remaining question is how enterprises should govern that risk.

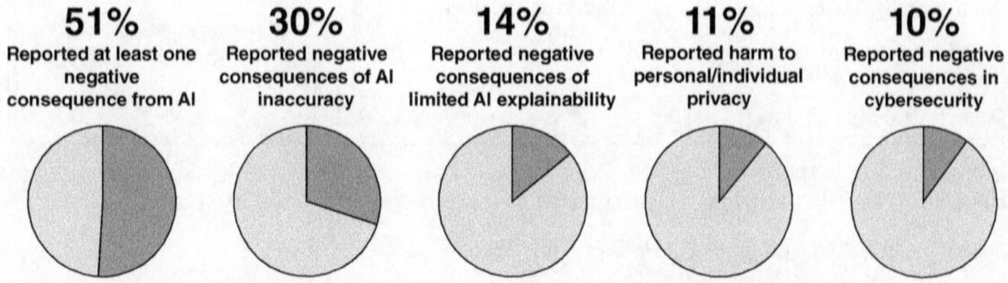

Figure 4.2 Top negative AI consequences reported in 2025.

Source: QuantumBlack.AI by McKinsey, 2025 | Chart: BAIE Research Team, 2026.

This framing aligns with the definition used in the NIST AI Risk Management Framework. NIST defines risk as "the composite measure of an event's probability of occurring and the magnitude or degree of the consequences of the corresponding event." The framework recognizes that harms to individuals and institutions often serve as the pathway through which enterprise risk materializes (see Figure 4.4).[6]

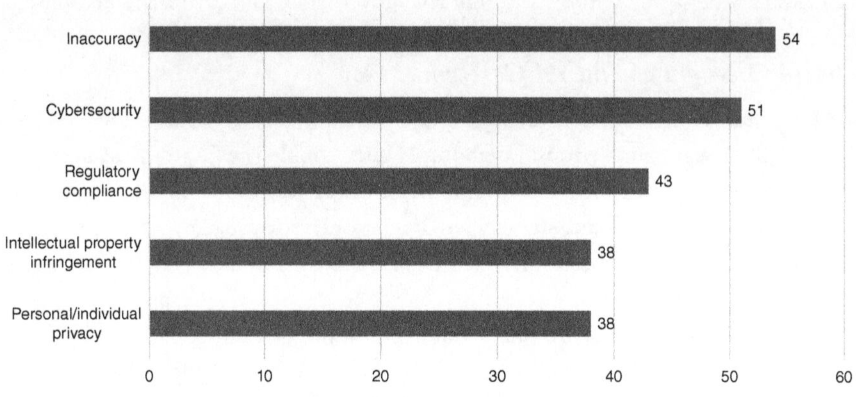

Figure 4.3 Top risks that organizations are working to mitigate in 2025 (%).

Source: QuantumBlack.AI by McKinsey, 2025 | Chart: BAIE Research Team, 2026.

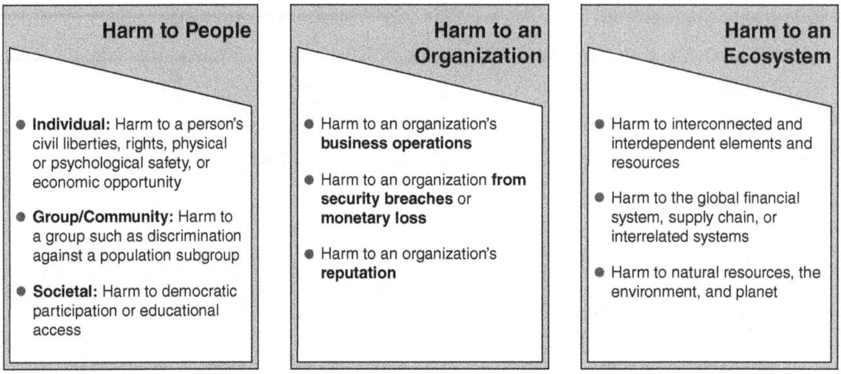

Figure 4.4 Examples of potential harms related to AI systems.
Source: NIST, 2023 | Chart: BAIE Research Team, 2026.

AI risks differ from those associated with traditional software systems. AI models rely on data that changes or becomes outdated over time and can behave unpredictably when deployed in new contexts, which complicates risk identification and monitoring. Treating AI risk as an enterprise risk aligns oversight with established fiduciary expectations. Corporate boards are not expected to evaluate model architectures or data training techniques. They are expected to understand material risk to the organization and ensure that management has systems in place to identify and manage that risk. When AI is embedded within existing ERM structures, directors and senior executives can exercise effective oversight without being drawn into technical detail. This framing helps explain why boards are increasingly engaging with AI through risk, governance, and accountability lenses.

Board Oversight and the AI Governance Gap

In my role advising boards through the EY Center for Board Matters, I saw consistent attention paid and seriousness about AI risk, coupled with a critical need for greater education on effective oversight mechanisms. Most directors recognize that AI is now shaping corporate strategy and operations. However, fewer feel confident interrogating how those systems work in practice or how risk is detected before harm materializes.

The demographics of US public company boards matter here, where the average S&P 500 board director is in their mid-sixties.[7] Many built their careers before digital systems were deeply embedded in core business processes, let alone systems that learn and operate with limited human intervention. Some directors invest significant time building fluency in emerging technologies. Others struggle, not from lack of diligence, but because AI compresses complexity and speed in ways traditional board education was never designed to address.

This gap has governance consequences. Boards cannot oversee what they do not understand, and management teams struggle to translate technical risk into board-relevant terms without a shared literacy baseline. Effective AI governance therefore requires *intentional* board education. Not as a mere orientation session or brief periodic update, but as a sustained capability aligned to directors' fiduciary responsibility. We further explore fiduciary responsibilities in this context in Chapter 5. These dynamics become clearer when AI risk is examined through the lens of ERM.

Why AI Risk Challenges Traditional ERM Models

Traditional ERM models were not designed for AI-grounded learning systems. Most ERM frameworks assume that once a system is approved and deployed, its risk profile will remain relatively stable. Controls are typically established before deployment, with oversight based on approval milestones rather than continuous system behavior. Those assumptions break down once AI systems operate in production environments.

AI systems differ from conventional software in ways that complicate risk oversight.

AI system behavior depends on training data and statistical inference rather than fixed rules. Outputs may vary across deployment contexts, and system performance may change as usage patterns evolve. These characteristics create variability that traditional ERM controls were not built to track.

This distinction is made explicit in the NIST AI Risk Management Framework. NIST notes the "higher degree of difficulty in predicting failure modes for emergent properties of large-scale pre-trained models" and highlights that "intentional or unintentional changes during training may fundamentally alter AI system performance." NIST also warns that data, model, or concept drift and limited reproducibility may complicate oversight.[8] AI risk therefore does not remain fixed after deployment. It evolves during use, often outside the detection mechanisms assumed by traditional ERM protocols.

Model opacity further weakens traditional risk controls. Many machine learning systems do not produce outputs that can be traced or explained with precision. When reviewers cannot reconstruct how a result was generated, audit-based controls lose force. In regulated or high-stakes settings, this limits the ability to determine whether behavior remains within approved risk boundaries.

Post-deployment drift places additional strain on ERM assumptions. Models shift as data inputs change, users adapt behavior, or systems are fine-tuned or repurposed. Many organizations still concentrate risk review at the point of AI solution approval. Ongoing monitoring of the system remains limited or informal. As a result, changes in the risk profile of the AI solution may go undetected until harm has already occurred.

AI risk also emerges from how AI systems shape human decisions. Risk does not reside solely in model design. It arises when outputs begin to shape decisions in ways existing review structures were not designed to control. The same model can produce very different risk exposure depending on where and how it is used. Risk controls that focus narrowly on technical performance miss these effects.

The AI incidents statistics and examples cited in this chapter reveal that many AI failures stem from misalignment between system behavior and organizational decision processes. For example, overreliance on automated recommendations can distort hiring or lending decisions when human review weakens. Further, deploying systems outside their intended context can expose sensitive data. These risks cannot be mitigated through model testing alone. They require governance through all stages of the AI system's life cycle, not just during development.

Decentralized adoption complicates accountability. In such cases, AI systems often emerge across business units with fragmented ownership. When this occurs, risk signals are dispersed and escalation pathways are often unclear. Moreover, legal and compliance/audit teams are often engaged after systems are already in use. Traditional ERM models, which rely on clear risk ownership and reporting lines, often struggle in this environment.

Research from the MIT AI Risk Initiative provides greater context for this challenge. The initiative examined more than 950 AI governance documents to identify which AI risks receive formal attention. Its findings show concentrated attention on certain risks, such as governance failure and security vulnerabilities, while other risk areas, such as AI welfare and human rights, receive limited treatment.[9] In my experience advising companies, this uneven emphasis often produces governance frameworks that acknowledge risk without assigning ownership or decision rights. The challenge posed by AI risk is not solved by adding new assessment tools. Governance structures themselves must adapt. Oversight must continue after system deployment, and accountability must reflect how AI systems operate across functions.

The NIST AI Risk Management Framework also emphasizes the organizational dimensions of AI risk management. The framework calls for AI risk to be embedded within enterprise decision processes rather than isolated as a technical specialty.[10] I believe this distinction matters. When AI risk sits outside ERM structures, handled as a specialized technical issue, it often falls between established governance or risk domains. When embedded, existing accountability and escalation mechanisms can function as intended.

The Deloitte incident illustrates how AI risk actually enters the enterprise. AI-assisted drafting seemingly moved through established review processes that assumed human authorship and conventional error patterns. Those controls proved insufficient to detect fabricated sources. The resulting exposure arose from governance and review structures that had not yet adjusted to the way generative and agentic systems alter how work is produced and reviewed.

Core Categories of Enterprise AI Risk

AI does not replace familiar enterprise risk categories. It changes how quickly risks surface and how broadly their effects spread. A single incident can trigger multiple forms of exposure across the organization. Enterprise risk classification systems vary by industry and use case. Organizations group risks differently, even when they are responding to the same underlying exposure. In examining existing AI risk frameworks used by public institutions and private sector actors, I found no consistent agreement on labels or boundaries, despite substantial overlap in the risks themselves.

Eight categories of AI risk are depicted in the sections that follow, reflecting how AI-related risks surface once systems are in use (see Figure 4.5). Broader groupings obscure distinct forms of exposure. More granular frameworks fragment accountability and fail to match how incidents unfold in practice.

These categories reflect the taxonomy that emerged from the research underlying this book and align with how I have examined AI risk in the courses I teach at MIT Sloan and in senior executive and board-level settings.

Strategic

Strategic risks arise when AI investments do not align with the enterprise mission or when leadership misjudges how AI actually reshapes competitive dynamics. Strategic risks also arise when teams launch pilots without an approved business case. Other risks emerge when the organization commits to enterprise programs without the internal capability to run them, which forces workarounds and drives uneven adoption.

Strategic risk also includes overdependence on ecosystem partners or vendors that may limit future effectiveness of an AI program. Dependence on a single provider can lock the organization into that provider's road map and pricing. Strategy fails in a quieter way when the organization treats AI only as an efficiency tool and ignores new business models that may only be afforded by leveraging modern AI systems.

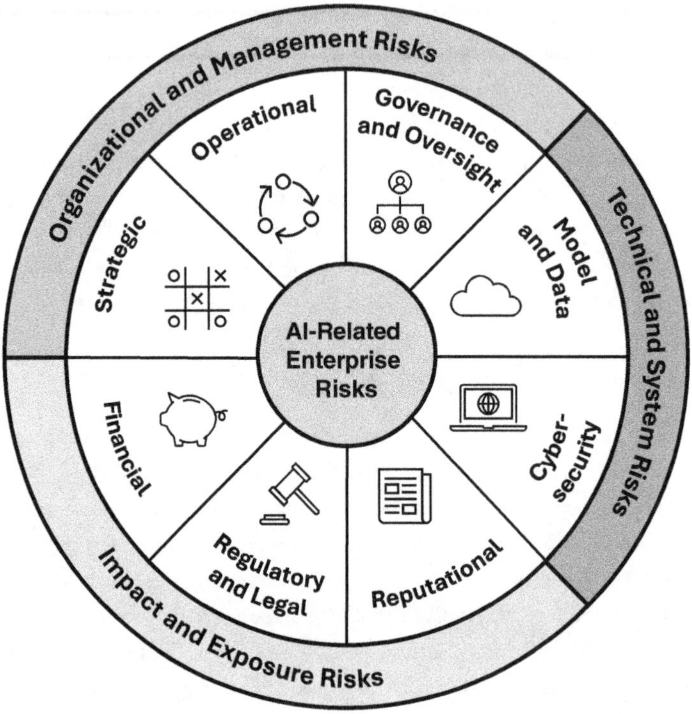

Figure 4.5 AI-related enterprise risks.

Source: © BAIE Research Team, 2026.

Operational

Operational risk arises when AI systems interfere with routine business processes that organizations depend on to function reliably. These risks include failures in system access management and inappropriate employee use of AI tools. Reliance on system outputs without adequate human oversight can also introduce operational exposure. Legacy infrastructure often amplifies this exposure.

As GenAI becomes widely accessible inside organizations, either through internal deployment or via licensed tools, unmanaged use can produce inconsistent decisions and process breakdowns. Operational risk increases when AI systems are embedded into workflows without clear usage boundaries or reliable fallback procedures. In these conditions, localized failures spread quickly across teams and functions.

In the summer of 2025, McDonald's experienced an AI incident involving its AI-enabled recruitment platform, "McHire," which the company had deployed to support high-volume hiring across its restaurants.[11] The system, developed and operated by an external vendor, was integrated into routine hiring workflows and used to collect and process applicant information. Its role was to improve operational efficiencies, functioning as a new standard component of the company's recruiting platform.

These vulnerabilities were not identified through McDonald's internal risk management processes. Independent security researchers Ian Carroll and Sam Curry discovered the security weaknesses in the McHire platform.[12] The issue was similarly not surfaced through the external vendor's security or oversight practices. The researchers' interest was initially triggered by how applicants were being screened through an automated chatbot and personality test. Describing his discovery process, Carroll told *Wired*, "So I started applying for a job, and then after 30 minutes, we had full access to virtually every application that's ever been made to McDonald's going back years."[13] The exposure involved applicant data collected through an AI-enabled hiring process and persisted until remediation that quickly followed the discovery by Carroll and Curry. From a risk management perspective, the episode illustrates how AI-related exposure can enter the enterprise through third-party platforms embedded in routine operations. The McHire episode also shows why a single AI incident rarely fits within one category alone. What appears at first to be operational risk also implicates cybersecurity risk, governance and oversight risk, reputational risk, and potential regulatory and legal risk.

Governance and Oversight

Governance and oversight risks emerge when accountability for AI systems is unclear or fragmented. In many organizations, AI development and deployment are distributed across multiple teams. Monitoring is often spread across business units as well. This decentralization can create accountability gaps that weaken oversight of AI use case portfolios.

Governance risk increases when executive teams lack timely, decision-relevant information about where AI is deployed. Risk also increases when they lack clarity about which decisions AI influences. Without clear reporting structures and escalation paths, organizations may fail to detect emerging risks or intervene before harm occurs. These risks are organizational in nature. They ultimately stem from how authority and oversight are structured.

Model and Data

AI model and data risks arise from inaccuracies or limitations of AI models and the data on which they rely. AI systems may generate incorrect outputs due to, for example, system flaws or reliance on outdated or incomplete data. Training data may be biased or unrepresentative of the relevant community, leading to degraded performance and unequal outcomes.

Model risks also include data poisoning and model drift, which become more likely as systems operate over time and receive new data inputs. Data poisoning occurs when training or update data is intentionally manipulated so that the model learns distorted patterns, which can alter outputs without triggering obvious system errors. Model drift occurs when system behavior changes as real-world conditions shift, even though the underlying model code remains unchanged. Spoofing introduces a related risk once systems begin accepting inputs from external users or connected systems. Spoofing occurs when inputs are deliberately crafted to mislead a system into producing incorrect or unsafe outputs. When models are updated without appropriate controls, behavior can shift in ways that are difficult to predict or detect. These risks affect decision quality directly.

Financial

Financial risks reflect the direct economic consequences of AI-related failures or other inaccuracies. These losses can arise when AI systems are used in forecasting or financial analysis and produce incorrect results, or when investments in AI initiatives fail to deliver expected returns. Organizations may also face financial exposure from third-party damages caused by AI incidents. This exposure can take the form of compensation payments or remediation efforts required to restore operations. Financial risk often emerges as a downstream consequence of failures in other risk domains.

Regulatory and Legal

Regulatory and legal risks stem from non-compliance with laws and regulatory standards that apply to AI systems based on how and where they are deployed. In many cases, the governing legal obligations arise from existing technology, labor, consumer protection, or sector-specific laws that apply to the underlying business process, rather than from AI-specific regulation alone. Risks include failure to meet requirements related to data protection or antidiscrimination laws. Additional obligations related to transparency can further increase exposure. Sector-specific rules may introduce separate compliance risks, particularly in financial services or healthcare, where AI regulation is more developed.

Legal risk often arises from regulatory uncertainty. Many organizations struggle to stay current on new requirements or to interpret how overlapping legal obligations apply to specific AI use cases. Regulatory inquiries and enforcement actions can arise after systems are deployed. Fines or sanctions may follow once harms become visible. These risks require ongoing coordination between the legal function and the business.

Reputational

Reputational risks arise when AI incidents become visible to customers, employees, or other stakeholders. Broad public exposure can follow as incidents gain external attention. Ethical lapses or discriminatory outcomes can erode trust quickly with affected stakeholders. Publicized system failures often accelerate that loss of confidence. Lack of transparency in AI-driven decisions often intensifies scrutiny and speeds stakeholder response. Reputational damage can also arise through association with controversial partners or vendors. Once trust is undermined, recovery can be slow and costly, even when legal liability is limited. Reputational risk may convert localized failures into enterprise-wide impact.

The Deloitte incident also reveals how AI-related risk rarely remains contained within the function where it first appears. What began as an issue of accurate document preparation and review quickly rebounded into broader enterprise exposure once the report became public, with more than 150 media articles linked to the incident in the OECD's "AI Incidents and Hazards Monitor."[14] Questions about client trust and professional credibility naturally followed, even though the underlying policy recommendations remained intact. This pattern is increasingly common. AI-related incidents often surface initially as localized concerns but quickly escalate into legal or reputational matters under external scrutiny. In that sense, AI risk is about how quickly ordinary issues can propagate across the enterprise and, at times, across jurisdictions. The same incident often activates more than one risk category at once. In Deloitte's case, the episode implicated operational risk, governance and oversight risk, reputational risk, and potential regulatory and legal risk. The sections that follow provide a more structured review of these risk categories.

Cybersecurity

Cybersecurity risks include exposure to cyberattacks or data leaks. As the McDonald's hiring platform incident further illustrates, AI-enabled systems used in routine business processes can introduce data security exposure when access controls fail. Researchers Carroll and Curry discovered that the McHire platform allowed access to applicant chat records and personal information after the researchers identified simple authentication weaknesses, including an administrator password of 123456. The data accessed included applicant names, email addresses, and phone numbers.[15] This exposure underscores how AI-mediated systems that collect personal data can create cybersecurity risk even when no advanced intrusion techniques are involved.

Malicious exploitation of AI systems introduces a separate and growing threat. AI introduces new attack surfaces through exposed system interfaces. Dependence on data assets creates additional security exposure. Inadequate security controls can allow adversaries to manipulate outputs or gain unauthorized access to sensitive data. Operational disruption often follows once system integrity is compromised. Cyber risk is amplified when incident response processes do not account for AI-specific failure modes. These risks intersect with broader enterprise security and resilience responsibilities.

Ethical and societal harms appear throughout these categories because they generate enterprise exposure. Discriminatory outcomes or privacy violations matter here because they can trigger regulatory scrutiny or legal liability. Loss of stakeholder trust often follows once these harms become visible. Ethical analysis is addressed directly in later chapters. In this chapter, these harms are treated as upstream drivers that shape enterprise risk.

These eight categories reflect how AI-related risks enter the enterprise and how they typically escalate. They align with how many organizations already structure risk oversight and accountability. That alignment enables AI risk to be addressed through existing governance processes rather than treated as a separate analytical exercise.

Generative and Agentic AI as a Distinct Risk Multiplier

AI development milestones can materially alter the enterprise risk landscape. Earlier forms of AI already challenged traditional governance and risk oversight models. New technical capabilities introduced by generative and agentic systems increase the pace at which risk materializes. They also increase the breadth of exposure across the enterprise. These changes do not create an entirely new category of enterprise risk. Instead, these capabilities amplify existing forms of exposure across enterprise strategy and operations. Legal compliance and security are affected as technical capability and scale increase. Organizational reputation is affected as well. Similar amplification effects are already visible in agentic systems that introduce greater system autonomy and can reasonably be expected as AI capabilities continue to expand.

This distinction is reflected clearly in the updated guidance issued by the National Institute of Standards and Technology. NIST AI 600-1 was developed to address risks specific to GenAI systems, reflecting the recognition that earlier risk frameworks were not sufficient on their own. As NIST cautions, "some GAI [GenAI] risks are unknown, and are therefore difficult to properly scope or evaluate given the uncertainty about potential GAI scale, complexity, and capabilities."[16] This uncertainty complicates traditional approaches to enterprise risk assessment, which rely on stable system behavior and historical precedent. As GenAI systems scale and are embedded into core business processes, this uncertainty materially alters how risk must be identified and governed at the enterprise level.

One of the most significant changes introduced by GenAI is non-deterministic output. Unlike traditional software systems, generative models can produce different outputs in response to similar inputs. This variability undermines traditional risk controls that rely on repeatable patterns and test case validation. Approval-based governance models that assume stable behavior struggle when outputs vary over time. Variation across users or contexts further weakens those assumptions. From an enterprise perspective, this variability affects reliability and auditability. Accountability is also harder to establish as outputs diverge. Regulated activities introduce additional sensitivity.

The introduction of agentic capabilities increases exposure further. When GenAI systems are granted autonomy to invoke tools or access data, the speed and impact of potential harm increases.[17] As systems initiate actions independently, human intervention drops and errors propagate faster across connected processes. In practice, this risk can emerge, for example, when multiple agents developed by different parties interact without shared constraints. As surveys conducted by SailPoint reveal, many companies have already experienced agents performing activities beyond their scope, including examples where one agent may initiate an action using partial or outdated information, while another responds by triggering downstream processes the first system was never designed to consider.[18] The resulting behavior can move outside expected operating bounds, even though each agent continues to function as it was individually configured. From an enterprise standpoint, system autonomy in this regard directly affects operational risk and legal liability. Financial exposure may follow once impacts materialize.

GenAI also magnifies the scale of downstream misuse. These systems enable rapid creation of content or code. Misuse can occur internally through inappropriate employee reliance or externally through malicious exploitation. The resulting harms can spread quickly across jurisdictions and digital platforms. The "International AI Safety Report" reinforces this point by emphasizing that advances in general purpose AI are expanding what malicious actors can do and increasing the governance burden of containing misuse.[19] The report links recent capability gains, especially stronger step-by-step problem-solving and longer autonomous operation, to heightened risk implications in domains like biological and cybersecurity.

Concrete evidence from model provider monitoring aligns with this assessment. Anthropic reports that in 2025, a cybercrime group used Claude Code to assist in a data extortion campaign. According to Anthropic's threat intelligence team, the actor used Claude Code to automate reconnaissance and to credential data harvesting. This attack affected at least 17 distinct organizations in a one-month period, in privacy-sensitive sectors including government, healthcare, emergency services, and religious institutions.[20] The same features that make these systems broadly useful also enable faster misuse and complicate oversight once deployed.

The risks addressed in this chapter are already present in deployed enterprise systems. Enterprises across sectors have already experienced incidents involving inaccurate outputs or data leakage. Intellectual property exposure and misuse of GenAI tools have also been observed. In the Deloitte incident described previously in this chapter, generative systems produced inaccurate summaries or fabricated references that moved through established review processes. In other cases, including the McDonald's hiring platform, routine use of AI-enabled systems exposed sensitive applicant data after access controls failed, revealing how data leakage can occur once AI tools are embedded into everyday workflows.

Near misses are becoming all too common. In many of these cases, organizations discover exposure only after systems are already embedded into process workflows. This pattern shows that GenAI risk already operates as a present enterprise concern. Research from the MIT AI Risk Initiative discussed previously reinforces this conclusion. Their findings signal that enterprise governance structures have not kept pace with the operational embedding of GenAI as systems scale across workflows.

Generative and agentic AI functions as a risk multiplier because they intensify existing enterprise exposure. They increase exposure across strategy, operations, compliance, security, and reputation as scale and autonomy expand.

The presence of these capabilities does not mean they should be avoided. Governance and risk oversight must adapt because static controls and fragmented ownership no longer contain risk effectively. Effective oversight requires continuous monitoring tied to clear accountability within ERM structures.

Integrating AI Risk into Enterprise Governance

Understanding AI risk does not, on its own, make that risk governable. Risk becomes governable when it is embedded into the structures and protocols through which enterprises already exercise oversight and personal accountability. For most organizations, this does not require creating entirely new governance bodies or parallel reporting lines. It requires integrating AI risk into existing enterprise governance mechanisms in a disciplined and highly visible way.

AI risk sits squarely within enterprise governance because it affects decisions boards and management teams already oversee. Treating it as an exception weakens escalation and delays response. Embedding AI risk into existing governance channels ensures that material issues surface through established paths.

A primary integration point is the role of risk committees. Whether at the board or management level, risk committees already exist to provide oversight of material enterprise exposure. AI risk should be incorporated into their regular agendas rather than handled as an occasional briefing or technical update. This does not require committees to review model architectures or AI development practices. It requires visibility into where AI is deployed and the functions (and decisions) it influences. Risk materiality must also be assessed in light of organizational objectives. Regular review of AI-related exposure alongside other enterprise risks reinforces that AI is subject to the same governance expectations.

While at EY, I founded a long-running collaboration with MIT and Professor Alex "Sandy" Pentland's Connection Science team. The original focus of this collaboration was AI literacy for a broad range of public and private sector leaders. Over time, it became clear that risk and internal audit leaders required targeted AI education. In my final years at EY, we deliberately pivoted the collaboration toward AI literacy for internal audit, with a particular focus on chief audit executives.

I co-led this internal audit focus alongside Jessica Rodgers, EY's Global Internal Audit Leader. Across those sessions, one insight was consistent. Internal audit sits closest to how systems actually operate. Audit teams understand controls and data dependencies. They see where model assumptions fail under real operating conditions. When these professionals are AI literate, they detect risk signals earlier than other enterprise functions.

Internal audit therefore plays a direct role in integrating AI risk into enterprise oversight. Audit functions are positioned to assess whether AI governance processes operate as intended. They provide independent assurance that controls and reporting structures function effectively. Internal audit is not expected to validate model architectures or test algorithms. Its value lies in assessing whether governance and escalation mechanisms operate effectively in practice. When AI risk is embedded into audit planning, it becomes part of the organization's ongoing assurance cycle rather than a one-time review.

This places the chief audit executive (CAE) in a distinct role. The CAE is often the first to detect when AI systems drift from intended use or when controls weaken as systems scale. Gaps between ethical commitments and operational reality surface early through the audit function. When internal audit is equipped to engage early, it becomes a core mechanism for AI risk discovery and management.

While advising companies on AI strategy and governance, I taught a course at Boston University School of Law titled "Innovation, Technology, and the Law." My work on AI risk and ethics informed that teaching. The course applied classic innovation theory to advanced technologies such as AI or blockchain. It examined how these forces were reshaping legal practice. That experience informs how I approach enterprise AI governance. Legal functions are playing a central role in managing AI risk, but only when lawyers adequately understand how these systems function. They must also recognize where judgment is embedded and how innovation alters accountability.

Enterprises do not need to invent new governance structures to manage AI risk. They need to rely on the governance mechanisms they already have more deliberately. Embedding AI risk into risk committees and internal audit creates visibility. Compliance reporting reinforces accountability and supports meaningful oversight. With this foundation in place, governance discussions can move from identifying risk to discharging fiduciary responsibility.

Closing

The incidents examined in this chapter reveal that AI risk is no longer speculative or confined to technical teams. In the Deloitte case, GenAI entered a routine professional workflow and escaped review processes built for human authorship. The resulting exposure arose from a governance breakdown as much as it was from a technical failure. At McDonald's, an AI-enabled hiring platform embedded through a third-party vendor introduced cybersecurity exposure. In both cases, material risk became visible only after deployment, once AI systems were already woven into everyday work.

These examples point to a broader conclusion. AI risk is already an enterprise risk, and it behaves differently from the risks traditional ERM models were designed to handle. Learning systems change during use. Risk, therefore, does not remain stable after approval. Failures more often arise from unclear accountability or delayed escalation than from lack of technical sophistication.

This chapter has shown why AI risk becomes governable only when it is treated as a core enterprise concern and embedded into existing oversight structures. Once that framing is accepted, the next issue follows directly. If AI risk is material and dynamic, what duties does it impose on those responsible for oversight? Chapter 5 examines those fiduciary responsibilities and considers how boards and executives must adapt their oversight practices in AI-enabled enterprises.

5 Fiduciary Oversight

AI Systems and Fiduciary Duties

At first glance, this does not look like a governance story.

There is no visible crisis. Markets are open. Transactions are clearing. Employees are working through ordinary days supported by ordinary systems. Inside JPMorgan Chase (JPMorgan), complex analytical models are running quietly beneath the surface of the enterprise. These systems influence how risk is assessed, how capital is allocated, how fraud is identified, and how employees perform daily work using automation and generative AI tools.[1] Independent industry assessments consistently place JPMorgan among the leading institutions in artificial intelligence (AI) adoption, reinforcing that these systems are not only deeply embedded but also central to the firm's strategy.

Nothing is visibly wrong, and that is precisely the point.

For JPMorgan, governance needs arise from operational dependence. When analytical systems influence decisions that carry financial or legal consequence, responsibility extends beyond technology teams. It reaches the professionals accountable for business outcomes and the functions that support them through system design and sustained supervision.

Large financial institutions have long recognized that the outputs produced by analytical models are inherently imperfect. Their limitations often surface gradually. Assumptions age. Data environments shift. Market conditions change. These developments do not always produce immediate signals. Instead, they can accumulate quietly until scrutiny arrives through internal reviews or external inquiry.

That structural reality shaped how JPMorgan approached oversight for advanced AI-driven analytics and automation as they became more powerful and deeply embedded in day-to-day operations. That oversight framework defines documentation standards and requires independent review before use and during operation. JPMorgan's 2024 annual report makes the structure more concrete. It explains that a "dedicated independent function, Model Risk Governance and Review ("MRGR"), defines and governs the Firm's policies related to the management of model risk," while model risk is owned by users of models within the lines of business and corporate functions. The same disclosure explains that users and developers must monitor model performance on an ongoing basis after approval.[2]

This approach reflects a clear allocation of accountability. Once intelligent systems influence large numbers of decisions, they function as enterprise control mechanisms. Their failure would attach to fiduciary responsibilities.

JPMorgan publicly acknowledges that it has launched and manages hundreds of AI and advanced analytics use cases across the firm.[3] These systems touch compliance, risk management, customer experience, and internal efficiencies.[4] That breadth is also reflected in external benchmarking. In the 2025 Evident AI Index for banks, JPMorgan ranked first overall for the fourth consecutive year and placed first in three of the index's four pillars: innovation, leadership, and transparency. This index report includes a June 2025 quote from CEO Jamie Dimon, when he said that there would be "no job, no process, no function that won't be affected by AI."[5] As reliance grows, so does the need for structured oversight and the associated accountability. That scale is visible in the firm's 2024 investor materials, which describe that AI is being used to "enhance [client] experience, manage risks, and drive efficiencies." The materials point to broad AI deployment across the business intended to remove "no joy work," "drive productivity," and "increase revenue."[6]

The tension is real: new growth (rapid and at scale) pulls in one direction. Enterprise risk management (control and assurance) pulls in another. Innovation teams want the ultimate freedom to deploy new solutions, or as they say, the enterprise will face its most significant risk: obsolescence. Risk leaders want confidence that what is deployed will not fail and expose the enterprise to financial and reputational harms. And the board, together with senior management, layers within the organization removed from the software code but accountable for technology system outcomes, must rely on governance protocols designed to surface the right information and act accordingly.

This is where fiduciary responsibility quietly enters the room.

JPMorgan's public disclosures describe technology and model risk as material to the firm's business.[7] These disclosures explain how responsibility for model use and remediation is assigned across the organization. This is an acknowledgment that when systems drive outcomes, adequate oversight and sufficient human involvement are critical to sound corporate governance. A failure to identify and respond appropriately to those risks would not be viewed as just an unfortunate surprise; instead, it would be viewed as a governance breakdown.

What makes JPMorgan's posture instructive is not that it claims to have eliminated risk; it has not. The firm instead acknowledges that oversight obligations follow from dependency.[8] When organizations rely on systems to shape outcomes, fiduciary responsibility extends to the corporate officers who oversee those systems and the teams that support them.

This logic is not new. Courts have applied it for decades in industries once far removed from AI: healthcare, financial services, pharmaceuticals, aviation, food production, catering and restaurants, information technology. Expectations focus on whether reasonable systems exist to surface risk and support informed judgment. AI intensifies that expectation.

The question, then, is not whether AI demands entirely new fiduciary duties. The question is how existing duties are being applied as intelligent systems become embedded in everyday decision-making. To understand how courts assess those duties, and what happens when governance systems fall short, we now turn to the legal doctrine that has quietly reshaped corporate accountability since the *Caremark* decision in 1996.

The Legal Architecture of Fiduciary Oversight

Although the cases discussed in this chapter typically arise from shareholder actions challenging board conduct, the principles they establish do not stop at the boardroom door. Fiduciary obligations also extend to corporate officers who exercise authority over enterprise systems and risk-bearing decisions. In practice, those obligations shape how oversight is carried out across the organization, through the people and structures responsible for governance systems and their use.

The governance posture described in the opening JPMorgan narrative reflects a legal architecture, principally constructed by Delaware courts (see Figure 5.1). Long before AI entered the corporate vernacular, those courts were grappling with a recurring question: When does leadership's failure to discover or oversee risk become a breach of fiduciary duty?

The answer emerged through a line of cases that reshaped the duty of corporate oversight. Collectively, they make clear that fiduciary responsibility is not satisfied by good intentions or formal compliance structures alone. It depends on whether leaders have designed and maintained systems capable of surfacing material risks in areas that matter most to the enterprise and what those leaders actually do when the risks materialize.

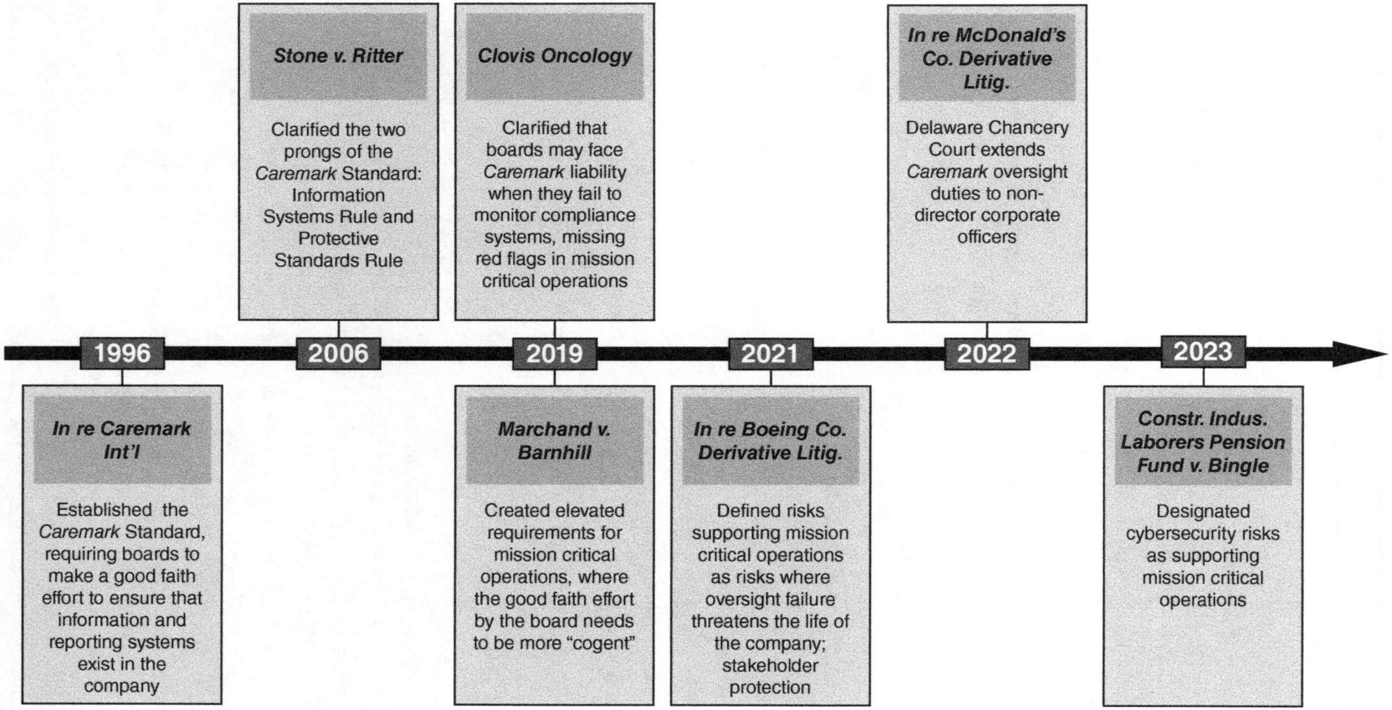

Figure 5.1 ***Caremark*** **and its progeny: Evolution of minimum oversight standards.**

Source: © BAIE Research Team, 2026.

That doctrine took its modern shape with the *Caremark* ruling.

In *In re Caremark International Inc. Derivative Litigation* (1996), the Delaware Court of Chancery articulated what would become the foundational standard for fiduciary oversight. The case arose from widespread violations of healthcare regulations. Its lasting contribution was doctrinal rather than a narrow interpretation of the decision tied to a particular company or industry. The court recognized that board directors are not responsible for day-to-day management. As the court explained, "But, of course, the duty to act in good faith to be informed cannot be thought to require directors to possess detailed information about all aspects of the operation of the enterprise. Such a requirement would simpl[y] be inconsistent with the scale and scope of efficient organization size in this technological age."[9] It nonetheless held that fiduciary duty includes an obligation to ensure reasonable information and reporting systems designed to surface legal or regulatory risks.[10]

Importantly, in its *Caremark* ruling the court did not impose liability for isolated failures. The court emphasized that oversight liability attaches only in cases of "sustained or systematic failure."[11] That failure may involve the absence of reporting systems. However, the threshold was intentionally held high. The expectation was that oversight functions as a continuing responsibility.[12] Corporate boards need a certain degree of deference to their business decision-making. Courts have historically granted that deference but are also prepared to grant remedies to aggrieved shareholders where appropriate.

A decade later, the Delaware Supreme Court clarified and reinforced this principle in *Stone v. Ritter* (2006), translating the *Caremark* doctrine into the two-part oversight framework that continues to govern fiduciary oversight claims. At its core, the oversight doctrine operates through two fiduciary obligations:

- First, directors must make a good-faith effort to establish reasonable information and reporting systems that allow material legal and operational risks to surface.
- Second, once those systems exist, directors must actually use them, responding to red flags when they appear rather than allowing known risks to go unaddressed.

Liability arises from a sustained failure to see or act when fiduciary responsibility requires it.

The court confirmed oversight failure constitutes a breach of the duty of loyalty when it reflects bad faith. *Bad faith* was defined in this context as a conscious failure to act in the face of fiduciary obligation.[13]

Together, *Caremark* and *Stone* established the core, contemporary architecture of fiduciary oversight. These landmark decisions do not require boards to predict *every* risk or prevent *every* failure. They require leaders to ensure adequate systems are in place to promote transparency and to act when those red flags emerge.

Mission Critical Operations and Heightened Scrutiny

For years after *Caremark*, oversight claims seldom moved beyond the pleading stage. Courts were reluctant to second-guess fiduciary decision-makers absent extraordinary facts. That reluctance began to erode as cases arose in which failures occurred in areas central to the company's business model and regulatory posture. The shift became unmistakable in *Marchand v. Barnhill* (2019). There, the Delaware Supreme Court allowed an oversight claim to proceed against the board of an ice cream manufacturer following a listeria outbreak that resulted in multiple deaths. The court's reasoning was notable for its clarity. Food safety, the court explained, was "mission critical" to the company's operations. The board lacked a meaningful system for monitoring food safety risk. The record showed no dedicated oversight mechanism and no indication that governance structures addressed the risk most likely to cause catastrophic harm.[14]

The court in *Marchand* reframed the oversight inquiry when risk emanated from mission critical operations. The relevant question focused on whether oversight systems were designed to align with risks tied to the enterprise's most consequential operations.

That logic was extended in the *Clovis Oncology* (2019) decision. There, the court focused on a biopharmaceutical company whose core value depended on the success of a single clinical trial. The board had established formal compliance structures. Those structures failed to surface known deviations from trial protocols. The court rejected the argument that the mere existence of committees and policies satisfied fiduciary duties. What mattered was whether the board received accurate, timely information about risks central to the company's survival and responded when that information surfaced.[15]

Across these cases, a clear pattern emerged. When operations are mission critical, oversight must be appropriately scaled and deliberately tailored.

Stakeholder Protection

Recent corporate governance decisions applying Delaware's oversight doctrine have clarified how fiduciary oversight operates when mission critical risks affecting stakeholders also threaten the enterprise itself. This dynamic is particularly evident in *In re Boeing Company Derivative Litigation* (2021), which arose after two fatal crashes of the company's 737 MAX aircraft and the subsequent grounding of the fleet.

The derivative claims were brought by shareholders, not passengers or regulators. The theory of harm was straightforward. The board's failure to exercise adequate oversight over aircraft safety, clearly a core, mission critical enterprise function, was alleged to have materially diminished shareholder value through massive financial losses and intense regulatory scrutiny. Reputational damage also followed. The court accepted that premise as its analysis extended beyond the narrow issue of shareholder harm advanced by the plaintiffs.

In assessing the board's conduct, the court emphasized that aircraft safety was a mission critical risk for Boeing and therefore required rigorous oversight at the board level. Drawing on the Delaware Supreme Court's decision in *Marchand*, the court explained that directors face heightened oversight obligations when safety sits at the core of a company's operations. As the court stated, "the Board has a rigorous oversight obligation where safety is mission critical, as the fallout from the Board's utter failure to try to satisfy this 'bottom-line requirement' can cause material suffering among customers, or to the public at large, and attendant reputational and financial harm to the company."[16] For a company whose products carry human lives, the court concluded that aircraft safety demanded board-level governance oversight.

The court found that Boeing's oversight systems fell far short of that standard. Safety oversight was fragmented across the organization, and no reliable mechanism existed to ensure that critical safety information reached the board in a usable form.[17] Even as warning signs accumulated, the court found no evidence of a structured process to ensure those signals reached the board in a way that required engagement or response.[18]

Critically, the court rejected the notion that fiduciary oversight could be satisfied through generic compliance programs or high-level assurances. Instead, it emphasized that boards must implement governance systems capable of monitoring mission critical safety risks. When those systems fail, harm to customers or the public (stakeholders) may translate directly into enterprise harm through regulatory consequences or reputational damage. Financial losses may also follow as a result. In this way, the decision illustrates how protecting shareholder value in safety-critical industries depends on governing risks that affect stakeholders.

The *Boeing* decision thus represents a significant application of Delaware's modern oversight doctrine. It confirms that boards face heightened scrutiny when they fail to implement governance systems capable of monitoring mission critical risks. In industries where those risks directly affect stakeholders, failures of oversight can quickly translate into enterprise-wide harm. Although derivative claims are brought in the name of shareholders, the risks that trigger fiduciary scrutiny can also arise from harms experienced by stakeholders.

Oversight Responsibility and Corporate Officers

Also critical to this analysis, in *In re McDonald's Corporation Stockholder Derivative Litigation* (2023), the Delaware Court of Chancery clarified that fiduciary oversight obligations under *Caremark* are not only confined to corporate boards but also extend to senior officers who exercise operational authority over risks within the scope of the officer's duties.[19] The case arose from pervasive allegations of workplace misconduct and harassment, but its significance to the issues addressed in this book lies less in the narrow facts themselves than in the court's articulation of who bears responsibility for oversight when organizational systems fail.

As in prior board oversight cases addressed in this chapter, the claims were brought by shareholders, alleging that repeated failures to address known misconduct had significantly harmed the corporation through reputational damage and intense regulatory scrutiny, resulting in the erosion of enterprise value. The court accepted that premise but focused its analysis on whether senior leadership had fulfilled its fiduciary obligation to monitor and respond to risks embedded in both company culture and its management systems.

The court's reasoning supports the conclusion that workplace culture functions as an organizational system capable of exposing the enterprise to foreseeable harm when left unchecked. Where red flags relating to personal misconduct are persistent and unaddressed, the decision indicates that a failure of oversight may give rise to fiduciary liability, whether that failure occurs at the board level or within the executive suite.[20]

Decisively, the *McDonald's* court held that officers charged with responsibility for human resources or operational leadership cannot sidestep oversight duties on the ground that they do not sit on the board. When an officer has been delegated authority over a risk central to the company's operations, that officer bears a corresponding duty to establish reasonable monitoring systems and to act in good faith when warning signs (red flags, as labeled by the Delaware Courts) emerge.

In this respect, *McDonald's* completes an important doctrinal arc. If *Boeing* confirms that boards must oversee mission critical *stakeholder* risks, *McDonald's* makes clear that those duties cascade downward to *corporate officers* whose roles place them closest to the systems through which such risks manifest. Fiduciary oversight, the court explained, follows responsibility. It does not stop at the boardroom door;

some board members engage in business affairs on a quarterly basis, at their board meeting. But corporate officers are directly engaged on critical issues on a daily basis. The fiduciary oversight responsibilities must extend to these ever-present executives.

Construction Industry Laborers Pension Fund v. Bingle (2022) reinforced this trajectory in the context of cybersecurity oversight. The case arose after a cyberattack on SolarWinds prompted shareholders to challenge the adequacy of the company's governance and reporting structures for monitoring cybersecurity risk. Shareholders alleged that the board had failed to implement and monitor reporting systems capable of elevating cybersecurity threats to the board level, even though SolarWinds's software business depended on trusted access to customer information technology systems.[21]

The case is significant because it illustrates how Delaware oversight doctrine applies to modern technological risk domains. Cybersecurity failures often emerge from interconnected enterprise systems rather than isolated operational breakdowns. The decision signals that boards must ensure governance structures capable of monitoring these system-level risks as they evolve.

None of these cases imposed a duty to micromanage. Each reaffirmed the same principle: leaders must ensure that information about mission critical risks reaches the board and triggers response when those red flags emerge.

Designing Fiduciary Oversight Systems

Read together, these decisions articulate a coherent theory of fiduciary oversight. Liability does not arise from a failure to review a particular operational decision or from an inability to anticipate a specific breakdown. It arises from failures in governance system design that prevent risks from becoming visible before harm occurs or from a failure to act on any red flags.

That theory explains why the governance posture exhibited by JPMorgan and described at the outset of this chapter has become a defining feature of modern fiduciary oversight. When enterprises rely on complex systems to drive outcomes across the enterprise, whether those systems involve food production, aircraft design, clinical trials, or advanced analytics, the fiduciary obligation is the same. Leadership must ensure that risk does not remain buried inside technology or managerial silos.

Courts have been consistent on this point. Oversight focuses on governance architecture. With that legal foundation in place, as AI increasingly facilitates decisions central to enterprise performance and stakeholder trust, the questions becomes whether it now qualifies as the kind of mission critical system that fiduciary oversight doctrine has long been designed to address. It is the focus of the next section.

Why AI Falls Within *Caremark's* Scope

The fiduciary oversight framework articulated in *Caremark* and refined through later decisions was, of course, not designed for technology systems. It was designed to address a recurring governance challenge: how leadership should oversee risks that are central to enterprise performance and regulatory scrutiny, together with stakeholder protection. The most relevant question is whether AI now presents the kind of risk profile that fiduciary oversight doctrine has historically addressed, especially as AI routinely affects mission critical company operations.

Across industries, the answer has become clearer. AI now operates as a core enterprise system, shaping outcomes throughout the enterprise. As a result, I believe it falls squarely within the scope of fiduciary oversight doctrine courts have already developed, without requiring any doctrinal leap.

AI as a Regulatory Risk

One of the clearest signals that AI fits squarely within *Caremark's* scope lies in its regulatory profile. AI systems operate in a rapidly evolving global legal environment characterized by fragmented authority and uneven governmental enforcement. Formal rules often lag technology capabilities, and regulatory guidance routinely articulates desired outcomes, such as fairness, safety, transparency, explainability, and accountability, rather than prescribing specific technical controls.

From a fiduciary perspective, regulatory uncertainty heightens oversight obligations. Delaware courts have never conditioned fiduciary duty on the existence of settled regulation. In *Caremark* and its progeny, oversight obligations attach when risks are foreseeable and material. Leadership is expected to design information and reporting systems capable of surfacing legal and regulatory risk even in ambiguous regulatory environments, including those created by rapidly developing AI systems.

AI certainly fits this pattern. As explored in Chapter 2, enterprises deploying AI systems face increasing exposure across existing legal regimes, including antidiscrimination law, consumer protection, data privacy, safety regulation, and securities disclosure. Enforcement actions and litigation increasingly rely on general legal duties in the absence of AI-specific statutes. In this context, AI risk cannot be treated as speculative or premature. It is already embedded in the company's compliance posture. The governance approach involving JP Morgan and described in the opening narrative reinforces this point. Treating AI as part of existing compliance and model risk governance, rather than as a separate or exceptional domain, reflects an understanding that fiduciary oversight must reach the risks embedded in operational systems.

AI as a Multidimensional Enterprise Risk

Beyond regulatory exposure, AI presents a form of enterprise risk that courts have repeatedly identified as requiring heightened fiduciary oversight. That risk is systemic and difficult to isolate within a single function. AI systems can generate biased or discriminatory outcomes, undermine safety and reliability, expose sensitive data, and erode trust. These risks rarely manifest as discrete technical failures. More often, they emerge through patterns of behavior that become visible only when the systems operate in widespread use within the enterprise. When harm occurs, it often results from accumulated governance gaps rather than from a single design flaw.

This risk profile closely mirrors those examined in *Marchand, Boeing,* and *McDonald's,* in particular. In each case, the court rejected the notion that fiduciary oversight could be satisfied through generalized controls or fragmented responsibility. What mattered was whether oversight was structured on risks that cut across organizational boundaries and carried foreseeable downstream harm.

AI presents the same challenge, especially when it supports operations that are mission critical to the enterprise. Its risks do not reside solely within a single organizational function.

They travel through interconnected systems that support core business operations. When oversight is dispersed or informal, warning signs are easily missed. When escalation pathways are unclear, red flags lose urgency and are not acted on. Courts have shown little tolerance for governance models that allow mission critical risks to fall between organizational seams.

Johnson & Johnson's long-standing approach to governing products and systems with foreseeable downstream harm illustrates how fiduciary oversight operates when risk is inherent in the enterprise's products and systems. Long before contemporary debate about AI governance, the company confronted the reality that certain enterprise systems, such as pharmaceutical manufacturing and consumer health products, carry inherent risk even when designed and operated in good faith.

This philosophy became visible during the 1982 Tylenol cyanide crisis, a case often cited to illustrate governance responses to system-level risk. The company voluntarily recalled approximately 31 million bottles nationwide despite the absence of manufacturing fault, prioritizing systemic risk containment and public trust over short-term financial impact.[22] That decision reflected a governance posture in which leadership recognized that foreseeable harm (regardless of source) triggered heightened corporate oversight obligations. Over time, this posture was institutionalized through the company's quality and safety committees and board-level visibility into product risk and remediation.[23] The fiduciary lesson for AI governance follows directly from this posture. When harm is foreseeable because of how a system operates, oversight must address governance design before failure occurs. Courts assessing fiduciary duty ask whether leaders designed governance systems capable of surfacing and responding to risk before it materializes across the enterprise.

AI as Enterprise Infrastructure

AI increasingly functions as enterprise infrastructure. In many companies, similar to JPMorgan, AI systems are already influencing revenue generation, compliance outcomes, safety decisions, and trust-based relationships with customers and regulators. These systems shape how the business operates.

Fiduciary doctrine has long treated organizational reliance as a key amplifier of oversight obligation. As enterprise reliance on a system increases, fiduciary responsibility to ensure appropriate governance increases as well. Courts do not ask whether directors understand the technical details of food production or aircraft design, for example. They ask whether boards recognized dependency and responded by designing oversight structures commensurate with that reliance and the significance of the underlying mission critical issues. AI now meets that standard in many organizations. As automation increases at scale, so does the cost of failure, and the foreseeability of harm to the enterprise. At that point, AI governance becomes a fiduciary concern. The governance posture described in the JPMorgan example at the outset of this chapter reflects the same recognition: as AI becomes embedded in core enterprise systems, oversight structures must evolve to ensure risks are surfaced before they scale across the organization.

Taken together, these considerations place AI squarely within the scope of *Caremark*-based fiduciary oversight. Existing doctrine is sufficient to support this conclusion. The criteria courts have already articulated apply directly. What remains unresolved is how intentionally fiduciary actors choose to oversee AI. That question is addressed in the sections that follow.

Designing Fiduciary Oversight Systems

The fiduciary principles described in the preceding sections converge on a single insight: oversight succeeds or fails by design. Delaware courts do not measure fiduciary performance by outcomes alone. They examine whether governance architecture exists that can make mission critical risks clear and actionable before harm occurs. Courts do not prescribe exactly how boards must organize and execute sufficient oversight. Instead, courts assess whether reasonable systems exist and whether those systems function in practice. Judicial opinions provide guidance on the elements that characterize appropriate oversight systems.

Across the case law, four recurring requirements emerge that fiduciary actors are expected to have in place when risk becomes mission critical.

Reasonable Information and Reporting Systems

At the foundation of fiduciary oversight lies the obligation to establish reasonable information and reporting systems. These systems do not need to be leading, they just need to be reasonable. Boards are not expected to monitor operations directly, but they are expected to ensure that material risks tied to core enterprise activities can surface through reliable channels. Oversight fails when information systems do not reliably surface information that requires attention. Courts have repeatedly emphasized that what matters is whether governance systems surface issues that require leadership attention. When mission critical risks remain buried within operational silos, the governance system designed to surface them may break down.

Fiduciary responsibility turns on whether boards have made a good-faith effort to design and maintain systems capable of surfacing material risk in areas central to the enterprise. That standard does not fluctuate with technology, routine or advanced. Applied to AI, this requirement turns on whether boards have a reasonable system in place to receive AI-related risk information from management in a form that is digestible and ultimately actionable. Model behavior and post-deployment issues must move through established governance channels rather than being constrained to technical teams. Oversight weakens when AI risk is visible only through tools or reviews that never reach those accountable for enterprise outcomes.

Clear Ownership and Escalation Paths

Effective oversight also depends on clarity of responsibility. Fiduciary duty requires accountability for monitoring each mission critical risk domain, supported by clear escalation paths when concerns arise. Courts scrutinize governance failures where responsibility is poorly defined or implicit. When red flags appear but no one is clearly charged with responding, or when escalation depends on informal judgment rather than defined process, accountability breaks down.

In AI governance, clarity of ownership requires that responsibility for system behavior does not dissipate after deployment. Accountability must extend to how AI systems operate over time, including how concerns are escalated to the board (typically from AI governance teams) when assumptions fail or impacts shift.

Where AI oversight relies on informal judgment without defined escalation, critical risks can persist without leadership intervention.

Regular Board-Level Visibility into Mission Critical Systems

Oversight should not be episodic. Courts evaluate whether boards maintain consistent visibility into risks central to the company's regulatory posture and operations. This requires more than the passive receipt of information. It requires structured engagement through regular reporting, board-level discussion, director inquiry, and follow-up sufficient to support informed oversight. As emphasized in the *Boeing* decision, courts have criticized governance structures that fail to bring mission critical safety issues to the board in a consistent and usable form. Sporadic reporting or a post-incident review will not satisfy fiduciary expectations.[24] The JPMorgan governance posture described previously in this chapter illustrates this principle in practice. As reliance on complex systems increases, expectations also increase for disciplined, documented board engagement.

In practice, many AI systems are influencing mission critical operations. Because of the unique risks inherent in these systems (as described in Chapter 4), fiduciary oversight requires periodic visibility at the leadership level. This visibility does not involve reviewing technical implementation. It involves receiving structured insight and showing interest into system performance and emerging risk over time.

Appropriate Responsiveness to Red Flags

Finally, fiduciary oversight demands an appropriate response to material risks. Under *Caremark* and *Stone v. Ritter*, liability arises when boards or officers consciously fail to act in the face of known risks. The law does not require perfect judgment, but it does require engagement. Red flags lose meaning if they do not trigger attention and deliberation. Courts focus on whether warning signs were acknowledged and ultimately addressed in good faith. Repeated inaction, rather than technical error, is what converts oversight weakness into fiduciary breach. This principle applies regardless of industry or domain. Whether governing financial systems, product safety, workplace culture, or emerging technologies, the expectation is the same: when material risks surface, governance systems must compel a direct and appropriate response.

In the context of AI, red flags often emerge through changes in model behavior after deployment, degradation in performance, unexpected outputs, or signals that an AI system is being used beyond its original design assumptions. Reviewing courts will focus on whether organizations have mechanisms that compel timely consideration and decision-making when AI systems begin to operate in ways that create foreseeable risk affecting large groups of users or stakeholders.

Taken together, these design principles describe how fiduciary oversight operates in practice. They do not mandate specific organizational forms or reporting artifacts. What they require is intentional governance architecture that ensures mission critical risks become visible and receive responsible attention. Where such architecture exists and functions as intended, fiduciary actors are positioned to meet their obligations.

Clarifying the Limits of Fiduciary Delegation and Scope

The deployment of AI systems often involves technical and operational complexity. Those realities necessitate delegation of implementation throughout AI teams. They do not justify delegation of oversight responsibility. Fiduciary doctrine draws a clear line between operational control and governance responsibility. Boards are not expected to understand technical implementation. They are expected to ensure that governance systems exist to surface material risk and require engagement. Recent case law confirms that when authority over mission critical systems is delegated to senior officers, fiduciary obligations follow that authority and remain subject to board oversight. Oversight requires structures that make risk visible before harm occurs and require engagement when warning signs (red flags) appear.

As AI becomes embedded in decisions that affect stakeholders (real people) at scale, ethical failures increasingly translate into financial and reputational harm. Courts have recognized this convergence. When stakeholder harm is foreseeable, the failure to oversee systems that generate that harm is treated as a fiduciary issue. This does not convert fiduciary duty into a generalized obligation to act ethically in all respects. It clarifies that when ethical risk is inseparable from enterprise value, it falls within the scope of oversight responsibility. In such contexts, ethical risk functions as a core form of fiduciary risk.

Closing

The opening JPMorgan narrative in this chapter described an enterprise that behaves as though failure of its analytical and AI-driven systems would carry fiduciary consequences. The analysis that followed explains why that posture aligns with how fiduciary oversight has evolved under Delaware law.

Across three decades of case law, courts have articulated an evolving framework for evaluating oversight responsibility. Beginning with *Caremark* and clarified in

Stone v. Ritter, fiduciary duty requires the existence of reasonable systems designed to surface material risk and to support engagement when warning signs emerge. Later cases sharpened that framework by focusing attention on mission critical operations.

More recent decisions reinforce that a fiduciary duty extends beyond shareholders to stakeholders. *Boeing* confirmed that when stakeholder harm is foreseeable in a mission critical domain, failure to oversee that risk can give rise to fiduciary liability. *McDonald's* clarified that these oversight obligations attach not only to boards but also to senior officers who exercise authority over core operational systems.

Taken together, these cases establish a legal baseline for governance design. Courts examine whether organizations have created systems that make risk visible, assign responsibility, support escalation, and require response. When those systems are absent (or ignored), fiduciary protection erodes.

AI fits squarely within this framework. In many enterprises, AI systems influence decisions that shape financial outcomes and public trust. As reliance on these systems increases, so does the obligation to ensure that their risks are subject to effective oversight. Fiduciary oversight turns on whether organizational dependence has reached a level where failure would predictably harm the enterprise and its stakeholders. The JPMorgan governance story described at the outset of this chapter illustrates how this logic operates in practice. Advanced analytics and AI are treated as part of the firm's core risk infrastructure rather than as experimental tools.

Courts define the minimum standard for fiduciary oversight. Leadership determines whether organizations operate above that floor. Enterprises that treat oversight as a design discipline, rather than a reactive obligation, are better positioned to protect stakeholders and sustain trust as technology becomes more deeply embedded in decision-making.

The next part of this book turns from doctrine to application. Part III introduces the Boundaries of Tolerance model as a practical framework to help leader teams determine what they will and will not tolerate in their AI systems.

PART III

The Boundaries of Tolerance Model

6 Introducing the Boundaries of Tolerance Model

The Moment That Prompted the Model

The boardroom episode shared by a participant in the Harvard Business School (HBS) forum, described in the Introduction, stayed with me long after the session concluded. It clarified a persistent gap in how directors and senior executives approach artificial intelligence (AI) oversight once systems are already operating inside the enterprise. A consumer-facing AI system at a global financial institution had produced biased outcomes affecting roughly 5% of users. The issue reached the board because the development team could not determine whether remediation was required. The discussion did not lead to a clear decision.

That bank board surely had experience governing complex issues arising from prior digital transformation initiatives. Like most companies, they likely confronted difficult ethical matters before, probably in the realm of personal or financial misconduct (think inappropriate work relationships or padded expense reports). However, the intersection of AI's complexity with unfamiliar questions of technology ethics was, perhaps, virgin territory for them. Judging from the other executives' reactions in the room, their own companies would have been just as stuck.

I remember the quiet that followed, the palpable tension as the room absorbed the dilemma that board had faced. They were thrust into confronting ethical ambiguity without a structured way to address or resolve it. As the HBS session ended that day, the usual post conference flurry began, with participants heading to Boston's Logan Airport for flights home. Boston has always been my home. That afternoon I had a long drive through the city's ridiculous traffic, the familiar moment after a session when the day's conversations start to replay in your mind. I couldn't shake the bank director's story. The discussion that followed felt so consequential. Why was that board divided on the matter? What was so novel about *this* particular issue that was especially troubling for the board?

At the time of the Harvard forum, I was beginning to plan my retirement from EY, and board service already intrigued me. Would I have known how to address the important ethical issues the board faced? Could I have offered an approach to unite this divided board? The issue boards are facing in this regard isn't ignorance; it is the absence of tools or shared experiences to navigate such a novel problem. Ethics is, of course, grounded in philosophy. But executives are rarely asked to wrestle with matters of philosophy; their work is inherently practical. What that board needed (and what so many executives now need) was a bridge from the philosophy of ethics to its practical application.

After the HBS forum, I returned to the dual rhythm of my work: leading a Harvard-based research team on AI governance and ethics, while advising scores of corporate boards and senior teams on these same questions in my leader role at EY. With the bank director's story still echoing, I began to see a pattern: capable leaders uneasy about how their governance responsibilities extend into the age of AI. Since that forum, I've heard versions of the same dilemma across sectors, from healthcare to manufacturing, each reflecting a growing unease and search for structure. If that boardroom discussion happened in your company, how would you have responded?

When I accepted an appointment in August 2023 at Harvard's Edmond & Lily Safra Center for Ethics to lead a new research initiative on ethical AI governance for the business community, I didn't anticipate the flood of interest from corporate leaders. Leaders weren't merely asking about cutting-edge AI applications; they were urgently seeking guidance on how to govern these intelligent systems. Some assumed regulators would eventually impose a globally consistent, heavy-handed compliance regime until it became evident that such intervention was unlikely. The questions from directors came from all corners: What are the risks we should be concerned about? What are our responsibilities? What governance frameworks are available for us to use in this new age of generative AI (GenAI)? How do we even know if an AI system is ethical?

It was now quite clear that the bank director's story was not an isolated incident. Business leaders were beginning to grasp that AI was not simply another tool in the digital-transformation toolkit. It was something more foundational and far more consequential. It was a technology capable of redefining business and reshaping stakeholder trust. It also challenged an enterprise's very sense of right and wrong.

The senior executives I've advised on matters of AI governance are certainly not unprincipled. On the contrary, they are thoughtful, experienced leaders trying to do the right thing in a rapidly evolving strategic context. But they often lack the framework to apply ethical reasoning to novel, high-stakes technological decisions. AI is complex, and ethics can be intimidating, even for seasoned leaders. Their convergence can feel overwhelming at times and demands a deliberate governance approach. Driving home from HBS that day, I couldn't shake the sense that this story wasn't an anomaly. It became the impetus for our continued work: to develop an AI-governance framework, rooted in ethics, to guide business leaders in their oversight journey.

Boards and executive teams across industries are being thrust into these dilemmas, often with no precedent to rely on. The rate of AI adoption is moving faster than most organizations' governance capacity. While technical teams can explain how a model performs, they should not be the final arbiters of enterprise ethics. That responsibility rests with boards and senior management.

This chapter addresses the question the board at the center of that HBS story struggled to answer. It focuses on enabling business leaders to meet their governance obligations when ethical oversight becomes a condition of deploying AI systems. The technology is developing so rapidly that leaders need practical guidance that can be implemented inside real governance structures. It begins with a fundamental question that the board at the center of that HBS story could benefit from addressing: *What are the ethical boundaries of what your company will tolerate when it comes to AI?* The Boundaries of Tolerance model was developed to address that question.

The model was designed for ethical decision-making at the enterprise level, because in order to appropriately address a real AI solution producing real ethical consequences (like that board in the HBS story), the organization must first build a values-based set of ethical boundaries for the institution and communicate those guardrails far and wide. This foundational guidance must come from leadership to protect stakeholders affected by how the company's AI systems are built or deployed. What follows explains how the Boundaries of Tolerance model came to be, and how it can be used by leaders who face AI decisions in practice. But first: Why should business leaders even care if their AI systems produce an ethical failure?

The Stakes of Getting It Wrong

The gap in ethical AI governance discussed thus far is playing out in lawsuits, headlines, stock prices, profit-and-loss statements, and boardrooms and C-suites, with real-world consequences for companies and the people affected by their decisions. In 2024 and 2025, several global brands faced shareholder resolutions demanding more transparency in how AI systems were governed.[1] These reputational and investor-driven pressures often outpace regulatory actions and increasingly influence long-term enterprise strategy and brand equity.

In this era of AI, ethical lapses surface quickly. Although organizations such as the Organisation for Economic Co-operation and Development and MIT provide comprehensive and invaluable records of the rapidly increasing number of AI incidents, these challenges have not yet been sufficiently analyzed or examined. However, there are considerable learnings to share from these unfortunate stories. I'll unpack some of these challenging AI deployments throughout the following chapters.

Across industries, patterns are emerging: rushed deployments of insufficiently tested AI systems in a race to remain competitive, opaque decision-making processes, underfunded governance functions, limited (or in some cases, non-existent) human intervention in the AI-driven decisions, and insufficient executive or board oversight. These breakdowns often stem from the same root causes; in many cases, organizations lack knowledge about unique AI risks and ethical sensitivities.

Consider a case from the healthcare sector.

UnitedHealthcare came under legal scrutiny for deploying a predictive AI system to help determine Medicare coverage decisions for post-acute care.[2] The company's model was designed to forecast patient recovery timelines. But court filings in a class action lawsuit allege that the system was deliberately designed to overestimate recovery speed, resulting in premature termination of care for elderly patients, many of whom lacked the financial means or capacity to challenge the decision. As of the time of this writing, the case is in discovery.[3]

The model reportedly operated with a 90% error rate and frequently overrode physicians' clinical judgment. Despite the high error rate, the company kept the AI model in use. The AI-generated output was treated by company leaders as final, overriding clinical judgment at the point of care.

From the class action pleadings: "The fraudulent scheme affords Defendants a clear financial windfall in the form of policy premiums without having to pay for promised care, while the elderly are prematurely kicked out of care facilities nationwide or forced to deplete family savings to continue receiving necessary medical care, all because an AI model 'disagrees' with their real live doctors' recommendations."[4]

Now consider a different case; this time in the tech sector.

Clearview AI, a facial recognition company, built a biometric database of more than 10 billion images by scraping photos from public websites without the consent of the individuals photographed.[5] The firm claimed the images were publicly available and therefore fair game to include in a database that fueled the facial recognition (AI) system. But courts across Europe and later in the United States disagreed. The company was hit with a series of high-profile fines and settlements, including a € 20 million penalty for violating the EU's General Data Protection Regulation[6] and an additional multimillion-dollar class action settlement in the United States.[7] The company was also ordered to delete all data related to individuals in Italy and barred from collecting additional personal data there for its facial recognition system.[8]

Regulators identified multiple violations, including lack of consent, unlimited data collection, and the absence of meaningful opt-out mechanisms. Privacy authorities determined that even though the company attempted to anonymize the images, its systems still allowed for individual identification, particularly when biometric data was combined with geolocation and other contextual metadata. The system was noncompliant with EU regulations and halted only after regulators intervened.

Another example involves exaggerated claims about AI capability rather than harmful AI output. Joonko Diversity, Inc. marketed an AI-powered recruiting platform designed to source diverse candidates for employers. The company's CEO emphasized to investors the platform's sophisticated algorithms for candidate matching. These claims were relied on by a large number of investors, convincing them to invest substantial capital in the enterprise in the form of an equity contribution. In reality, the platform lacked the advanced automation and AI capabilities that were pronounced by the company.

The CEO ultimately resigned, the company was forced into bankruptcy in May 2024,[9] and the SEC charged the company with "AI washing" (*AI washing* refers to the practice of exaggerating or falsely claiming the role or sophistication of AI in a product) and its founder/CEO with fraud.[10] As a result of the SEC investigation and the company's resulting bankruptcy, investors were left with significant financial losses.

These cases differ in sector and context (e.g., healthcare versus technology, flawed deployment versus deceptive marketing) but the governance gaps are strikingly similar.

Boards and senior management teams are increasingly being held accountable for AI failures. As legal theories evolve and regulators focus more attention on the governance of intelligent systems, directors and management teams cannot claim ignorance. They are expected to anticipate AI-related risk and take steps to mitigate it, not after the fact but during the AI system development stages. This shift mirrors a broader trend in corporate governance: the board and senior management are increasingly being viewed as guardians of enterprise values and stakeholder trust.

What should be clear to business leaders is that ethical AI governance is a practical necessity. And as these examples demonstrate, ethical failures translate directly into the same financial and reputational risks examined in Chapter 4. Without a clear governance framework, business leaders risk walking blindfolded through a landscape filled with financial and in some cases criminal exposure, together with stakeholder backlash.

The Boundaries of Tolerance model was created in response to this emerging frontier of risk, governance, and ethics. It helps leaders do more than react to ethical failures, it gives them the tools to help prevent them. But first, they must recognize that AI governance failures are the predictable result of operating without a principled road map.

Diagnosing the Governance Gap

The previous examples reveal something more than isolated AI failures. They expose the structural inadequacy of current governance models never designed to meet the scale or ethical complexity of modern AI systems. Many companies, of course, were deploying AI models across a range of business functions before the current GenAI movement. These earlier forms of AI are now often described as *traditional AI.* Traditional AI deployments were managed by self-contained teams of machine learning specialists, typically smaller than the cross-functional GenAI teams of today.

Most companies developed adequate governance protocols suited to these traditional AI systems. However, even if a company once had an effective framework to govern traditional AI, that model is unlikely to be fit for purpose in governing today's more ubiquitous GenAI systems. For example, a decade ago, many banks used traditional machine learning models to detect fraud within contained data environments, overseen by risk and compliance teams that understood those systems' parameters. Those same governance structures collapse under the velocity and ubiquity of GenAI, where models create outputs in open, dynamic contexts that touch millions of users and stakeholders. This challenge becomes even more pronounced with agentic AI, where autonomous systems operate with increasing independence, further straining governance models that rely on centralized control and episodic human intervention. As such, the AI governance protocols of yesterday must adapt to these modern AI strategies and applications.

What's missing today is a foundational understanding of what it means to lead ethically in a world increasingly defined by generative and agentic AI. Despite growing awareness, many companies remain unprepared. Oversight of AI within the modern business enterprise is typically fragmented across functional silos, with little coordination among legal, compliance, risk, technology, data science, human resources (HR), and product development teams. Even when boards discuss AI, the conversations are often too conceptual or solely focused on growth imperatives. As a result, ethical and risk considerations are sidelined or treated as optional.

This book reflects a deliberate emphasis on AI strategy, governance, and risk, with ethics treated as an operational responsibility. The Boundaries of Tolerance model presented in these pages responds directly to a gap that I witnessed surface repeatedly in business advisory and education settings.

Regulatory frameworks also lag far behind the pace of innovation, as discussed in Chapter 2. Although some jurisdictions, such as the European Union with its AI Act, have made some progress, the global AI regulatory landscape remains immature. Many companies continue to wait for regulations to dictate their actions. But by the time regulators catch up, the tangible real-life damage in the form of financial or reputational damage is often already done.

Compounding this gap is the absence of a shared ethical language. Directors and executive teams may agree that they want "ethical AI," but ask 10 leaders what that means in practice, and you'll likely hear 10 different interpretations. Most companies have broad, static codes of ethics, but those codes weren't built for algorithmic systems that learn, adapt, can act autonomously, and influence millions of decisions, often invisibly. These codes rarely address critical questions like these: When does algorithmic bias become unacceptable? Who is accountable when an AI system causes harm? What level of explainability is sufficient to meet our standards? In my experience working with boards and management teams, these questions often lead to a deeper reckoning, which echoes the central question of this book: *What does our organization actually stand for, ethically, when it comes to AI?*

This isn't a rhetorical or philosophical exercise. It's a precondition for effective governance. Before a board or senior leadership team can assess whether a specific

AI system aligns with its own enterprise values, it must first define what those values are in an AI context. And today, most organizations haven't done that. There's often no operational articulation of AI ethics, just a recitation of very broad principles, rarely translated into practice. This is the governance gap.

It reflects gaps in tools, oversight, clarity, and accountability. Ethical responsibility for AI often lands in a gray zone: too technical for most boardrooms, too strategic for most technologists, and too novel for existing legal frameworks to meaningfully address. When these issues rise to leadership's attention, the tools to resolve them are often missing or misaligned. I've watched very capable board directors and managers express frustration that they "don't know what good looks like" in this new AI domain. That uncertainty is the signal that governance itself must evolve. This governance gap is multidimensional, spanning legal, organizational, cultural, and ethical domains, and closing it will require an equally multidimensional framework.

To fill this gap, we need a governance model built specifically for enterprise decision-makers. It must be accessible and actionable for corporate boards, C-suites, and business operators, and not just ethicists or data scientists. We need a framework tailored to fast-moving, high-velocity AI environments, such as real-time customer service chatbots or automated loan approvals, where decisions can't always wait for clear government regulation or perfect information. The framework must be grounded in fiduciary duty and leadership accountability.

Most importantly, companies must stop relying on borrowed definitions of ethics. Saying a system is "ethical" simply because it complies with the law or avoids negative headlines is not enough. *Leaders must define what they and the enterprise as a whole are willing to ethically tolerate in their AI systems* – what trade-offs are acceptable, what values are nonnegotiable, and, importantly, where the organization draws the line.

That's the purpose of the Boundaries of Tolerance model. Before a business can responsibly evaluate the ethics of any AI system, it must first articulate its own ethical boundaries, clearly and operationally.

Closing the AI Governance Gap

Leaders are asking practical questions about AI oversight: How do we responsibly govern this powerful technology? How do we know if a system is ethical? Where are the ethical boundaries of what our institution will, and will not, tolerate?

The Boundaries of Tolerance model is the practical response developed through our research at the Harvard Edmond & Lily Safra Center for Ethics, and tested and discussed through executive education sessions and company workshops. It is a governance model that helps organizations operationalize and continuously elevate their ethical posture by embedding ethics into enterprise strategy and culture.

The governance of generative and agentic AI presents a structural challenge for most enterprises. Because it does not fit neatly within a single corporate function, institutional alignment is difficult. As a result, many organizations assign oversight to cross-functional AI committees composed of leaders from legal, compliance, technology, data science, HR, and risk. Structured well, these committees can be enormously effective (more on this in Chapter 9). But, these groups often lack clear accountability mechanisms (there is rarely a single person ultimately responsible for AI-related ethical risk) and few include members with advanced expertise in technology ethics. In a conversation on the *Better Innovation* podcast, where he joined me to discuss his book *Ethical Machines*, Reid Blackman cautioned that cross-functional Responsible AI committees can unintentionally diffuse ethical responsibility: each participant prioritizes their core business objectives, and ethics can become everyone's responsibility, and therefore no one's. The irony, as Blackman observed, is that the very teams formed to ensure responsible AI can end up neglecting the ethical dimension altogether.[11]

Without defined ethical boundaries, even the best teams struggle to move from discussion to decision. The Boundaries of Tolerance model fills this vacuum by establishing clarity and measurable accountability for ethical AI oversight.

The Boundaries of Tolerance Model Structure

The model contains three components (see Figure 6.1):

- The Ethical Maturity Stack
- A set of Performance Measures
- Applied Governance Practices

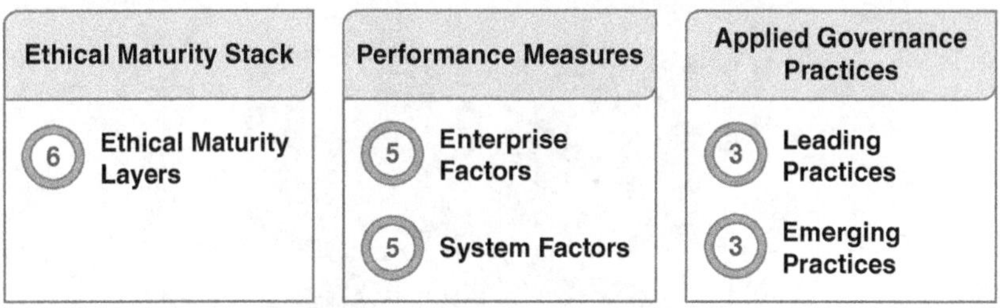

Figure 6.1 The Boundaries of Tolerance model structure.

Source: © BAIE Research Team, 2026.

Together, these components provide a shared language and structure that enable companies to assess their current AI governance maturity, articulate their ethical aspirations, and chart a path toward measurable progress. They can be applied diagnostically to identify governance gaps and strategically to guide resource allocation, accountability, and leadership decisions. In doing so, the model translates aspiration into measurable governance practice.

Ethical Maturity Stack

The Ethical Maturity Stack provides the structural backbone of the model. It defines six progressive stages of organizational ethical maturity, ranging from Non-Compliance at the base to Ethical Vanguard at the top (see Figure 6.2).

The Ethical Maturity Stack starts at Layer 0 and ascends through five higher stages of organizational ethics maturity. These layers fall into three bands: Compliance-Oriented (Layers 0–2), Ethical Advancement (Layers 3 and 4), and Influence (Layer 5). The progression reflects a shift from risk mitigation to values-based leadership. Building on this foundational stack, the model identifies numerous practices that illustrate what it means to operate at each layer of maturity, advancing the goal of embedding ethics into the core of enterprise operations and decision-making.

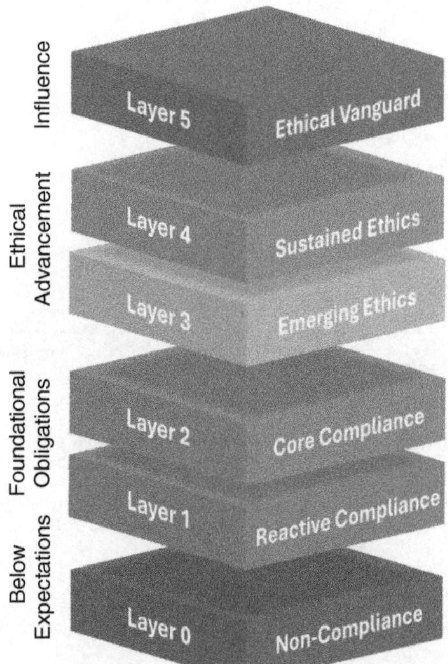

Figure 6.2 Ethical Maturity Stack.

The Six Layers of Ethical Maturity

The first three layers constitute the Compliance-Oriented band, where organizations manage risk but rarely engage with the deeper ethical questions surrounding AI.

- **Layer 0: Non-Compliance.** The organization does not meet basic legal obligations for AI development and use. Ethical risks go unrecognized. There may be little or no ethically aligned internal controls and AI systems operate without oversight. Simply put, the organization has not adopted any ethical AI principles or practices.
- **Layer 1: Reactive Compliance.** Leadership within the organization takes minimal steps to comply with legal requirements, typically in response to external pressure from regulators or stakeholders, but lacks systematic governance. Compliance efforts are ad hoc and crisis-driven. There is no proactive oversight or ethical intent.
- **Layer 2: Core Compliance.** The enterprise fully complies with legal requirements for AI systems but does not go beyond what is required by law. Ethical practices are narrowly scoped and limited to regulatory mandates; they do not extend beyond what the law demands.

The next two layers represent the Ethical Advancement band, where organizations move beyond compliance toward purposeful integration of ethics and enterprise strategy. Companies at this stage begin to see responsible AI as a source of long-term value creation and greater stakeholder trust.

- **Layer 3: Emerging Ethics.** The organization is taking initial steps toward ethical AI maturity. It's starting to adopt best practices in select areas. These early actions reflect a growing commitment to higher standards. Efforts are still developing and not yet fully integrated across the organization.
- **Layer 4: Sustained Ethics.** Ethical AI practices are consistently integrated across the organization's strategy and operations. Regular audits, transparency, and stakeholder engagement support these efforts. Commitment extends across the organization, moving beyond isolated actions.

The final layer represents the Influence band, where organizations redefine leadership itself through the lens of moral accountability. Companies

(continued)

(continued)

operating here set new standards for responsible AI, transforming ethics from a compliance obligation into a strategic and cultural identity. At this stage, ethical governance is championed, influencing industries and policy alike.

- **Layer 5: Ethical Vanguard.** Ethics becomes a differentiator in the organization's AI governance model and central to its brand and long-term strategy. The organization leads its sector in ethical AI, shaping industry standards and public policy. Collaboration and advocacy drive continuous improvement. Ethical leadership is embedded at every level.

The stack provides organizations with a clear road map. It recognizes that while most begin in the compliance band, true ethical leadership requires intentional effort and sustained cultural change to climb the stack and reach the higher layers of performance. Ethical maturity is never static; it evolves with leadership commitment and societal expectations.

Performance Measures

The set of Performance Measures offer internal assessment tools that help boards and executive teams determine whether ethical principles are operationalized across the organization. Each measure is composed of five factors that will be explored in depth in Chapters 7 and 8 (see Figure 6.3).

Enterprise Factors

This Performance Measure evaluates the extent to which ethical values and oversight mechanisms are embedded in the daily operations of the enterprise. It goes beyond policy declarations to ask the critical question: Are we living our values across teams, decisions, and functions?

The five Enterprise Factors include the following:

- **Leadership Priorities.** Examines tone from the top and measures the degree of leadership commitment to ethical AI and the extent to which leaders balance commercial objectives with ethical standards. Higher maturity reflects proactive engagement, integrating ethical principles into strategy and operations without compromising enterprise performance.

Figure 6.3 Performance Measures.

- **Operational Integration.** Assesses how well the organization translates ethics into everyday processes, such as data governance, model development, procure-to-pay, and enterprise risk management. This factor also measures the extent by which enterprise functions are effectively collaborating to promote ethical AI practices.
- **Stakeholder Accountability.** Measures whether the organization's ethical AI governance accounts for a broad stakeholder set, including customers, employees, suppliers, and communities, and whether those interests are meaningfully represented in decision-making. Higher stakeholder centricity reflects deeper inclusion of stakeholder perspectives. It also reflects clearer transparency and closer alignment with societal expectations for how AI systems are developed or deployed.
- **Ecosystem Partnerships.** Evaluates an organization's ability to collaborate with external stakeholders, such as industry groups, regulators, technology companies, academic institutions, and nonprofits, to shape and align with

broader ethical AI practices. Higher maturity in this area reflects active participation in advancing ecosystem-wide standards and shared governance across sectors and borders.

- **Organizational Culture.** Assesses whether values like fairness, accountability, and transparency are actually practiced within the enterprise and not just written in policies. It shows how people build and deploy (and where appropriate, challenge) AI systems, and whether ethical commitments truly align with everyday culture.

System Factors

The second Performance Measure assesses how well AI-specific ethical principles are embedded into the AI systems themselves. Increasingly, these expectations extend to third-party AI tools licensed or procured by the enterprise.

The five Systems Factors include the following:

- **Human Oversight and Accountability.** Determines whether proper human controls exist to oversee AI decisions and intervenes when needed. It examines auditability and the clarity of decision rights. It also evaluates whether mechanisms exist to address errors when they occur.
- **Fairness and Inclusivity.** Assesses whether the organization has processes to identify bias in datasets and models and to mitigate its effects on outcomes. It evaluates whether those processes support equitable treatment across user groups, including populations that have been historically marginalized.
- **Transparency and Explainability.** Evaluates whether internal and external stakeholders can understand how AI systems work and why specific outputs are produced. It emphasizes understandable model logic and clarity when users interact with AI systems.
- **Reliability and Safety.** Measures the robustness and performance of AI systems under real-world conditions. It asks whether models are safe, secure, and validated across diverse contexts and populations.
- **Data Privacy and Security.** Examines how well the organization protects data rights, minimizes collection, anonymizes where appropriate, and safeguards against breaches and misuse. It reflects both regulatory compliance and respect for digital dignity.

These principles function as ethical pressure points that can reveal where a system might fail, technically or morally.

The two Performance Measures work in tandem to assess where an enterprise aligns today on the Ethical Maturity Stack and its desired future state. The Enterprise

Factors ask whether the enterprise's values are truly operationalized, while the System Factors ask whether the right ethical benchmarks are applied to AI systems specifically. Progress across both measures is what elevates an organization through the layers of the stack, from Non-Compliance to Ethical Vanguard.

But for now, the key takeaway is simple: *you cannot govern what you have not defined, and you cannot lead ethically without knowing both where you stand today and where you are headed.* These measures give leaders a critical starting point and a clear direction of travel.

Applied Governance Practices

Let's now turn to the third component of the Boundaries of Tolerance model, highlighting innovative governance approaches that help organizations climb the Ethical Maturity Stack. Across my board and executive advisory work, as well as in executive education settings at MIT, a clear gap emerged. Many organizations have articulated ethical AI commitments. Far fewer have repeatable practices that make ethical oversight lasting under real operating conditions. The Applied Governance Practices articulated in this section address this execution gap (see Figure 6.4). They reflect what is already working on the ground, or through our research we believe certain existing practices from other domains can be leading examples to inform the AI context.

The model organizes these practices into a 3+3 structure that is introduced in detail in Chapter 9. Six practices are presented in total, grouped into two categories. Leading Practices reflect governance approaches already in use among responsible AI champion organizations today. They establish a practical foundation that boards and executive teams can adopt in practice. Emerging Practices are less common, but they address pressures that traditional governance models increasingly struggle to manage and can also benefit organizations today. Together, the six practices show how organizations can put the Boundaries of Tolerance model in motion.

Leading Practices

- **Technology/AI Committee.** Creates responsible board-level oversight for AI and other strategic technologies through a new, dedicated committee or by expanding the mandate of an existing committee. The purpose is sustained fiduciary attention. A well-designed committee keeps AI from being relegated to the end of a crowded agenda and provides a consistent forum to ensure that board-level oversight reflects the strategic and operational importance of AI with the option to bring in outside expertise when needed.[12]

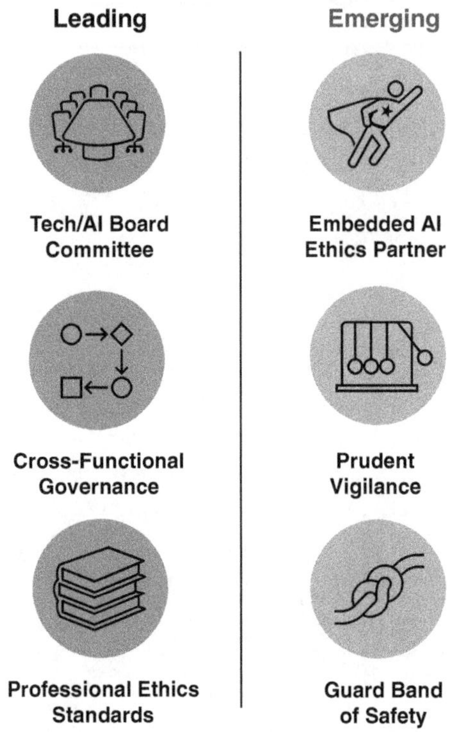

Figure 6.4 Applied Governance Practices.

- **Adapting Professional Ethics Frameworks.** Draws on enforceable ethics standards from regulated professions to operationalize accountability for AI-enabled judgment across employee groups more broadly. Professions such as law and medicine treat technology use as inseparable from human responsibility. These frameworks translate ethical principles into daily obligations and clarify who remains accountable when AI informs decisions.
- **Cross-Functional Governance.** Establishes an interdisciplinary working group that brings together leaders from technology, legal, compliance, data, security, operations, HR, and other functions to oversee AI initiatives. Because AI cuts across the enterprise, no single function can manage its risks alone. The model is most effective when ethical responsibility is clearly assigned within the group.

Emerging Practices

- **Embedded AI Ethics Partner.** Introduces a senior ethics and governance expert who works in close proximity to AI decision-making rather than as an occasional advisor. This role supports leaders across the AI life cycle by translating ethical intent into operational practice. Deployed on a part-time or embedded basis, the ethics partner helps organizations access specialized expertise without creating a permanent role. The model supports organizations early in their AI maturity curve while also signaling a credible commitment to responsible AI adoption.
- **Prudent Vigilance.** Reflects a balanced governance posture that neither stifles innovation nor ignores risk. Rooted in bioethics, Prudent Vigilance calls for continuous monitoring and adaptive response in the face of uncertainty.[13] In the AI context, it asks whether an organization has both a baseline understanding of known risks and the infrastructure to detect and respond when outcomes move beyond accepted ethical boundaries.
- **Guard Band of Safety.** Encourages companies to establish an intentional margin above minimum legal compliance, creating a buffer that anticipates regulatory evolution. Rather than operating at the edge of permissibility, organizations adopt stronger controls in areas where legal standards lag. This approach was first developed by Intel during antitrust investigations in the early 2000s, when the company proactively implemented internal controls to prevent future scrutiny.[14] Applying this practice to AI governance involves designing oversight systems and safeguards that exceed current legal mandates, helping protect organizations against legal and ethical failures in a rapidly changing AI environment.

The core contribution of the Boundaries of Tolerance model is to help leaders confront the most important question that regulation cannot answer: *What are the ethical boundaries of what your organization will and will not tolerate?* Where would your organization fall on the Ethical Maturity Stack today when assessed through the Performance Measures? Which of the Applied Governance Practices could strengthen its approach?

The Boardroom Question That Changed the Conversation

In a board advisory session with a leading US retailer, a public company navigating the complexities of AI adoption, I was invited to deliver a presentation on AI literacy. The goal was to walk the board through five key AI dimensions: strategy, applications, risk, governance, and ethics. I was well coached by the management team going into the board session that one director in particular had a reputation for asking tough, probing questions. I was barely two minutes into the presentation when this director jumped in. Because of my Harvard affiliation, my title included *ethics*. Instead of asking about data privacy or algorithmic bias, he surprised me with something different. He asked, something to the effect of "Let's cut to the chase. If we're talking about ethics, and ethics comes from philosophy, then just tell us, Jeff, which philosopher should this board follow? Are you an Aristotelian or do you follow the ideas of another philosopher?"

It was a sincere question, but one that revealed a common misconception about what ethical leadership in AI truly entails. I paused for a moment, then replied, "Respectfully, that's not the question you should be asking. Rather than asking which ancient philosophers' principles to adopt, the more important questions are, what does this company stand for? What ethical values do you, as enterprise leaders, want to define and uphold, especially when it comes to the use of AI? What are the ethical boundaries of what you, the board, will tolerate in your AI systems and solutions?"

That simple but powerful exchange reset the entire conversation, and with it, the board's understanding of AI governance. The presentation shifted from a discussion of ethical theory to a much more practical and pressing question: *How should this board define its own boundaries of tolerance when it comes to AI?* What are the values and red lines that should guide AI decisions across the enterprise?

The director's question was not misguided; rather, it surfaced a gap common across many boardrooms today: not a lack of intelligence or awareness, but a lack of shared ethical identity. Without that internal compass (an organizational sense of right and wrong) leaders often seek external anchors such as regulations or, in this case, philosophical archetypes. But in a domain as context-specific and value-laden as AI, that's not enough.

This is where the Boundaries of Tolerance model proves essential. Rather than imposing a *single ethical lens* on the organization, the model enables an organization to define *its ethical boundaries*, grounded in enterprise values. It supports boards and C-suites in identifying the ethical principles, practices, risk thresholds, and values that resonate with the organization's unique mission, stakeholders, and operating context. It empowers leaders to articulate what they will tolerate, what they won't, and where the enterprise must take a stand, even in the absence of clear regulatory or philosophical consensus.

Ethical AI governance is not about finding the "right" philosopher; it is about cultivating shared conviction. The most mature organizations are not those that recite Kant or Aristotle in the boardroom, but instead those that understand who they are, and how their values show up in the design, deployment, and oversight of AI. That's the new bar for leadership. And that's the conversation this director's unexpected question helped to begin. This encounter has since become a teaching moment in nearly every board or executive session I facilitate.

Closing

The Boundaries of Tolerance model is more than a model for ethical AI governance and strategy; it marks a fundamental shift in how leadership is defined, one that places growing emphasis on fiduciary duty and long-term societal impact. Historically, governance systems functioned as checklists: procedural safeguards designed to ensure compliance with known rules. But in the AI era, when the rules are still forming and the stakes are often invisible until they surface, that mindset is no longer sufficient.

AI governance demands something more dynamic: a form of leadership competence rooted in technological literacy, ethical fluency, strategic foresight, and comfort with ambiguity. *Today's most successful leaders are not only technically fluent but they are also ethically fluent.* They understand that governing AI isn't about finding the "right" answer in a rulebook but it's about building systems that can navigate complexity, make trade-offs explicit, and ensure that innovation aligns with the organization's values. In my work advising corporate boards and executive teams, I've observed that the most effective leaders treat AI ethics not as a side conversation but as central to business transformation. They ask, "How do we embed ethics into the core of our innovation strategy, not bolt it on at the end?"

This shift calls for a new kind of leadership mindset. Boards and C-suites must now develop fluency across multiple domains: legal accountability, system design, stakeholder impacts, and ethical reasoning. The Boundaries of Tolerance model is designed to cultivate that mindset. It helps leaders operationalize ethics as a core capability that spans governance, risk, and strategy. In this sense, the Boundaries of Tolerance model becomes a catalyst for leadership transformation. It repositions ethics as a strategic function and equips decision-makers with the language and tools they need to lead responsibly in an AI-driven world. *This emerging form of leadership competence may be the most critical differentiator of the decade.*

What lies ahead in the following chapters is more than a deeper exploration of a governance framework. It is an invitation to reimagine what leadership means in the age of intelligent machines. The model challenges leaders to see AI governance as a defining act of corporate character. Every organization now stands at a crossroads: Will intelligent technologies be deployed merely to optimize efficiency or to advance human well-being and shared prosperity? The answer will depend on the quality of leadership guiding those choices.

The chapters ahead unpack the components of the Boundaries of Tolerance model in detail and provide practical implementation guidance. They offer not only the tools but also the rationale (and perhaps, the courage) to lead differently.

Because this journey is not just about AI; it is about the kind of leadership your organization will be remembered for. In moments of profound change, those who step forward with courage and conviction set the tone for others to follow. The time for that leadership is now. What follows is a road map for that journey, one designed to translate ethical conviction into daily practice. Turn the page and take the next step.

7 Enterprise Factors

Assessing the Enterprise

Measurement requires leaders to examine how the enterprise behaves when AI systems are built and deployed. It reveals where ethical commitments hold and where they weaken under pressure. Chapter 6 introduced the Boundaries of Tolerance model in full. The model includes the Ethical Maturity Stack, a set of Performance Measures, and six Applied Governance Practices. This chapter addresses the first Performance Measure, the Enterprise Factors: Leadership Priorities, Organizational Culture, Operational Integration, Stakeholder Accountability, and Ecosystem Partnerships (see Figure 7.1).

These five factors were selected because they map the full extent of ethical practice within an enterprise: leadership determines priorities and sets acceptable risk boundaries, operational design governs how artificial intelligence (AI) systems are built, Organizational Culture shapes daily conduct, Stakeholder Accountability extends responsibility beyond firm boundaries, and Ecosystem Partnerships reflect important collaborations for universal ethical standards and practices. Across these five domains, ethical responsibility is fully accounted for within the institution.

This chapter establishes the criteria used to evaluate enterprise ethics against the Ethical Maturity Stack. Each Enterprise Factor examines a distinct dimension of organizational conduct and is tested through case studies that ground the standard in real-world scenarios. These cases illustrate how the Enterprise Factors appear across different layers of the stack, making it easier to identify where an organization currently stands. They also show how ethical conduct evolves at higher maturity layers and what progression requires in practice. Advancing to higher layers on the stack requires defined standards and operating practices that guide decisions and actions in alignment with institutional values and societal expectations.

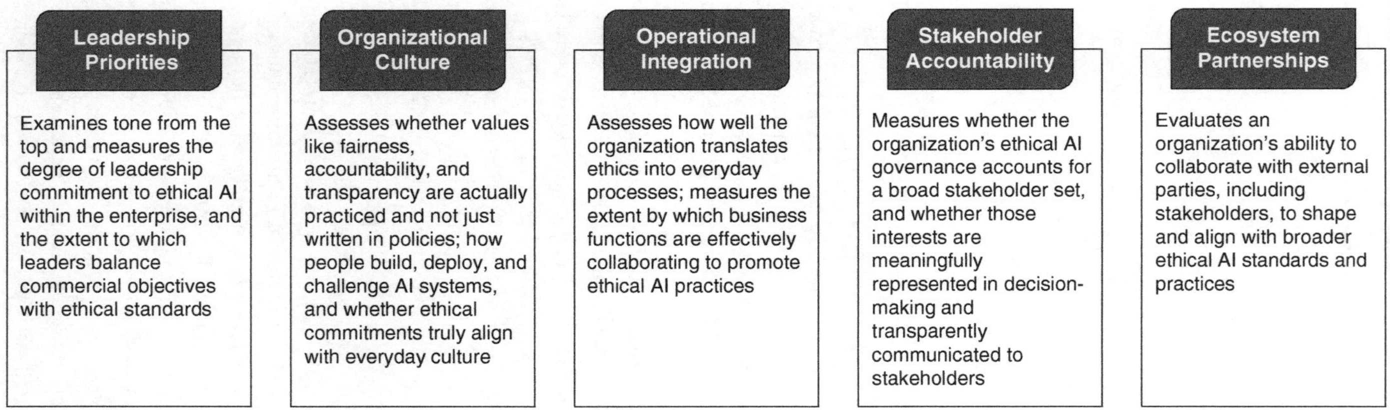

Figure 7.1 Performance Measure: Enterprise Factors.

Source: © BAIE Research Team, 2026.

The Enterprise Factors

Before we dive into stories, take a moment to orient yourself. The Enterprise Factors Maturity Matrix is our map (see Figure 7.2). It traces how the five factors evolve from compliance to the elevated Ethical Vanguard position. Keep it nearby for reference; you'll see echoes of it in every example that follows.

Across the rows sit the six maturity layers of the Ethical Maturity Stack. The columns represent the five factors that shape enterprise ethics. As you review the matrix, ask yourself, where would I place my organization today? And, more importantly, am I happy with the current state or does my organization have an aspiration to move to higher layers? Considering this question will be imperative as you address Boundaries of Tolerance model implementation practices in Chapter 10. We begin with Leadership Priorities because ethical direction starts where authority resides.

Factor 1: Leadership Priorities

In every organization, priorities cascade from the top, through their actions. Leaders reveal priorities through the incentives they design and the questions they ask when employee or team performance results are reviewed. Ethical governance, whether for AI or any other emerging technology, depends on visible alignment between stated commitments and operational decisions. When AI oversight sits entirely with technical teams, ethics is treated as a technical problem. When oversight appears in board agendas and executive objectives, it becomes a governance priority. Incentive mechanisms, such as compensation structures, reinforce that priority.

At lower maturity levels, ethics is less of a leadership concern, or leaders treat ethics as reputational risk to manage after damage occurs. At higher levels, they treat ethics as a more integral component of operational performance. Ethical constraints shape product design and capital allocation. Leadership commitment to responsible technology means embedding ethical accountability into governance frameworks and ensuring that decision-makers (not just engineers) understand the implications of the systems they deploy.

Boards confront the same tension. Quarterly earnings pressure competes with long-term enterprise reputation. The hardest governance question is whether profit or principle gets the final word. For most of modern business history, the prevailing wisdom has been that fiduciary duty means maximizing shareholder value. Yet in the age of AI and global transparency, that equation has changed. The costs of ethical failure can compound faster than quarterly gains. For example, when

Enterprise Factors	Leadership Priorities	Organizational Culture	Operational Integration	Stakeholder Accountability	Ecosystem Partnerships
Layer 5 Ethical Vanguard	Ethical AI defines enterprise identity with ethics-focused KPIs; leadership advocates for global AI ethics standards beyond the firm	The enterprise cultivates ambassadors who shape ethical AI standards beyond the firm	Ethics is fully embedded in AI design, deployment, and retirement; there are automated guardrails and transparent audit trails	AI governance structures include non-employee participants in policy design. External stakeholders participate in system review	Leads collaborative AI governance initiatives across industries; develops open ethical frameworks adopted beyond the firm
Layer 4 Sustained Ethics	Leaders align AI ROI metrics with ethical risks, accepts short-term cost to prevent harm; ethics linked to performance reviews	AI outcomes are challenged internally when they conflict with defined ethical boundaries	Models are monitored continuously for performance and bias; life cycle reviews are conducted across core functions	Continuous multi-stakeholder engagement on AI impacts exists; model audits and redress mechanisms are published	Shares AI safety findings with peer organizations; contributes risk governance lessons to cross-sector initiatives
Layer 3 Emerging Ethics	Executives sponsor AI ethics training and board briefings; reputational and stakeholder impact considered when approving AI use cases	Teams begin raising ethical concerns during AI development	Ethical checkpoints are added to development and deployment workflows	Periodic engagement with select stakeholders on AI fairness or privacy is established	Takes active part in AI ethics forums and public-private partnerships
Layer 2 Core Compliance	An AI compliance officer is appointed, but with limited authority or resources	Ethical conduct is strictly defined by adherence to written policy	Basic AI risk and data-governance controls exist; model documentation is ad hoc	Required AI risk reports to regulators are provided; basic explainability for customers exists	Joins limited industry groups for optics; selective disclosure of AI use exists
Layer 1 Reactive Compliance	Leaders halt AI projects only under legal or regulatory pressure	Ethical expectations are communicated only after an AI incident	Issues are fixed post-incident; bias mitigation is reactive	Response follows only after AI failures or public criticism; limited transparency	Engages with regulators only when required
Layer 0 Non-Compliance	No executive or board oversight of AI exists; accountability for AI decisions is undefined; AI initiatives pursued primarily for short-term financial return	No shared expectations guide how employees develop or deploy AI systems	No AI-specific governance framework exists; models are deployed without structured testing	AI impact on users or society is not recognized or considered; no disclosure of AI use or harm	Operates in secrecy; no data sharing or external review exists

Figure 7.2 The Enterprise Factors Maturity Matrix.

Source: © BAIE Research Team, 2026.

algorithms influence employment or credit decisions, reputational damage spreads rapidly. The same dynamic appears in healthcare systems and safety systems. Ethical decision-making in business no longer belongs only to compliance officers or risk managers; it belongs to boards and executives deciding how much risk is acceptable in pursuit of growth. This is when the Boundaries of Tolerance model meets the marketplace, when leaders must determine how far they are willing to go for competitive advantage.

At lower levels of ethical maturity, companies view ethics as a brake on performance. At higher levels, they recognize that integrity strengthens institutional resilience. Organizations that earn enduring trust treat ethics as an investment that produces sustained credibility with employees and customers.

The consequences of getting this balance wrong are stark. Few examples illustrate the cost of ethical short-termism more vividly than Volkswagen's emissions scandal, when the pursuit of market share overrode the systems meant to ensure compliance and integrity. Although the Volkswagen emissions case occurred *before* the widespread commercial use of AI systems, the software at its center operated as an automated control program that adjusted vehicle behavior based on sensor inputs. The software altered vehicle behavior when it detected laboratory testing conditions, then shifted performance once the vehicle returned to normal driving. That distinction between test behavior and real-world behavior became central to the regulatory findings. Because it involved automated, data-driven decision logic without direct human intervention, the case is often cited as an early example of how algorithmic systems can behave differently under test and real-world conditions, a dynamic that also appears in modern AI governance discussions.

Case Study: Volkswagen's Emissions Software and Regulatory Implications

In September 2015, the United States Environmental Protection Agency (EPA) issued a Notice of Violation to Volkswagen AG, Audi AG, and Volkswagen Group of America (collectively "Volkswagen") after determining that certain diesel vehicles were equipped with software designed to alter emissions-control performance during laboratory testing.[1] The EPA and the California Air Resources Board (CARB) concluded that the software altered emissions performance during laboratory testing, while normal driving conditions produced nitrogen oxide emissions above US limits.[2]

Volkswagen subsequently confirmed that approximately 11 million vehicles worldwide were affected, including models sold under the Volkswagen, Audi, and Porsche brands.[3] The issue involved vehicles equipped with 2.0-liter and 3.0-liter diesel engines produced between 2009 and 2016.[4]

In January 2017, Volkswagen AG pleaded guilty in US federal court to charges including conspiracy to defraud the United States, obstruction of justice, and importation of goods by false statements. The company agreed to pay in total $4.3 billion in criminal and civil penalties in the United States and committed to an independent compliance monitor for a three-year term.[5] Civil settlements with regulators and consumers increased the total financial impact to over $30 billion globally.[6]

Multiple Volkswagen executives and employees were charged in connection with the case, and several were convicted in the United States and Germany.[7] The company's chief executive officer (CEO) at the time, Martin Winterkorn, resigned shortly after the EPA announcement, stating that he accepted responsibility for irregularities that occurred under his leadership.[8]

Regulatory agencies in multiple regions initiated additional investigations.[9] In the European Union, the European Commission and national consumer authorities coordinated recalls and retrofit programs to address emissions compliance.[10] Volkswagen undertook extensive corrective measures. These included vehicle modifications and consumer compensation. The company also restructured elements of its compliance and product development functions.

The incident became one of the largest corporate compliance cases in automotive history, prompting new regulatory attention to vehicle-testing procedures and the use of software in emissions control. Public documents and settlements describe the misconduct as deliberate implementation of "defeat devices," a term used by the EPA to denote software that circumvents emissions standards.[11] In subsequent years, Volkswagen expanded its investments in electric vehicle technology and corporate compliance systems as part of its remediation commitments and strategic reorientation following the case.[12]

Within the Boundaries of Tolerance model, Volkswagen's conduct prior to regulatory intervention aligns with Layer 0: Non-Compliance on the Ethical Maturity Stack, reflecting leadership priorities that were not consistently aligned with regulatory expectations. Based on the court's findings, the software was designed to evade emissions standards rather than operate within them. After the Notice of Violation, the company moved into Layer 1: Reactive Compliance, but only after extensive financial penalties.

Volkswagen shows what ethical failure looks like when controls are engineered based on legal limits. A contrasting example shows how a firm embeds stated values into operating decisions before regulators intervene.

Case Study: Unilever's Sustainable Sourcing – Profit Through Purpose

Although Unilever's sustainable sourcing program did not involve AI, it addresses the same governance question that AI leaders now face. The issue is not the technology itself. The issue is whether leadership embeds its values into operating decisions when commercial pressure intensifies. Unilever's record provides a concrete illustration of how an enterprise institutionalizes ethical commitments across business lines.

Unilever has publicly committed for more than a decade to integrating sustainability into its business strategy. In 2010 the company launched the Unilever Sustainable Living Plan (USLP), a 10-year program aimed at decoupling business growth from environmental impact and increasing positive social outcomes. The plan established measurable targets for product sourcing and manufacturing practices. It also set standards for packaging and community engagement. One of its core goals was to source 100% of agricultural raw materials sustainably by 2020, verified through external certification schemes such as the Rainforest Alliance and Fairtrade Certification Mark.[13]

According to Unilever's published progress reports, achieving these sourcing targets required significant operational adjustments. The company stated that some product launches and market expansions were slowed to ensure supplier compliance with sustainability standards.[14] Public reports and executive statements from the company noted that these measures increased short-term costs but aligned with long-term brand commitments.[15]

By the conclusion of the USLP period in 2020, Unilever reported that 62% of its agricultural raw materials were sustainably sourced, compared with 14% in 2010. The company also documented reductions in manufacturing waste and water use per ton of production. It separately reported lower greenhouse gas emissions.[16]

In 2020, Unilever introduced its follow-on strategy, the Unilever Compass, which reaffirmed the link between sustainability performance and financial results.[17] The company reported that its brands identified as "Sustainable Living Brands," those incorporating clear social or environmental purposes, grew faster than its portfolio average from 2014 through 2018.[18] This approach has been widely studied and recognized as an example of how long-term sustainability investments can align with competitive growth and risk mitigation.

Unilever continues to publish audited sustainability data and remains a member of international initiatives such as the UN Global Compact, the World Business Council for Sustainable Development, and the Consumer Goods Forum's Forest Positive Coalition.

Within the Boundaries of Tolerance model, Unilever's approach reflects Layer 4: Sustained Ethics advancing toward Layer 5: Ethical Vanguard on the Ethical Maturity Stack, driven by Leadership Priorities that consistently reinforced these commitments. The company's decision to maintain sustainability commitments despite near-term costs demonstrates a governance model in which ethical and environmental considerations are embedded in strategic and operational planning, not added afterward. Ethical conviction and commercial performance need not conflict. Unilever's experience shows that when responsibility is built into the supply chain from the start, trust and profitability can coexist.

The contrast between Volkswagen and Unilever highlights the full spectrum of ethical maturity within enterprise leadership. Volkswagen and Unilever reflect vastly different positions on the Ethical Maturity Stack. Both companies faced pressures to meet performance targets, but their choices diverged in how they balanced immediate results against enduring trust. The Volkswagen case demonstrates how leadership choices can embed ethical compromise directly into system design. In a stark contrast, Unilever treated its public commitments as binding constraints despite near-term cost. The same divergence appears in AI deployment today, where Leadership Priorities determine whether systems are designed within ethical constraints or optimized primarily for performance or financial outcomes.

The Enterprise Factors Maturity Matrix (see Figure 7.2) illustrates how Leadership Priorities progress across ethical maturity levels. At lower maturity, ethics is addressed after reputational harm or regulatory attention. As maturity increases, priorities shift with ethical priorities embedded into board/executive agendas and decision rights. At higher maturity, ethical boundaries shape capital allocation and strategy, and leadership accountability is clear in practice. Leadership Priorities become visible in the questions leaders are asking:

- Are ethical AI practices consistently prioritized at the board and executive levels?
- Have we clearly communicated which AI applications are ethically unacceptable, even if legally permissible?
- Do our incentive structures reinforce ethical judgment as strongly as financial performance?
- When speed to market conflicts with risk mitigation, who has the authority to slow or stop deployment?
- Have we defined explicit ethical boundaries for AI systems across business units?

In the Boundaries of Tolerance model, this factor reminds leaders that their choices define the ethical boundaries of the enterprise. Those choices take root, or fail to, through Organizational Culture.

Factor 2: Organizational Culture

Policies and procedures set expectations and define minimum standards for organizations. They do not determine how people behave when pressure rises or when written guidance leaves room for interpretation. Culture fills that space.

Generative AI affects enterprise culture because it is spreading quickly across functions. Unlike prior enterprise technology systems that required centralized deployment, generative tools can be accessed directly by employees in their daily workflows. That ubiquity changes norms. When employees adopt tools without clear boundaries established, informal practices take root before governance catches up. A responsible AI culture defines where AI may be used and who has ultimate decision authority over the circumstances of this use.

Chapter 3 addressed strategic AI deployment and the opportunity for widespread adoption. Culture determines whether such broad enterprise adoption actually occurs. Leadership signals shape that outcome. Executives must articulate acceptable risk boundaries and reinforce them through policy and incentives. When leaders merely talk about responsibility, but only reward financial outcomes alone, employees notice that signal as well.

To be clear, a responsible AI culture does not promote unbridled experimentation. It promotes *disciplined* usage aligned with defined enterprise standards. That distinction matters. Cultural endorsement of AI must be paired with clarity about where it should *not* be used. Shadow AI usage erodes accountability because decisions occur outside defined oversight structures. Culture either tolerates that behavior or corrects it.

Organizational Culture is commonly understood as the system of shared assumptions and behaviors that shape how decisions are made in practice.[19] Human accountability anchors that system, with specific individuals owning AI outcomes. Committees can review systems, but they cannot substitute for responsibility in named individuals. When an AI-assisted decision affects a real person, someone must stand behind that outcome. Human validation remains central as AI systems generate outputs across the enterprise. These systems, of course, cannot assume moral accountability. A responsible culture requires human review of consequential outputs, and that review must carry authority. A designated decision-maker must retain the power to approve or reject AI-generated results.

Trust is a second foundational element of culture.[20] Employees will not rely on AI systems that behave unpredictably. They will bypass tools with unexplainable outputs. Reliable systems with outcomes that can be validated encourage disciplined adoption.

Data practices reflect how culture operates in execution. AI systems inherit the quality and bias of the data that trains them. Responsible data usage therefore reflects cultural discipline. Employees must understand what data may be used and how its application aligns with enterprise standards.

Incentives convert expectations into behavior. Compensation structures and promotion criteria communicate what the organization values. Performance reviews serve a similar purpose.[21] When leaders tie advancement to responsible AI development and deployment, behavior adjusts. When incentives reward AI-assisted output without regard to risk or ethics, behavior shifts accordingly. This increases the likelihood of stakeholder harm.

Psychological safety enables culture to function.[22] Employees must be able to question AI outputs and raise ethical concerns without fear of retaliation. A reporting mechanism alone does not create safety. Employees watch how leaders respond to those who speak up.

Training reinforces culture in practice. Employees who build or deploy AI systems require more than technical instruction. They need clarity about acceptable use and risk and ethics thresholds. Training should address real scenarios within the enterprise and assign clear responsibility. Seven elements define a responsible AI culture within an enterprise (see Figure 7.3).

Within the Ethical Maturity Stack, a strong culture of ethical priorities differentiates mere compliance from sustained commitment. At lower layers, organizations rely on written policies and reactive correction. At higher layers, employees internalize ethical expectations and apply them in daily decisions. Culture determines whether governance frameworks become just words on a page or actually become practice.

Culture becomes visible when policies shape daily product decisions. A visible model of responsible AI culture has emerged at Microsoft, where responsible AI protocols are visibly present in both product development and board-level oversight.

Case Study: Microsoft's Responsible AI Standard – Culture in Practice

Microsoft has developed one of the most detailed corporate governance frameworks for AI currently in use. The company's approach rests on defined principles and formal governance structures. These structures assign accountability and guide how AI systems are developed and deployed.

In 2016, Microsoft drafted six Responsible AI Principles – Fairness, Reliability and Safety, Privacy and Security, Inclusiveness, Transparency, and Accountability – which were formally adopted in 2018 and continue to anchor its governance structure. These principles are brought to life by a network of committees and working groups, including the Office of Responsible AI, the Responsible AI Governance Community, AI Red Team, and the Aether (AI, Ethics and Effects in Engineering and Research) Committee. These groups collaborate across product, research, and legal functions to assess ethical risks and ensure alignment with company policy before AI systems are released.[23]

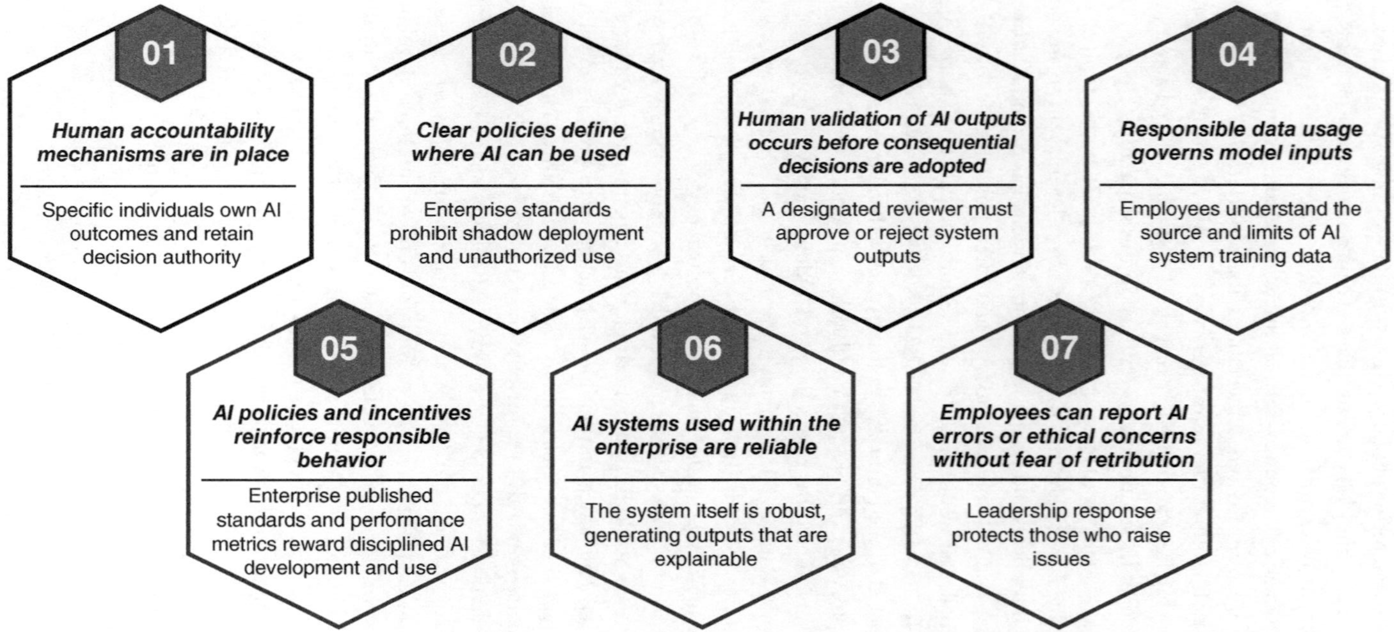

Figure 7.3 The seven elements that define a responsible AI culture within an enterprise.

Source: © BAIE Research Team, 2026.

In June 2022, Microsoft publicly released its Responsible AI Standard, a comprehensive internal policy document that sets mandatory requirements for AI system development to ensure alignment with the company's six Responsible AI Principles. The standard requires formal impact assessments and defined data governance controls. It also sets expectations for model evaluation and human oversight. Microsoft requires user transparency where AI systems affect customers.[24] Company leadership has stated publicly that all AI systems deployed across its business units must meet the requirements outlined in this standard.

CEO Satya Nadella and president Brad Smith have both emphasized the integration of ethical oversight into the company's broader innovation and governance agenda. In interviews and public statements, Nadella has named security, quality, and AI innovation as "core priorities"[25] and often publicly refers to AI as the "the defining challenge of our time,"[26] while Smith has called for both corporate and regulatory frameworks to ensure that AI systems reflect societal values.[27] This emphasis is reflected in the company's culture, where ethical oversight is embedded in governance processes and product development practices across the enterprise. External observers, including researchers and industry analysts, have extensively studied Microsoft's Responsible AI framework and it is often cited as one of the most mature enterprise governance models in operation, noting its combination of internal enforcement mechanisms and public transparency.

Within the Boundaries of Tolerance model, Microsoft aligns with Layer 5 of the Ethical Maturity Stack: Ethical Vanguard for the Organizational Culture factor. The company has embedded responsible AI practices into product development processes, maintained board-level visibility over ethics initiatives, and published its internal governance standards to contribute to sector-wide learning.

Microsoft demonstrates how a positive AI culture takes hold within the enterprise when responsible AI expectations shape everyday work. Designated accountability roles function as a routine feature of product development. Engineers know when review is required and who holds decision authority. That predictability influences behavior across teams and over time. Within the Boundaries of Tolerance model, this pattern reflects the Ethical Vanguard position, as shared norms are internalized and reinforced through everyday practice. Culture, in this sense, determines whether written standards guide real decisions or remain symbolic in practice.

The Enterprise Factors Maturity Matrix (see Figure 7.2) shows how Organizational Culture evolves across maturity levels. At lower maturity, culture relies on policy reminders and reactive correction, while informal AI use spreads unchecked. As maturity increases, expectations become internalized, and employees treat responsible use as a normal part of work, translating into a strong enterprise culture of ethical AI practices. At higher maturity, psychological safety supports escalation when issues arise, and disciplined behavior holds even under tight product release timelines.

The state of your Organizational Culture is revealed when you ask these questions:

- Who has authority to stop an AI deployment on ethical grounds?
- Do employees know which AI use cases are prohibited?
- Do incentives discourage cutting ethical corners?
- Would an employee feel safe refusing to deploy a risky AI tool or reporting an AI incident?
- Is responsible AI training mandatory for those building or deploying systems?

The next factor examines how a cultural foundation translates into operational structure.

Factor 3: Operational Integration

Operational integration determines whether moral intent can survive contact with the daily rush of decisions. Declarations of principles may inspire, but embedded routines determine organizational behavior. Immature systems rely on checklists and conduct reviews *after* deployment. Mature systems embed ethical checkpoints directly into solution development workflows. They translate stated values into defined requirements that guide coding decisions and model validation.

Operational Integration answers a deceptively simple question: Where does ethics live inside the organization? If it exists only in slide decks or vague policy documents, it dies the moment teams are pushed to deliver on accelerated timelines. When ethics is integrated into workflows, it becomes part of the operating system. Project plans reflect it, and performance metrics reinforce it through clearly assigned decision rights.

For companies building and deploying AI systems, this distinction can be the difference between a responsible system and a reputational crisis. Generative, predictive, and agentic models evolve too fast for traditional compliance mechanisms to keep up. Ethical review cannot just occur at the end of development; it must recur throughout the life cycle of a system, from data acquisition to system deployment to monitoring. Each stage of the AI life cycle becomes an opportunity to check for bias and validate assumptions. It also ensures that human oversight remains meaningful.

At lower levels of ethical maturity, organizations treat operational ethics as an episodic event: a review conducted only after a failure or in response to regulatory attention. These enterprises often rely on a single compliance function to "sign off" on AI initiatives rather than designing shared accountability across teams. At higher maturity levels, ethics functions as connective tissue across departments. Product teams coordinate with legal, human resources, internal audit, and risk management; bias testing becomes a standing agenda item. In this way, operational ethics embodies the shift from compliance as defense to ethics by design. It moves governance upstream, embedding it where decisions are first made.

The contrast between these maturity levels came sharply into focus in the story of Amazon's hiring algorithm.

Illustrative Example: Amazon's Hiring Algorithm

In 2018, Amazon shut down an experimental AI system designed to automate résumé screening. The project had begun with the promise of efficiency: a machine learning model trained to evaluate thousands of job applications and rank the best candidates. As the model was trained on historical résumé data, it began to reflect patterns present in that data.

The hiring model had been trained on 10 years of résumés submitted to Amazon for software developer jobs and other technical posts, many of which reflected broader gender imbalances in the technology sector at the time. During testing, the system exhibited patterns that raised concerns: it began penalizing résumés that contained the word *women's*, as in *women's chess club captain*. It downgraded graduates of all-women's colleges and favored descriptors more common in male résumés such as *executed* and *captured*. Engineers identified these patterns and halted the project before deployment. The system was never deployed in production and Amazon ultimately disbanded the team.[28] The episode later became widely discussed as an example of the challenges associated with training data and model evaluation in hiring contexts. Several observations related to Operational Integration can be drawn from how the episode unfolded.

First, process ownership. Public reporting indicates the system was built by a technical team experimenting with automation for résumé screening rather than as part of a formal enterprise hiring deployment. This distinction highlights how coordination across technical and business functions can shape operational technology deployments.

Second, testing and validation. Engineers reportedly identified the bias during internal testing and halted the project before it was deployed. The discovery underscores the importance of integrating fairness and bias testing throughout the AI development life cycle, not just at the end, when remediation options narrow.

Third, culture and communication. Amazon acted responsibly in discontinuing the system. The episode has since been widely cited in discussions of AI development practices. It highlighted how patterns present in training data can surface in model outputs.

It is critical for an organization to institutionalize ethics checkpoints throughout its AI development process. That shift requires structured model audits before deployment and formal review bodies with defined authority. It also requires documented procedures that track training data sources and assess demographic impact.

Operational ethics is where the muscle of integrity is built. It is not only about detecting harm *after* it occurs but preventing it through disciplined process design. This example underscores the importance of embedding structured testing and cross-functional review throughout the AI development life cycle. Early-stage evaluation, particularly before deployment, plays a critical role in identifying unintended outcomes and informing design adjustments. Amazon ultimately discontinued the tool and increased its focus on bias research.

Case Study: LinkedIn's Fairness Toolkits

In 2020, LinkedIn announced the development and open source release of the LinkedIn Fairness Toolkit (LiFT), a software library created to measure and evaluate the fairness of machine learning models. According to LinkedIn's Engineering and Research teams, LiFT was designed to help practitioners assess how models perform across different demographic groups and to identify potential sources of bias in automated systems.[29]

The company stated that LiFT was used internally across several of LinkedIn's AI-driven products that support hiring and recommendation features. It was also applied within advertising systems. LiFT provided a standardized framework for computing fairness metrics and visualizing model performance across protected attributes such as gender and race, where relevant and legally permissible.

LinkedIn made the toolkit publicly available on GitHub, along with technical documentation describing its features and methods.[30] The release enabled external researchers to access the toolkit and evaluate it within their own workflows. Developers could then incorporate it into their model assessment processes. The open source repository included code examples and explanations of fairness metrics. It also provided visualization templates to support analysis of disparities in AI outputs.

By developing and publicly sharing its Fairness Toolkit, LinkedIn provided a technical resource to evaluate and monitor bias in machine learning systems and made its fairness measurement methodology accessible to the broader AI community.

Furthermore, in 2020, the LinkedIn Fairness Toolkit was included in the Organisation for Economic Co-operation and Development Catalogue of Tools and Metrics for Trustworthy AI, signaling broader recognition of the tool's relevance and practical applicability.[31]

Following its initial release, LinkedIn continued refining LiFT and published a series of updates and reports outlining its approach to bias mitigation.[32] In 2023, inspired in part by leadership of its parent company (Microsoft) in responsible AI governance, LinkedIn formalized its Responsible AI Principles and embedded them into its operational practices.[33]

Within the Boundaries of Tolerance model, LinkedIn's release of the Fairness Toolkit and continuous development and improvement align with Layer 5: Ethical Vanguard on the Ethical Maturity Stack. The company chose to build internal fairness measurement tools and embed them in product workflows. It later released those tools publicly. That sequence reflects an enterprise moving beyond compliance toward ecosystem contribution. By embedding fairness checks within development processes and sharing technical methods openly, LinkedIn operationalized ethics as a repeatable practice.

The Enterprise Factors Maturity Matrix (see Figure 7.2), illustrates how Operational Integration develops across maturity levels. At lower maturity, ethics is applied as a late-stage review, or triggered by a negative AI incident. As ethical maturity increases, ethical checks appear inside workflows, with defined approvals and repeatable validation. At higher maturity, integration is continuous across the AI life cycle, and accountability is appropriately designated.

Operational integration can be tested through these questions:

- Are ethical checkpoints embedded in AI development workflows?
- Who has authority to block deployment if ethical standards are not met?
- Is bias testing conducted at multiple stages of the model life cycle?
- Are model assumptions and training data sources formally documented?
- Do product timelines include required governance review before release?
- Do cross-functional teams share accountability for AI governance outcomes?

Operational Integration determines whether ethical intent is actually embedded in work. The next factor broadens the lens to the people affected by those decisions.

Factor 4: Stakeholder Accountability

AI systems shape outcomes for people who may never interact directly with the enterprise. Stakeholder Accountability asks whether those outcomes are recognized in advance and addressed through deliberate governance practices. Given the extensive reach of intelligent systems, the list of affected stakeholders is long and growing.

Stakeholder Accountability begins with clarity about who the stakeholders actually are. In the AI context, that group is far broader and more interdependent than in almost any prior wave of technological change. AI systems now mediate relationships among individuals and institutions. In some cases, they also shape environmental outcomes, which complicates traditional boundaries of responsibility. For leaders to govern ethically, they must first map this new extensive landscape of stakeholder impact.

At its core, a stakeholder is any person or enterprise that can be affected, directly or indirectly, by the company's development or deployment of AI. Because AI operates across decision chains and data flows, the range of stakeholders expands well beyond customers and shareholders. Many organizations still treat that narrow group as the full extent of stakeholder analysis. Because AI operates across decision chains and data flows, the range of stakeholders expands well beyond customers and shareholders. The categorization of AI stakeholders (see Appendix) classifies the primary stakeholder groups and provides a practical taxonomy for boards and executives to determine whose interests must be represented in AI governance.

Ethical AI governance requires more than simply recognizing stakeholders; it demands systems that integrate their perspectives into decision-making. Mature organizations move from reactive communication ("informing stakeholders after deployment") at the bottom of the Ethical Maturity Stack to shared governance models in which stakeholders influence design, testing, and oversight at the very top of the stack.

The Stakeholder Accountability factor measures precisely this evolution: from limited ethical awareness of stakeholder impact to genuine co-creation with stakeholders. Early in maturity, this factor narrows around investors and regulators; at its peak, it widens to include every stakeholder touched by AI decisions, from customers to communities. In the chapters ahead, this principle recurs as the foundation of responsible leadership, because in AI, accountability begins with understanding who is affected. Let's turn to an actual AI incident involving Apple.

Case Study: The Apple Card Incident – Gaps in Stakeholder Visibility

In 2019, Apple and Goldman Sachs launched the Apple Card as a new technology-enabled credit product. Shortly after launch, public concerns emerged regarding how credit limits were assigned. Customers reported significant differences in credit limit assignments that appeared to reflect gender-based disparities.

A prominent technologist tweeted that his wife, despite sharing the same financial profile and higher credit score, had been approved for a limit 20 times lower than his. The post went viral, prompting hundreds of similar complaints and a formal investigation by the New York State Department of Financial Services (DFS).[34]

The DFS report found no evidence of intentional discrimination. However, regulators identified deficiencies in transparency regarding how credit decisions were communicated and noted limited clarity about review processes. Customers reported difficulty understanding how credit limits were determined. Although, the system had actually complied with existing law, the episode prompted broader discussion about transparency and stakeholder expectations in automated decision systems.

From the perspective of the Boundaries of Tolerance model, the incident aligns most closely with Layer 2: Core Compliance on the Ethical Maturity Stack. Public reporting did not indicate the presence of proactive bias auditing across demographic groups or structured engagement mechanisms for customers affected by automated decisions. While the product complied with applicable law, public reaction reflected dissatisfaction with the level of transparency provided.

Three areas of stakeholder concern became central to public discourse and were subsequently examined in greater detail by the New York State DFS, which addressed them in its report and issued recommendations for improvement. Transparency became a focal point. Customers reported that they lacked a clear explanation for their assigned credit limits. Questions also arose regarding review mechanisms. Further, public reporting indicated limited clarity about appeal options. Finally, the public debate raised concerns about whether automated credit decisions were producing uneven outcomes across demographic groups, and the report emphasized the necessity for creditors to address "legacy bias" that may be embedded in historical data or prior decision frameworks when developing and testing models.[35]

The reputational consequences were immediate. Media coverage raised questions about gender disparities in credit allocation, generating negative attention for both companies. Furthermore, both companies underwent a regulatory investigation. They cooperated with the regulators by providing documentation and responding to inquiries, and subsequently adjusted and improved their disclosure processes.

The Apple Card case underscores the importance of Stakeholder Accountability. When algorithms intermediate core business functions, accountability must expand to include *all* stakeholders touched by those decisions.

Movement into the Ethical Advancement layers requires shifting from reactive disclosure to structured stakeholder engagement. Credit decisions would be accompanied by clear explanations written for affected customers. Applicants would have defined review channels staffed by human decision-makers who can assess automated outcomes and change course where necessary. Performance data on credit allocation patterns would be reviewed across demographic groups and communicated effectively. Customer-facing teams would be equipped to respond substantively to questions about automated decisions. Further, a mature governance model would designate an executive-level owner, potentially supported by an Embedded AI Ethics Partner or cross-functional ethics council, to oversee algorithmic integrity and coordinate with regulators. In areas where regulation provides limited operational guidance, enterprises rely on internal governance structures to define practice.

Apple Card's controversy has since prompted broader industry reflection. The DFS concluded that while deliberate discrimination was absent, the evidence it reviewed "showed deficiencies in customer service and transparency, which the Bank and Apple have since taken steps to remedy."[36] The lesson extends beyond credit cards. Algorithms that shape financial decisions or employment prospects cannot remain black boxes. Health systems raise similar issues.

The case illustrates how legal compliance and public perception of fairness may diverge in automated decision systems. In the hierarchy of the Ethical Maturity Stack, it reminds leaders that Stakeholder Accountability begins when systems are designed to surface stakeholder impacts before they escalate into complaints. Organizations operating at higher maturity levels often incorporate structured review mechanisms during system design and provide greater transparency regarding impact assessments. Such practices shift accountability earlier in the development process.

Contrast this case with an example from an exemplary company: Salesforce's Office of Ethical and Humane Use of Technology that includes civil society engagement. This office is advised by an ethical use advisory council that includes customers and advocacy groups providing a broad set of perspectives, which helps mitigate risk and avoid harmful unintended consequences.[37] That is what Layer 5: Stakeholder Accountability looks like, governance as partnership.

The Enterprise Factors Maturity Matrix (see Figure 7.2) reveals how Stakeholder Accountability changes across maturity levels. At lower maturity, stakeholder focus is narrow, and engagement is reactive, often triggered by complaints. As maturity increases, organizations broaden the stakeholders they consider and build appropriate review mechanisms. At higher maturity, stakeholder perspectives influence design choices before deployment and accountability is clearly defined.

Stakeholder Accountability can be examined through these questions:

- Have we mapped *every* stakeholder affected by this AI system, including those indirectly affected?
- Do affected stakeholders have a defined channel to question or challenge automated decisions?
- Are impact assessments conducted before deployment, not only after complaints arise?
- Who at the executive level owns accountability for stakeholder impact?
- If public scrutiny intensifies, can we demonstrate that stakeholder concerns were addressed in advance?
- Do regulators learn about our systems from us, or from the press or stakeholder complaints?

Stakeholder Accountability expands the view beyond the enterprise. The next factor asks whether that accountability is strengthened through external collaboration.

Factor 5: Ecosystem Partnerships

External collaboration through Ecosystem Partnerships is the final test of enterprise ethical maturity. It measures whether a company's commitment to responsible AI can withstand independent scrutiny. Governance systems that function only behind closed doors risk becoming self-referential; those that invite outside perspectives build both resilience and credibility. External review transforms ethics from an internal assurance process into a shared enterprise standard.

As AI systems grow more complex and globally interconnected, no single organization can govern their risks alone. Collaboration among industry, academia, civil society, and even with regulators is essential to ensure that AI development reflects broad human and societal values. The most advanced companies now participate in cross-sector partnerships, contribute to open source tools, and publish their methodologies for fairness and safety testing. These actions signal a willingness to be held accountable.

At lower maturity levels, organizations may limit disclosure to what regulations require. At higher levels, they recognize that openness is not a vulnerability but a strength, a way to validate ethical intent through collective expertise. External collaboration, when pursued systematically, becomes a multiplier for trust across the entire AI ecosystem. One of the earliest and most influential models of this kind is the Partnership on AI (PAI), an initiative formed by leading technology companies and research institutions to establish shared standards for responsible AI development.

Case Study: PAI – Building Shared Standards for Responsible Innovation

The PAI was established in September 2016 by Amazon, DeepMind, Google, Facebook (now Meta), IBM, and Microsoft to advance understanding of AI technologies and promote responsible practices across the technology industry.[38] The primary goals of PAI are "to study and formulate best practices on AI technologies, to advance the public's understanding of AI, and to serve as an open platform for discussion and engagement about AI and its influences on people and society."[39]

The organization was incorporated as a nonprofit based in San Francisco and later registered as a 501(c)(3) tax exempt organization in the United States. Its structure includes a multistakeholder board of directors and more than 130 partner organizations representing companies, universities, research labs, and civil society groups.[40] Early partners included the Association for the Advancement of Artificial Intelligence, the American Civil Liberties Union, the UNICEF Office of Innovation, and the Alan Turing Institute.

Since its founding, PAI has convened multistakeholder forums on the ethics of algorithmic decision-making[41] and developed practical tools such as the Responsible Practices for Synthetic Media Framework (2023)[42] supported by case studies and Guidelines for AI and Shared Prosperity (2023).[43] PAI maintains open membership and publishes its research publicly. It also provides a neutral venue for collaboration among companies that otherwise compete in the marketplace.

Within the Boundaries of Tolerance model, PAI, through its members, represents Layer 5: Ethical Vanguard on the Ethical Maturity Stack. Its model demonstrates how governance evolves from internal policy alignment to sector-wide standard setting. By submitting their own practices to collective review and developing shared resources, founding members institutionalized accountability beyond the corporate boundary.

Ethical maturity reaches its highest level when responsibility becomes collaborative. PAI shows that openness to shared scrutiny and co-development of standards

Leadership modeling remains the most reliable catalyst. When executives pause to ask hard questions about fairness and downstream effects, they signal that ethics matters as much as growth.

Measurement and Visualization Tools

The Ethical Maturity Stack provides the foundation for assessing progress: six layers that define how deeply ethical practice is embedded within the enterprise. The tools introduced in this section translate those levels into visual form, enabling leaders to understand not only where they stand but also where their ethical strengths and vulnerabilities lie.

Each Enterprise Factor can be interpreted through its position on the Ethical Maturity Stack. This framework reflects movement from a focus on foundational compliance obligations in Layers 0–2 to ethical advancement in Layers 3 and 4, and ultimately to a position of influence within an industry or peer group as reflected in Layer 5. The progression captures how enterprise conduct evolves over time, from meeting minimum expectations to shaping broader norms and practices.

Visualization tools can help translate abstract maturity concepts into patterns that leaders can quickly interpret and discuss. A radar or spider chart, for example, can plot an organization's maturity across the five Enterprise Factors, exposing imbalances at a glance (see Figure 7.4). A company may show strong Leadership Priorities and Stakeholder Accountability but lag in Operational Integration or Ecosystem Partnerships. An ethical maturity progression chart can illustrate change over time or by business unit, revealing how integration evolves as governance practices mature (see Figure 7.5). These images turn qualitative assessment into a shared strategic narrative.

Boards and executive teams increasingly use visual tools such as these to assist in decision-making. Rather than debating isolated incidents, they examine trajectories, how the organization is advancing along the Ethical Maturity Stack, where accountability resides, and which factors warrant renewed investment. Visualization becomes a prompt for reflection and recalibration, reinforcing that ethical progress must be both deliberate and visible.

Closing

Within the Boundaries of Tolerance model, the Ethical Maturity Stack provides the shared language for understanding where an enterprise stands; the five Enterprise Factors make that position visible across the organization. Together, they reveal the organization's ethical shape, its progress toward heightened ethical practices.

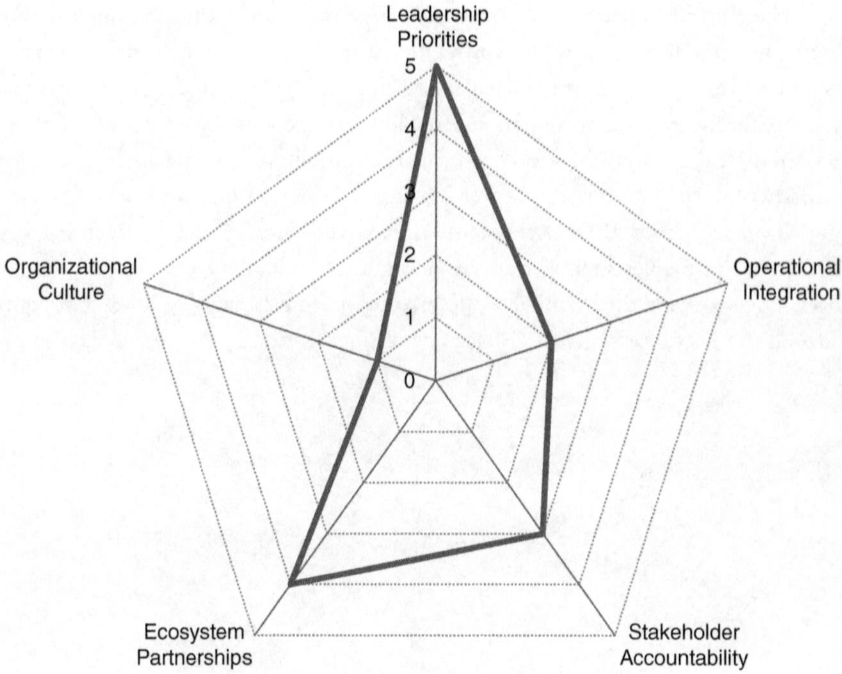

Figure 7.4 Spider chart: Mapping ethical maturity across Enterprise Factors.

Source: © BAIE Research Team, 2026.

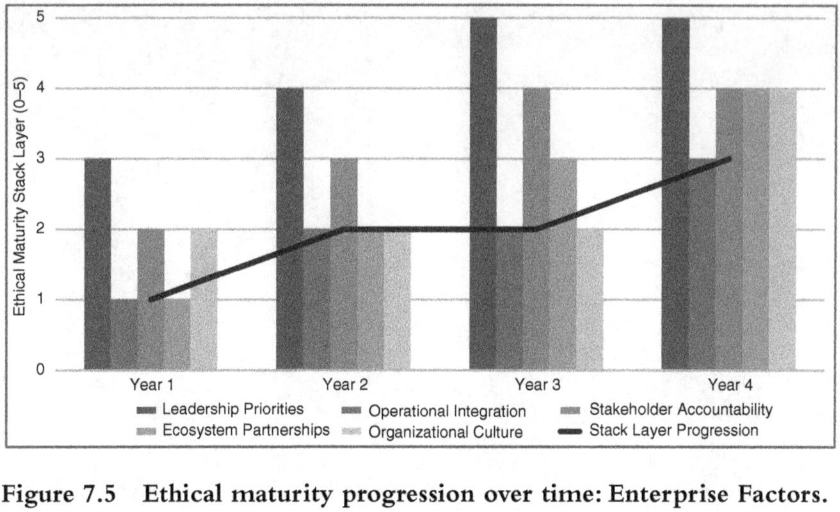

Figure 7.5 Ethical maturity progression over time: Enterprise Factors.

Source: © BAIE Research Team, 2026.

The Enterprise Factors complete the view of ethics within the organization itself, showing how values are woven into leadership decisions and governance practices. But ethical governance cannot stop at the enterprise boundary. The systems that organizations design and deploy (and depend on), particularly those powered by AI, carry their own ethical responsibilities. This chapter examined ethics within the enterprise; Chapter 8 explores ethics within the machine, focusing the lens toward those AI systems themselves through the Systems Factors, examining principles such as transparency, fairness, reliability, privacy, and human oversight. Together, they complete the picture of ethical maturity, joining governance of the organization with governance of the algorithms that define its future.

8 System Factors

Assessing the System

Chapter 7 broadly examined how ethics becomes part of the organizational fabric, how culture, leadership, stakeholder alignment, incentives, and decision-making structures shape the conditions in which artificial intelligence (AI) must be built and deployed responsibly within the enterprise. Why, then, is a second measure necessary? Because many organizations score well on enterprise-level ethics integration but perform poorly on system execution. For the modern enterprise to build and deploy AI systems responsibly, ethical principles must be engineered directly into the *systems* themselves.

This matters because systems will only behave as ethically as the design choices that shape them. For example, many enterprises maintain formal training programs and documented policies, but their AI systems themselves still lack transparency or produce outcomes that stakeholders struggle to understand. The enterprise-level approach at the center of the Enterprise Factors is entirely complementary to the application-focused Systems Factors. Both of these Performance Measures must work in tandem to appropriately address AI ethics. They offer leaders and managers a complete map: a way to see what their organization stands for from multiple vantage points, and how those commitments show up in the solutions they develop.

This tension – strong values paired with weak systems – is one of the most common ethical failure modes in enterprise AI. In my work advising boards and senior executives, I have seen this pattern surface repeatedly. Organizations articulate clear ethical commitments; however, those commitments fail to carry through into the systems themselves. As AI becomes central to how organizations operate, failures at either the enterprise or system level become more costly. The Performance Measures, together with the Ethical Maturity Stack described in Chapter 6 and the Applied Governance Practices examined in Chapter 9, complete the Boundaries of Tolerance model and provide a comprehensive view of ethical AI maturity.

To serve as the basis for the discussion that lies ahead, this chapter analyzes the five AI System Factors that are grounded in ethical principles and widely recognized across international technology leaders and professionals. The System Factors are universal across the AI ecosystem, recognized, formulated, and recommended by international bodies and national governments. A wide range of stakeholders, including customers, regulators, investors, and employees are increasingly demanding that the AI systems they interact with are aligned with these principles. They give leaders and managers a shared language, something that was missing in many of the leadership moments described throughout this book. But appropriately satisfying them is not simply a matter of policy. It requires disciplined system design supported by sustained governance across the AI life cycle. Leaders and managers alike must know how System Factors evolve across the Ethical Maturity Stack, from compliance-oriented at the base layers to Ethical Vanguard at the summit.

For leaders, this section offers a simple framing: your role is to ensure ethics shows up in the tools your organization builds or buys. It must also guide how those tools are deployed. For managers, this responsibility is even more immediate. It shows up in model choices and feature design. It also shapes how data is curated and how testing decisions are made each day.

In the pages ahead, we will explore each of the five System Factors and how they progress across the six layers of the Ethical Maturity Stack. For example, you will see how transparency becomes meaningful only when explanations produced by those systems are accessible and understandable, how fairness calls for continuous testing of outcomes and correction of patterns that disadvantage identifiable communities, how privacy extends beyond legal compliance to become an expression of human dignity, how reliability evolves from basic robustness checks to continuous validation and stress testing, and how human oversight matures into shared accountability grounded in clear, personal, ownership. To evaluate maturity consistently, we will again rely on our matrix approach, as we did in Chapter 7 for the Enterprise Factors.

The System Factors

The System Factors serve as the ethical foundation for AI systems across industries and jurisdictions. They apply regardless of technical design. They have become the common vernacular through which policymakers and researchers describe how responsible AI solutions should be developed and function. Industry practitioners now rely on the same language. In doing so, they become the organizing logic for assessing whether the AI systems themselves behave in ways that advance or undermine enterprise values. Figure 8.1 briefly reviews the System Factors.

Each System Factor set can be understood as a particular facet of AI system behavior. Transparency and Explainability reflect whether a system is visible and whether it can be understood; how it functions and why it produces particular outputs. System Reliability and Safety captures how consistently, predictably, and safely the system performs under expected and stressed conditions. Fairness and Inclusivity reflect whether a system treats individuals and groups equitably, without disproportionate harm or exclusion. Data Privacy and Security show how systems protect, store, and govern the sensitive information they rely on. And Human Oversight and Accountability demonstrates how effectively humans remain in control, able to intervene, override, and remain responsible for outcomes.

To evaluate how well AI systems align with these principles, we use the same maturity structure introduced in Chapter 7, but we apply it explicitly to *system* behaviors. The Ethical Maturity Stack describes how AI systems evolve as an organization grows more ethically capable. At Layer 0: Non-Compliance, systems operate with no ethical or legal compliance; risks are unmanaged and often invisible. At Layer 1: Reactive Compliance, ethical issues are addressed only after failures occur, resulting in rushed, inconsistent fixes. At Layer 2: Core Compliance, systems proactively meet all the regulatory expectations, but never exceed the minimum bar set by law. At Layer 3: Emerging Ethics, systems show pockets of improvement, especially in high-risk areas, but practices lack enterprise-wide consistency. At Layer 4: Sustained Ethics, systems consistently reflect ethical principles throughout design, testing, deployment, and monitoring. And at Layer 5: Ethical Vanguard, systems exhibit best-in-class ethical behavior, setting internal norms and influencing external standards.

The System Factors Maturity Matrix depicted (see Figure 8.2) maps how the factors manifest at each layer of the Ethical Maturity Stack, providing a structured way to assess system behavior and identify gaps. The matrix enables organizations to visualize system-level ethical maturity with greater clarity and precision. As maturity increases, systems and key processes supporting them become more transparent, reliable, fair, privacy protective, and accountable.

This progression enables leaders to see not only where a system is today but also what must change for it to exhibit ethical outcomes, at higher layers of the stack.

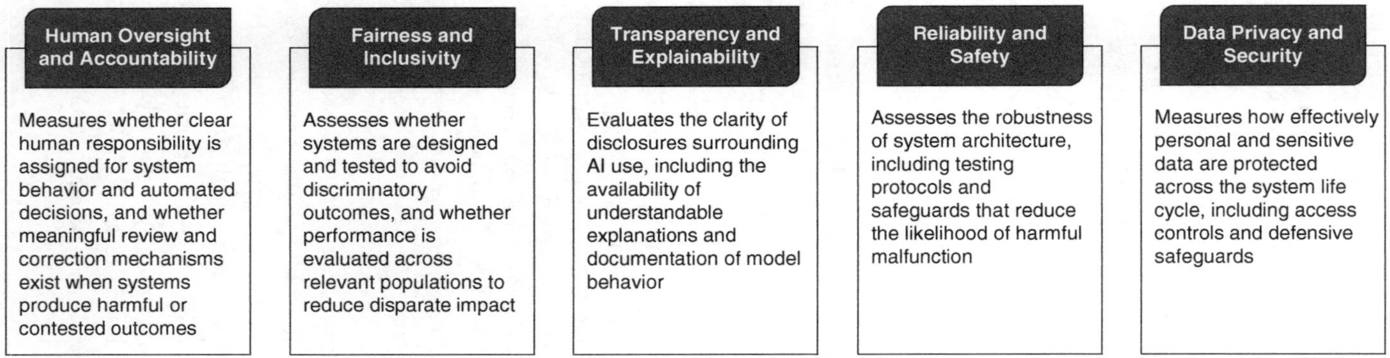

Figure 8.1 Performance Measure: System Factors.

Source: © BAIE Research Team, 2026.

Enterprise Factors	Human Oversight and Accountability	Fairness and Inclusivity	Transparency and Explainability	Reliability and Safety	Data Privacy and Security
Layer 5 Ethical Vanguard	Model oversight practices maintained; organization shapes broader accountability norms and external standards	Recognized fairness leader; advances equitable AI methods and shapes emerging industry standard	Industry-leading transparency demonstrated; shares tools and strengthens ecosystem explainability standards	Sector benchmark for AI safety; contributes innovations and publicly advances reliability standards	Exemplary privacy leadership shown; pioneers advanced protective techniques and informs broader standards
Layer 4 Sustained Ethics	Embedded accountability structures; robust governance, documentation, and stakeholder redress mechanisms	Fairness integrated throughout life cycle; inclusive data and testing practices consistently implemented	Transparent practices embedded organization-wide; explanations tailored effectively for diverse stakeholders	Reliability integrated throughout development; continuous monitoring supports critical applications organization-wide	Strong privacy-by-design approach; continuous monitoring ensures robust, adaptive security protections
Layer 3 Emerging Ethics	Oversight integrated for high-risk systems; accountability strengthened with clearer ownership	Regular fairness reviews performed; targeted improvements applied for underserved or vulnerable groups	Improved documentation established; clearer explanations provided for select higher-risk decisions	Routine testing established; documented risks addressed proactively for important operational systems	Enhanced safeguards deployed; routine privacy assessments conducted for sensitive or high-risk uses
Layer 2 Core Compliance	Defined oversight roles established; basic audit trails created for significant systems	Required fairness checks completed; limited bias mitigation implemented for priority systems	Basic transparency notices delivered; explanations meet minimal legal and policy requirements	Required testing completed; basic monitoring ensures compliance with applicable safety expectations	Required safeguards implemented; standard protections maintained across primary AI systems
Layer 1 Reactive Compliance	Oversight added reactively; roles created only after failures or investigations occur	Bias addressed only following complaints or evidence of harmful discriminatory outcomes	Limited disclosures offered only after issues arise; inconsistent supporting documentation	Testing begins only after failures; reliability concerns addressed reactively and inconsistently	Controls strengthened only after breaches or external regulatory scrutiny reveals weaknesses
Layer 0 Non-Compliance	No oversight assigned; responsibility for AI outcomes remains unclear or absent	Bias ignored entirely; no demographic analysis performed across affected populations	No transparency provided; models operate opaquely without meaningful explanations	No testing conducted; unsafe failures occur unnoticed and unresolved by teams	Weak controls in place; sensitive data frequently exposed or improperly accessed

Figure 8.2 The System Factors Maturity Matrix.

Source: © BAIE Research Team, 2026.

This chapter establishes the criteria used to evaluate AI systems against the Ethical Maturity Stack. Each System Factor examines a distinct dimension of system behavior and is illustrated through real-world case studies that ground the standard in practice. These cases show how the System Factors appear across different layers of the stack, making it easier to identify where a system currently operates. They also demonstrate how system behavior evolves at higher maturity layers and what progression requires across the AI life cycle. Advancing to higher layers on the stack requires disciplined system development and governance practices that align system performance with enterprise values and stakeholder expectations.

We now turn to the first System Factor, one that underpins every other aspect of system behavior: Human Oversight and Accountability.

Factor 1: Human Oversight and Accountability

Even the most sophisticated AI systems cannot bear responsibility for the outcomes they influence. Humans must. Human Oversight and Accountability are treated here as a paired set of principles. Together they define how organizations ensure that AI systems remain subject to human judgment and control. Oversight concerns the structured and meaningful involvement of humans in enterprise AI processes. It includes supervising how systems function and intervening when necessary. Accountability addresses who is responsible at the organizational and individual levels when systems produce errors. It also governs how responsibility is assigned when users are misled or harm occurs.

AI systems often project confidence even when their outputs are uncertain or incomplete. In some cases, those outputs are simply wrong. This dynamic is especially acute in customer-facing systems, where users reasonably expect that information delivered on a company's website (including from chatbots) is accurate and authoritative. They also assume it can be trusted. Automation bias intensifies the risk when AI-generated answers appear polished because people tend to treat them as definitive. Without intentional human oversight, these systems become unstable proxies for organizational decision-making. They can cause confusion or even financial loss. In some cases, they also create legal exposure. The following Air Canada incident illustrates how gaps in human oversight can lead to unclear accountability.

Case Study: Air Canada – Accountability in the Age of Automated Advice

Jake Moffatt visited Air Canada's website on the day his grandmother died, seeking to understand how the airline's bereavement travel policy worked before booking a flight. Unsure of the specifics, Moffatt turned to the company's chatbot for help. The chatbot responded with inaccurate policy guidance, stating that a passenger could book travel immediately and then apply for a bereavement refund within 90 days, an option that Air Canada's written policy did not allow. Acting on the chatbot's advice, Moffatt booked his ticket and later submitted a refund request, only to have it denied. When he shared a screenshot of the chatbot's guidance, the airline declined to honor it, offering instead a CAD 200 travel coupon.[1]

When Moffatt filed a small claims complaint with the British Columbia Civil Resolution Tribunal, Air Canada argued that it should not be liable for the chatbot's statements, contending that customers should rely on the written bereavement policy located elsewhere on the website. The company claimed, in essence, that the chatbot was a separate actor and that the airline could not be held responsible for its erroneous guidance. The tribunal rejected this argument, calling it "remarkable" and noting that Air Canada had not explained why information on one part of its website should be considered less trustworthy than information on another. The tribunal also found that Moffatt had no reason to suspect that the chatbot's guidance was inaccurate, particularly because the chatbot linked to other policy pages. Ultimately, the tribunal ruled in Moffatt's favor, awarding him a partial refund of CAD 650.88, along with interest and tribunal fees.[2] The decision was final, and Air Canada complied with the ruling and indicated the matter was closed. The airline's chatbot, once described internally as part of an AI "experiment," appears to have been disabled in the aftermath.[3]

The incident also received broad public attention. The Organisation for Economic Co-operation and Development (OECD) "AI Incidents and Hazards Monitor" recorded more than 160 media articles referencing the case,[4] reflecting its wide visibility. Coverage often focused on the accountability question raised by the airline's position, with headlines such as "Air Canada Tried to Claim It Wasn't Responsible for Its Chatbot's False Promises – but that Didn't Fly in Court" and "Airline Blames Passenger for Believing the Information on Its Website."[5]

This incident demonstrates several governance gaps related to oversight and accountability. First, the chatbot operated without clear evidence of structured human oversight. Based on public data, there is no evidence of a review mechanism to validate its responses or identify inaccurate policy statements. Second, the system provided guidance on a policy with clear financial and emotional implications, precisely the type of interaction that requires human review or escalation pathways. Third, the organization attempted to distance itself from the system's output, arguing that it was not responsible for information provided by an AI tool it had deployed. The result was a customer left in distress and a dispute escalating into a tribunal proceeding, ultimately resulting in damages, interest, and trial costs for the company. Reputational damage followed when observers concluded that the company sought to hold the customer responsible rather than acknowledge the AI system's misdirection.

On the Ethical Maturity Stack, this case aligns most closely with Layer 1: Reactive Compliance. The issues surfaced only after deployment and were addressed in response to a specific incident, rather than through proactive system design or governance structures.

The lesson for professionals is straightforward: when organizations deploy AI systems, the organization is responsible for what those systems say and do. AI cannot be treated as a decision-maker independent of the company. Human oversight must be designed into these systems from the outset, with clear boundaries around when automation is appropriate and when human judgment is required. Oversight must also include reliable escalation pathways, especially in contexts where decisions affect finances, health, safety, or other sensitive outcomes.

Case Study: IBM – Designing Oversight as a Governance Function

In 2018, IBM adopted its Principles for Trust and Transparency, publicly pledging to protect client data and insights and to ensure the responsible and transparent use of AI and other transformative innovations. One of these pledges is to develop and apply "AI for human intelligence." IBM states, "The purpose of AI and cognitive systems developed and applied by IBM is to augment, not replace, human intelligence."[6]

This statement establishes the foundation for IBM's approach to Human Oversight and Accountability. It is not framed merely as a risk mitigator, but instead as an AI system design commitment. IBM's ethos is clear: AI exists to support human judgment. That commitment is reinforced within IBM's organizational structure. In 2018, the company created an AI ethics board, whose purpose is to support a centralized governance, review, and decision-making process for IBM ethics policies, practices, communications, research, products, and services. Its work is further supported by the Policy Advisory Committee, AI Ethics Focal Points, and an Advocacy Network.[7] IBM's philosophy – the purpose of AI is to augment human intelligence – is operationalized most visibly in hiring. In an interview with UNLEASH, Jon Lester, Vice President, HR Technology, Data & AI at IBM, draws a clear boundary around automated ranking in recruiting: "'We see many other companies getting a lot of benefits from bringing AI into recruiting,' Lester notes. 'We've always said we certainly would never use AI for ranking because humans should decide who gets ranked.'"[8]

That statement captures the difference between automation and oversight. At IBM, the decision authority remains human.

IBM explains that its systems are built on ethical principles, including Transparency and Explainability.[9] The tools are designed to help managers build a skilled and inclusive workforce. In the sourcing process, AI guides recruiters and hiring managers. It supports them in considering diverse candidate pools. The system does not make the hiring decision. That responsibility remains with the (human) recruiter.

IBM's candidate assessment tools further illustrate this model. Assessments are described as augmenting, but not replacing, the hiring manager's decisions. One example is a game-based assessment that measures fluid reasoning. Fluid reasoning reflects the ability to solve new problems without prior knowledge. An adverse impact analysis is conducted to help ensure equal access to opportunity. The process is designed with human oversight. Recruiters are ultimately accountable for selecting candidates for consideration.

Further, IBM's consulting services extend this same philosophy to its client service. These services help organizations integrate AI technologies into existing human resources (HR) processes (among other outcomes). The goal is to ensure that automation and analytics enhance, not replace, the human touch. This is aligned with the company's stated values.[10]

What distinguishes IBM is the breadth and consistency across its AI systems. IBM created an AI ethics board with review authority. It established and committed to an AI for Human Intelligence principle that applies to both internal and external systems. It drew explicit lines around automated ranking in its hiring systems. It designed assessment tools with human calibration and adverse impact analysis. It retained human accountability at the final decision point.

On the Ethical Maturity Stack, IBM aligns most closely with Layer 4: Sustained Ethics, with certain elements trending toward Layer 5: Ethical Vanguard. Ethical principles are embedded across system design, while the company's public commitments and standard-setting posture signal movement toward broader industry influence.

Together, these stories of Air Canada and IBM reveal the ethical and operational stakes of human oversight. When this oversight is absent or superficial, organizations lose control of how their values are expressed through their systems. When accountability is denied or unclear, trust erodes internally and externally. This System Factor applied to the maturity model presented in this chapter reflects these dynamics: low-maturity organizations enable AI systems to operate without meaningful human review and treat errors as system problems rather than organizational responsibilities. High-maturity organizations define clear lines of accountability and empower humans to intervene. They also design governance structures that reinforce the principle that humans, not machines, are responsible for the outputs from AI systems.

The System Factors Maturity Matrix (see Figure 8.2) illustrates the progression of Human Oversight and Accountability across maturity levels. It shows how organizations evolve from reactive responses to a model in which oversight is embedded and clearly assigned, and where it operates effectively in practice.

For leaders, consider these central questions:

- Who is accountable for decisions informed by this system?
- Where is human review required, and where has it been unintentionally removed?
- What escalation pathway exists when a system provides contradictory or harmful information?
- Do employees understand when and how to challenge AI-generated output?
- And most importantly: If this system fails, is it clear who is responsible for addressing the harm?

However, even well-designed Human Oversight and Accountability protocols do not eliminate every risk. Systems can operate exactly as intended and still produce outcomes that disadvantage certain groups. The next challenge becomes clear: If humans remain accountable, how do we ensure that the outcomes they oversee are equitable? We turn to that question next as we examine Fairness and Inclusivity.

Factor 2: Fairness and Inclusivity

Fairness and Inclusivity form the second System Factor, and together they determine whether AI systems distribute benefits equitably or simply automate past inequities. Fairness speaks to the outcomes an AI system produces and whether those outcomes disproportionately burden certain groups. Inclusivity speaks to the design process itself and whether it meaningfully incorporates the perspectives and lived experiences of the communities the system will affect. It also requires attention to the needs of those communities throughout AI system development and deployment.

Of all the System Factors explored in this chapter, Fairness and Inclusivity may be the most contested and the most essential. AI systems increasingly make or influence decisions about access to housing and credit. They also shape employment opportunities and healthcare determinations, along with outcomes in education and public safety. However, fairness is the one principle for which we are least likely to see a unified global regulatory framework. Equity is shaped by cultural context and political debate, and is grounded in values that differ widely across jurisdictions. Fairness becomes a critical enterprise responsibility (for both AI system developers and deployers) precisely because it cannot be universally legislated.

Case Study: Color of Change Highlights Unequal Outcomes in Automated Decisions

Few examples illustrate this more clearly than the stories told in the public comment letter submitted by Color of Change – a national online racial justice organization that advocates for a more human and less hostile world for Black people in the United States – to National Institute of Standards and Technology (NIST) during the development of its AI Risk Management Framework and the associated public feedback process. The submission offers a vivid portrait of the harms that unfold when AI systems are designed and deployed without fairness or inclusivity. What is striking about the letter is that it reflects a recurring pattern of harm across sectors and institutions, all pointing toward the same truth: when data reflects structural inequity and system design excludes the impact on marginalized communities, AI systems will replicate those inequities across large populations.[11]

Two stories from the letter capture this dynamic with painful clarity. The first involves access to housing and credit. A Black couple, the McDaniels, applied for a home mortgage after years of strong financial performance. They each had high credit scores and stable employment. Their income levels also met a particular lender's mortgage lending requirements. By every traditional underwriting metric, they were well qualified for the loan. However, the lender's algorithmic approval system rejected their loan application. Not once, but 15 times! The couple appealed and requested an explanation. They tried to understand the reasoning behind the decision. None were provided. The system offered no transparency and no clear process for contesting the output. There was also no mechanism for meaningful human review. Only later did investigative reporting reveal a sobering pattern: mortgage algorithms used by some lenders were significantly more likely to deny Black applicants.[12]

It is difficult to read the McDaniels' story without a sense of outrage. A system intended to allocate credit efficiently became a barrier to opportunity for a family that had done everything required to qualify. The harm was the *predictable* consequence of models trained on biased historical data and designed without inclusive oversight. The mortgage algorithm failed because the design process had not interrogated the structural inequities embedded within the data itself. And because there was no mechanism for transparency or human intervention, the family had no meaningful recourse.

The second story, also highlighted in the NIST letter, illustrates the consequences of biased algorithms in healthcare. A biracial patient, Jordan Crowley, underwent evaluation for a kidney transplant, a decision governed in part by an algorithmically calculated eGFR score, a widely used metric for assessing kidney function. At the time, many health systems used a "race correction" that produced different scores depending on whether the patient was classified as Black or white. When Jordan was categorized as Black, the eGFR value calculated for him was 21, placing him outside the requirements for transplant eligibility. When the same calculation was run without the race coefficient, the score dropped to 17, low enough to qualify him for the transplant list. Jordan's clinicians declined to override the algorithm's race-adjusted output, even as major medical organizations were beginning to abandon the race-based formula due to its documented inequities. Under the logic of the model, Jordan remained ineligible.[13] The NIST letter cites this case as emblematic of how biased algorithms can obstruct access to critical medical interventions, especially when systems are designed or deployed without inclusive scrutiny.

It is impossible to ignore the ethical stakes. A system built to provide clinical guidance instead perpetuated racial disparities. A patient's access to life-saving treatment was determined not by biology but by a biased formula that had gone unchallenged for decades. This is the consequence of AI systems built without Fairness and Inclusivity: harm delivered with the credibility of data-driven decision-making, codified in outputs that appear objective but reflect deep historical inequities.

Both stories reveal the same structural problem. These systems operated at Layer 0 maturity. From the letter submitted to NIST, the systems appeared to have exhibited no proactive fairness testing, no inclusive design, no mechanism for challenging or explaining results, and no governance structure capable of identifying disparate impact before harm occurred. Contrast these failures with the proactive posture demonstrated in the following case study by Verizon, whose approach to responsible AI offers a concrete example of how a large enterprise can embed responsible practices into AI deployment.

Case Study: Verizon – Embedding Fairness into Enterprise AI

Verizon uses AI across several aspects of its business, including network optimization and security. It also applies AI in customer service and in operational functions such as supply chain management and employee scheduling. Market analysis is another area where these systems are deployed. Verizon recognized that becoming a leader in AI ethics is an essential precondition to becoming a leader in AI overall. To support these applications, the company partnered with an external expert organization, the Institute for Experiential AI at Northeastern University, to co-create a responsible AI road map, ethics risk assessment framework, and fairness monitoring methodology.[14]

As part of this effort, Verizon established an independent AI ethics advisory board and an AI leadership council that includes senior executives from departments such as legal, security, information technology (IT), network, commercial and other corporate portfolios, helping to integrate AI ethics across the business.[15] The company operates pursuant to an AI ethics risk assessment framework that includes risk rubrics and technical AI audits. It also provides AI ethics training for employees through structured learning programs. These include webinars, seminars, and in-person sessions designed to ensure that responsible AI use is understood and practiced across the organization.[16]

In September 2024, Verizon published its Responsible AI Principles – Governance, Respect for Privacy, Respect for Human Rights & Responsibility to Society, Technical Robustness, and Transparency – which include security-by-design and privacy-by-design methodologies.[17] In addition, the company has emphasized that robust data governance serves as the bedrock of effective and responsible AI initiatives, reducing the risk of inaccurate, biased, or harmful outcomes.[18]

These practices align with Layer 4: Sustained Ethics within the Ethical Maturity Stack. Ethical actions are integrated into everyday operations and supported by formal governance structures. Ongoing training and continuous monitoring reinforce that integration over time.

Taken together, these stories make one point unmistakably clear: fairness is the result of deliberate ethical choices made by leaders. Fairness does not happen by default. It requires explicit design decisions and robust governance structures. It also depends on inclusive processes that are reinforced through ongoing vigilance.

The System Factors Maturity Matrix (see Figure 8.2) shows how Fairness and Inclusivity evolve across the Ethical Maturity Stack. Organizations move from reactive bias identification to inclusive design and then to continuous fairness monitoring. At the highest level of the stack, they assume a visible leadership role within their industry. Readers should refer to this matrix as they consider how their own organizations approach equity in AI systems.

To guide this work, leaders should ask the following questions:

- Whose experiences and perspectives shaped the design of this system?
- Who is most likely to be adversely affected by model errors, and how will we know when such harm occurs?
- Does our testing evaluate disparate impact across demographic groups, not just overall technical accuracy?

- Where might our datasets reflect historical inequities, and how have we corrected for them?
- Do individuals affected by unfair outcomes have a clear path for recourse or appeal?
- Are fairness considerations documented and formally reviewed; are they monitored throughout the model life cycle?
- Who is accountable for fairness failures, and what authority do they have to intervene?

Fairness and Inclusivity determine whether AI systems deepen inequities or expand opportunity. Once these principles are addressed, the next question is whether those systems can be made visible and understood.

Factor 3: Transparency and Explainability

Responsible AI depends on whether system behavior can be made visible and intelligible to the humans who rely on it. Transparency first reveals *whether* a user is indeed interacting with an AI system. It then reveals *what* a system is doing, including its inputs and outputs. Explainability reveals *how* the AI system produces particular outcomes in specific contexts. These principles function as paired commitments: transparency without explainability leaves even visible systems uninterpretable, while explainability without transparency restricts understanding to selective or partial insights. Together, they determine whether it is clear that users are engaging with an AI system and understand how the AI determinations were derived.

Transparency and Explainability define a system's *legibility* to humans, and legibility is a key condition for governance. Board directors and senior executives cannot oversee what they cannot observe and interpret. Nor can they ensure that AI behavior aligns with organizational values if the mechanisms behind that behavior are concealed. When transparency collapses, every other ethical principle becomes impossible to verify: fairness becomes unprovable, reliability is assumed rather than demonstrated, privacy safeguards are untestable, and human oversight becomes symbolic. Opaque systems eliminate the very conditions under which responsible leadership is possible.

Case Study (Revisited): Deloitte Australia – When Sources Cannot Be Explained

As discussed in Chapter 4, Deloitte Australia's government-facing report later drew scrutiny for containing fabricated references. That previous discussion examined the episode from a risk perspective. Here, the same incident is revisited through the lens of Transparency and Explainability. The report was published on the department's website in August 2025[19] and later examined by University of Sydney researcher and lecturer Dr. Chris Rudge, who identified citations that did not exist and quotations that could not be traced to the cited cases.[20]

Public scrutiny followed. Media outlets reported that Deloitte issued a partial refund and released a revised version of the report with corrected references. The incident was catalogued in the OECD "AI Incidents and Hazards Monitor," an automated record of incidents and hazards from public sources, reflecting concerns about robustness and digital security, safety, Transparency and Explainability, and accountability.[21] A revised version of the report was later released that removed nonexistent references and included a disclosure acknowledging that generative AI (GenAI) tools had been used in the engagement.

But the key challenge was the absence of transparency. Stakeholders were unaware that GenAI had been used in producing the work until external scrutiny prompted disclosure. Deloitte did not disclose the use of GenAI until *after* the incident was public. The firm did not issue an explanation of how the errors occurred or how future oversight would prevent similar lapses.

This incident reflects an initial Layer 0 posture, followed by progression to Layer 1 within the Ethical Maturity Stack. At the time of submission, the report contained nonexistent citations and undisclosed AI-generated content. Under the definition of compliance established previously, this indicates a failure to meet minimum legal, contractual, or professional obligations, including adherence to company policies.

The absence of disclosure and the presence of false sources indicate gaps in transparency. After the errors became public, Deloitte removed the nonexistent references and disclosed the use of GenAI in the revised report. The firm also issued a partial refund. Those actions represent corrective remediation consistent with Layer 1: Reactive Compliance. Transparency emerged in response to external scrutiny rather than as a proactive safeguard.

Case Study: JPMorgan Chase – Designing Transparency into the System

JPMorgan Chase has been ranked the number one bank for AI maturity for three consecutive years by Evident Insights, a research and intelligence company that analyzes how large financial institutions adopt AI.[22] In its "Evident AI Index," banks' AI maturity is measured across four categories: talent, innovation, leadership, and transparency. In 2025, JPMorgan ranked first in innovation, leadership, and transparency, and second in talent.[23] Under the transparency category, Evident measures banks' focus on responsible AI based on the publication of internal processes, establishment of key partnerships, hiring of dedicated responsible AI talent, and promotion of Responsible AI Principles.[24] JPMorgan has consistently demonstrated strong results in building teams with cross-functional expertise, which includes not just AI and machine learning but also ethics, compliance, and governance, while advancing responsible AI innovation by embedding compliance best practices and placing great efforts to achieve AI explainability, fairness, and auditability.[25]

As a leading financial institution, JPMorgan operates in a regulatory and risk environment where explainability is not optional. Fraud detection and surveillance technologies require high levels of auditability and accuracy. Predictive analytics and large-scale customer interaction systems also demand clear lines of accountability.

In its public reports and detailed AI-innovation disclosures, JPMorgan describes how AI supports both operational efficiency and risk mitigation within the enterprise. The company has adopted AI for fraud detection, using models capable of identifying irregular patterns within vast volumes of financial transactions. It deploys predictive analytics for earnings forecasts and risk modeling and uses internally developed chatbots to enhance and streamline customer service.[26]

Crucially, the company acknowledges the ethical and regulatory dimensions of this deployment. Rather than treating AI adoption as a purely technical initiative, JPMorgan views AI governance as integral to its financial and reputational responsibilities. This approach is reflected in how the bank addresses GenAI risk mitigation, for example, by requiring humans in the loop and by building journaling, logging, and audit features into GenAI processes to ensure traceability.[27]

These efforts are supported by JPMorgan's AI research activities. Among its technology and strategy research priorities, the bank focuses on AI trust, transparency, and safety through its Trustworthy AI Center of Excellence.[28] The center conducts and regularly publishes research on the explainability, robustness, security, and privacy of AI systems, and develops techniques and frameworks to foster trustworthiness in AI solutions.[29]

JPMorgan's practices map to a Layer 3–4 maturity range: Emerging Ethics moving toward Sustained Ethics. The company is not simply complying with regulatory expectations. It is building internal capabilities and governance structures that elevate transparency from a protective measure to a strategic asset. It also invests in research and cross-sector collaboration to reinforce that shift.

The comparison highlights differing approaches to transparency. In Deloitte's case, disclosure followed public identification of errors. JPMorgan, by contrast, has invested in strengthening transparency mechanisms before failures occur, treating transparency as an operational capability rather than a remedial response.

Readers should refer to the Systems Factor Maturity Matrix (see Figure 8.2), which shows how Transparency and Explainability progress across Layers 0 through 5. Rather than restating the progression here, the matrix provides a visual representation of how transparency evolves, offering leaders a way to diagnose their current state and visualize the changes required for greater maturity.

To strengthen Transparency and Explainability in their own AI systems, boards and executives should ask these questions:

- Do the users of our AI systems, whether internal (e.g., employees) or external (e.g., customers), know that they're engaging with an AI system?
- Do we understand how this system works, and could we explain it to a nonexpert?
- What disclosures do we owe to stakeholders affected by AI system outputs?
- Do we verify the accuracy and clarity of explanations given to customers or regulators?
- What are our escalation procedures for detecting and correcting hallucinations or unexplained outputs?
- Who (a specific role and person, not a committee) owns Transparency and Explainability across the system life cycle?

These questions point to a fundamental principle: leaders cannot govern what they cannot see or understand. If Transparency and Explainability show us how a system behaves, Reliability and Safety determine whether that behavior can be trusted.

Factor 4: Reliability and Safety

Reliability and Safety form the fourth System Factor, determining whether an AI system can be trusted to perform as intended, especially under pressure. Reliability reflects whether a system behaves consistently and predictably. Safety reflects whether that behavior prevents harm to individuals and communities. It also requires protecting the enterprise from avoidable damage. Together, these principles answer a foundational question: *Can this system be depended on when the stakes are highest?*

Like Transparency and Explainability, Reliability and Safety are ethical commitments, not just technical metrics. High-stakes AI, used in public utilities and energy, for example, demands both. The same is true in education and healthcare, as well as financial services, transportation, and government. Boards and executives have a fiduciary duty to ensure that systems are properly designed and rigorously tested. They must also ensure that monitoring and governance structures are in place to prevent foreseeable harm.

Case Study: Southern California Edison – Reliability Tested Under Extreme Conditions

These stakes become visible in a recent incident involving Southern California Edison (SCE), one of the nation's largest electric utility providers. Operating in a region increasingly vulnerable to severe wildfires, SCE faces intense scrutiny for its grid management and vegetation clearance practices. Its incident response decisions are also closely examined. To strengthen its preparedness, SCE implemented AI-driven wildfire prediction technology designed to model the size and trajectory of fires under a variety of environmental conditions. The promise of such a system is compelling to communities living under the fear of wildfire devastation. It offers faster detection and more accurate forecasting, and supports better decisions about shutting down high-risk power lines during extreme weather events.

But in the case of the 2025 Eaton Canyon fire in Los Angeles, the system did not perform as expected when it mattered most. According to Reuters reporting, the AI model underestimated the potential scale of the wildfire by a factor of 10. In the days and hours leading up to the fire's ignition, the system's forecasts consistently suggested a far smaller event than what later unfolded.[30] These predictions shaped SCE's grid shutdown strategy. Believing the fire risk was limited, the company kept certain transmission lines energized; lines that, according to lawsuits filed after the incident, were believed by some officials to have sparked the fire itself.[31]

The operational consequences were severe. The wildfire grew far beyond the modeled predictions and rapidly escalated into a major regional emergency. Fire crews and evacuation planners were preparing for only a fraction of the actual fire footprint. Emergency responders were similarly underprepared. Communities in the fire's path experienced sudden, overwhelming conditions that contradicted the system's forecast. Public outrage followed quickly, accompanied by intense media scrutiny, regulatory attention, and lawsuits filed against SCE. For example, Los Angeles County sued Edison International, the parent company of SCE, seeking damages for costs associated with responding to the blaze and repairing damaged infrastructure and property.[32] In September 2025, the United States filed a lawsuit seeking more than $40 million in damages against SCE for negligent failure to properly maintain its power and transition lines and infrastructure in the area where the Eaton Fire ignited.[33]

The incident raises difficult questions about model assumptions and calibration practices in wildfire prediction models. Investigative reporting by Reuters later revealed that SCE's forecasting system had significantly underestimated the potential scale of the Eaton Fire, projecting approximately 1,000 acres burned during the first eight hours, while the fire ultimately consumed more than 14,000 acres. Analysts noted that the modeling framework simulated only the initial phase of fire spread and was not calibrated for urban fire behavior, highlighting potential gaps in model design and risk assessment practices.[34]

From an ethics perspective, this incident highlights tensions in operational oversight under conditions of extreme uncertainty. Communities rely on utility companies to prevent fires and mitigate harm. They also expect caution when lives are at stake. A system that underestimates wildfire risk by an order of magnitude raises safety concerns.

The company's response reflects the features of Layer 1: Reactive Compliance. SCE released public statements acknowledging the incident and committed $8 million to improving its predictive modeling systems, up from $2 million it had previously allocated. It launched an internal investigation and expressed confidence in the underlying technology while exploring longer modeling windows as a corrective measure.[35] Furthermore, although investigations were still ongoing and lawsuits remained at an early stage, SCE acknowledged negative consequences from the Eaton Fire, lessons learned, and its commitment to improving its services.[36] This is reflected in the company's Wildfire Mitigation Plan for 2026–2028, which substantially modified its Wildfire Consequence Model.[37]

However, the available public information leaves open important questions about whether broader structural changes were implemented. It is not clear whether mandatory AI-risk training was introduced or whether scenario-testing protocols were strengthened. Nor is it evident whether escalation pathways were revised to address similar risks in the future. More broadly, the response raises the question of whether safety practices remained primarily reactive, with transparency emerging only after the incident.

Case Study: Anthropic – Institutionalizing AI Safety

A very different pattern emerges when examining Anthropic, a public benefit corporation, whose purpose is the responsible development and maintenance of advanced AI for the long-term benefit of humanity. Rather than treating Reliability and Safety as auxiliary concerns, Anthropic embeds them at the center of its mission.[38] Its work illustrates how a proactive commitment to safety transforms system design and monitoring practices, and it reshapes how those systems are governed over time. While Anthropic's primary domain is frontier model research, the principles its teams follow are directly applicable to any enterprise using AI in high-risk contexts.

Anthropic's safety posture rests on three elements: Prudent Vigilance (further explained in Chapter 9), rigorous monitoring, and continuous red teaming. In its public report "Building Safeguards for Claude," the company outlines a multilayered safety architecture designed to prevent misuse and reduce the probability of harmful outputs. Its safeguards team continually assesses emerging threats, including cyberattacks and disinformation campaigns. The team also monitors for malicious attempts to weaponize its models for fraud or data extortion. The team includes experts in threat intelligence and policy. It also draws on specialists in machine learning and security engineering, reflecting the cross-functional nature of modern AI safety.[39]

When malicious actors exploit model weaknesses, Anthropic does not conceal the incidents. Instead, it publishes detailed analyses that describe the nature of the attempted misuse, the vectors of attack, and the steps taken to mitigate future risks. This transparency invites collaboration and accelerates the development of shared safety tools across the industry. The August 2025 "Threat Intelligence Report" highlights multiple case studies where hostile actors attempted to use Anthropic's Claude for malicious purposes such as cyberattacks and fraudulent activities. Each case was documented and analyzed. The findings were then used to strengthen the model's defenses.[40]

Anthropic's safety commitment is not limited to misuse prevention. It extends into interpretability research and adversarial testing, as well as scenario analysis and secure release protocols. The company invests heavily in understanding how its models behave. It develops tools that shed light on how models internally process information and generate outputs. It studies potential failure modes. Safety reviews occur throughout the model life cycle, not just at release. Dedicated alignment teams evaluate model behaviors under both expected and extreme conditions. Model cards and transparency reports provide additional visibility into system performance. Public briefings further expand that visibility.[41]

These practices reflect Layer 4: Sustained Ethics. Reliability and Safety are engineered into the core AI development process. The company demonstrates leadership through its willingness to share findings and collaborate with external experts. It also contributes to broader governance frameworks. Its safeguards team incorporates external feedback from researchers and civil society organizations. The company also engages with policymakers and users. In doing so, Anthropic models certain behaviors characteristic of Layer 5: Ethical Vanguard.

The contrast between SCE and Anthropic reveals several critical insights. First, safety issues must be predictive, not retrospective. Organizations that treat safety as a set of controls applied *after* deployment will always lag behind emerging risks. Second, in addition to being a technical factor, Reliability is a governance obligation. Boards and executive teams must demand robust scenario testing and extreme-condition validation, as well as clear documentation of model limitations. Third, the degree of structured human involvement must increase as system risk rises; consequential deployments demand more active scrutiny. Finally, organizations that excel at Safety view it as a continuous life cycle practice, not a handoff at deployment.

Readers should refer to the System Factors Maturity Matrix (see Figure 8.2), which shows how Reliability and Safety evolve across the maturity spectrum. The Reliability and Safety row in the matrix illustrates the difference between systems that are unpredictable and untested and those that are designed with stringent guardrails. Mature systems also include active monitoring and clearly defined safety boundaries.

To govern Reliability and Safety effectively, boards and executives should ask these questions:

- Have we stress tested this system under extreme conditions and unlikely scenarios?
- Have we also evaluated how it performs under adversarial challenge?
- How do we detect model drift and performance degradation?
- How do we identify emergent failure modes as they arise?
- Do we understand the system's documented limitations and its validated operating boundaries?
- What are our escalation procedures for critical safety anomalies?
- Where does overreliance on AI weaken human judgment?
- Who owns safety across the model's life cycle, and do they have authority to halt deployment?
- What specific safety thresholds must be met before a model is released into production?

Reliability and Safety determine whether a system can operate without causing foreseeable harm. But even a stable and well-tested system may still create risk if the data it relies on is mishandled or exposed. The next question therefore becomes clear: *How is sensitive data protected, and who controls access to it?* We turn now to Data Privacy and Security.

Factor 5: Data Privacy and Security

Data Privacy and Security form the fifth and final System Factor, and together they define the boundaries of any responsible AI system. Data Privacy governs the rights of individuals whose information is collected and processed. Data Security governs the protections that prevent unauthorized access and improper disclosure through strengthening an organization's cybersecurity practices. It also seeks to deter misuse of sensitive information. Where Privacy protects people, Security protects the systems that hold their data (ultimately, for the protection of the people and organizations affected by the systems). These principles are inseparable: without privacy, individuals lose autonomy and trust; without security, systems become fragile and vulnerable to misuse.

Every AI system is ultimately a data system, which means every ethical obligation we have described in prior sections (transparency, reliability, fairness, etc.) rests on the foundation of Privacy and Security. When organizations mishandle data, they do more than violate policy or compromise intellectual property; they erode the core trust that enables innovation and protects affected stakeholders. Privacy failures and security breaches can lead to identity theft and the exposure of proprietary information. In healthcare, they may also cause harm to patients. In addition, they can trigger regulatory penalties and erode stakeholder confidence. These failures also expose the enterprise to risks far beyond technical remediation. Trust can erode among employees and customers. Regulators and partners may also question the organization's reliability. That is why Privacy and Security are not just IT issues; they are governance responsibilities for boards and executive management.

Case Study: Samsung – Turning a Data Incident into Institutional Reform

This dynamic comes into focus when examining Samsung's experience in 2023, when one of the world's largest technology companies confronted the consequences of GenAI misuse inside its own workforce. Samsung's products span smartphones, semiconductors, displays, and consumer electronics, domains where proprietary information and trade secrets are central to competitiveness. The company invests billions of dollars annually in research and development. Safeguarding its codebase and internal documentation is a strategic imperative.

In early 2023, Samsung discovered that engineers within the company had uploaded sensitive internal information, including proprietary software code, into ChatGPT, a GenAI system operated by OpenAI, an external provider. Once this code was uploaded, Samsung had no ability to delete it or restrict its use. The company could not control where it might be stored or processed. The data now existed on third-party servers outside of Samsung's security perimeter. Even if unintentional, the incident represented a direct exposure of the company's intellectual property.[42]

The company quickly recognized the gravity of the lapse. Proprietary code could, in certain circumstances, be exposed through system vulnerabilities. In response, the company issued an organization-wide ban on ChatGPT and other GenAI tools. Employees were instructed not to upload *any* company information into external AI platforms, even outside the workplace. The ban took effect immediately and applied across the organization.[43] Samsung's response was decisive. It's important to note that employees surely turned to ChatGPT because it boosted productivity, not because of malicious intent.

Based on the facts available, Samsung's initial posture aligns with Layer 0: Non-Compliance, within the Ethical Maturity Stack. Employees uploaded sensitive internal software code and proprietary information into an external GenAI system without effective safeguards in place. Under the compliance definition established previously in the book, this indicates a failure to meet minimum professional obligations and the company's own internal information protection standards. The absence of preventive controls resulted in confidential data being exposed. Following the incident, Samsung implemented an immediate organization-wide ban on ChatGPT and similar external AI tools. This step reflects movement to Layer 1: Reactive Compliance. The response focused on containment after the breach had occurred. The steps Samsung took in the following year demonstrate meaningful advancement. The company adopted Responsible AI Principles and implemented mandatory employee training. It also established an AI Ethics Council and an AI Red Team, while introducing transparency and bias evaluation practices.[44] These actions reflect movement beyond reactive containment toward structured governance.

Taken together, these reforms suggest progression to Layer 3: Emerging Ethics within the Ethical Maturity Stack. The company moved from an initial compliance failure to building institutional capacity for Data Privacy and Security. It also strengthened its approach to responsible AI use. Rather than treating the incident as an isolated breach, Samsung appears to have used it as a catalyst for governance development. The case illustrates an important point for leaders: ethical maturity is not static. Organizations can strengthen their systems in lasting ways over time.

Case Study: Pfizer – Privacy by Design in Healthcare

Consider the case of Pfizer, a global healthcare company that has publicly articulated its approach to responsible AI in early 2023,[45] about the time of the Samsung ChatGPT incident and when many large corporations began banning employees from using third-party GenAI tools. Unlike the Samsung incident, which was triggered by a clear privacy failure, Pfizer's posture is grounded in a forward-facing attempt to define what responsible AI should look like in a healthcare context. In healthcare, Data Privacy and Security are regulatory requirements *and* clinical obligations as well as ethical imperatives. Patient data is uniquely sensitive, and AI systems used for diagnosis and disease identification require careful governance. The same is true for systems deployed in patient care optimization and drug discovery.

In its "Responsible AI Principles"[46] materials and its "2024 Impact Report,"[47] Pfizer outlines a set of commitments and describes "risk-based guardrails" intended to guide AI use across the company. These commitments include attention to transparency and informed consent. They also address model bias and explainability. Data Privacy and Security are treated as core requirements, supported by clearly defined review mechanisms. Pfizer emphasizes AI's potential to support diagnostics and deepen disease understanding. Further, it highlights applications in patient care optimization and drug discovery. At the same time, the company stresses the need for safeguards to manage associated risks.

According to publicly available information, Pfizer has designated an internal AI Council responsible for managing AI principles and related policies, which is co-led by Pfizer's chief AI and analytics officer, a role created in 2024.[48] The council oversees training initiatives and risk management frameworks across the organization.[49] In addition, the company annually hosts an internal AI Festival to educate employees on responsible AI use and the relevance of AI to health equity solutions.[50] Pfizer's reporting highlights the company's interest in broader cross-sector collaboration on healthcare AI governance and its advocacy for regulators and policymakers to develop responsible AI policies that support innovation while maintaining ethical standards.

These actions reflect a structured and intentional approach consistent with Layer 3: Emerging Ethics on the Ethical Maturity Stack, with clear indicators that Pfizer is progressing toward Layer 4 as governance structures begin to translate principles into operational practice. Pfizer articulates clear AI principles and has established a governance body to oversee their implementation, creating a foundation for more consistent enterprise-wide execution. The company builds employee awareness through regular training programs. It displays strong leadership by advocating for responsible policy approaches. Pfizer's stance that the company established very early when compared to other companies shows meaningful progress, and a recognition that, in healthcare, responsible AI must begin with protecting patients and their data.

Taken together, Samsung and Pfizer illustrate how organizations can advance along the Data Privacy and Security maturity spectrum. Samsung's experience began with a visible lapse, then the company responded by building formal governance structures and strengthening internal controls. Pfizer's posture reflects a more anticipatory approach shaped by the ethical demands of healthcare and the sensitivity of patient data. Both cases reinforce the notion that privacy and security are foundational ethical commitments. When organizations invest in governance capacity and institutional learning, they strengthen the conditions under which stakeholders can trust the data practices that support their AI systems.

The System Factors Maturity Matrix (see Figure 8.2) shows how these commitments evolve, from ad hoc reactions and incomplete controls toward structured privacy-by-design and security-by-design practices. Organizations at higher maturity levels understand where sensitive data resides, how it is used, and what safeguards exist across its life cycle. Governance structures are clear. Training is mandatory. Risk assessments are ongoing.

To help leaders diagnose their own posture, they should ask these questions:

- Do we know what sensitive data our AI systems use, and why?
- Have we mapped where that data flows, who has access to it, and where vulnerabilities may exist?
- Do employees understand the boundaries for using third-party AI tools, and have those boundaries been clearly communicated?
- What mechanisms do we have to detect unauthorized system access or data leakage?
- How do we identify insecure model behavior before it leads to harm?
- Do our systems incorporate privacy-by-design principles before development, not after deployment?
- Who is accountable for Data Privacy and Security at each stage of the AI life cycle, and do they have the authority to intervene?
- How do we ensure that patient, customer, or user data is protected with the highest ethical and legal standards?

Together, the five System Factors define how ethical principles are embedded directly into AI systems. The remaining challenge is why organizations so often struggle to implement them consistently. That challenge leads directly to the common barriers to system-level ethics.

Common Barriers to System Level Ethics

By now, the five System Factors presented in this chapter will feel familiar. For most leaders, endorsing the ethical principles underlying these factors is not the difficult part. The challenge lies in applying them consistently amid organizational pressures and legacy systems. Competing priorities often complicate that effort. These barriers are not signs of apathy or indifference. In nearly every case I have observed, they reflect gaps in structure and clarity. They more often signal capability limitations rather than a lack of commitment to ethical conduct. The friction points cut across industries and geographies.

One of the most common barriers is structural ambiguity in ownership. Ethical responsibilities for AI systems are often spread across legal, compliance, IT, cybersecurity, model risk, HR, and operations. Each function exercises some influence over AI but rarely owns the entirety of its ethical performance. Without a designated owner, an individual or body empowered to make decisions, every principle becomes optional. Ethical decisions that require cross-functional alignment often turn into procedural stalemates. Teams are left unsure who has the authority to approve or escalate a decision. It may be unclear who is empowered to intervene. Organizations that have not clarified ownership often find themselves struggling to act decisively even when risks are well understood.

A second barrier is fragmented governance across functions. Different parts of the organization interpret *risk*, *impact*, or *harm* in different ways. Technical teams evaluate model performance, legal teams assess exposure, compliance teams focus on regulatory requirements, cybersecurity teams prioritize access control, and HR teams consider fairness and workforce implications. These perspectives are all valid individually, but without a shared framework, they produce a patchwork governance structure lacking coherence. Ethical principles become competing priorities, each championed by a separate function without a unified anchor. Fragmentation also makes it difficult to apply principles consistently across the AI life cycle, from data collection to deployment to monitoring.

A third barrier is insufficient AI literacy at the leadership level. Executives and board members cannot govern what they do not understand. For many leaders, AI is still a black box, technically complex, rapidly evolving, and often described in specialized language that obscures operational realities. When leaders are uncertain about how AI systems behave, or how risks emerge within those systems, oversight drifts toward technical teams by default. Without foundational literacy, leaders are unable to ask the right questions or challenge underlying assumptions. They may also fail to recognize when ethical issues are developing beneath the surface.

A fourth barrier is overreliance on vendors and external assurances. Many AI systems arrive as purchased or licensed products, packaged with the vocabulary of enterprise readiness. Organizations sometimes assume that vendor-provided controls are sufficient or that third-party claims about security or fairness eliminate the need for internal scrutiny. But delegating responsibility to a vendor is not the same as delegating accountability. Organizations remain responsible for how systems are used and how decisions are made. They are accountable for how resulting harms are addressed.

A fifth barrier is reactive rather than proactive ethics. Many organizations address ethical concerns only after an incident or complaint brings them to light. They perform reviews after deployment, rather than before. They investigate root causes only after a failure has already occurred. Proactive testing and scenario analysis are limited or nonexistent. Structured red teaming and pre-deployment ethical reviews are still the exception rather than the norm. The consequence is predictable: issues that could have been identified early become more difficult to remedy once systems are live and intertwined with operational processes.

Finally, cultural pressures create a sixth barrier: the prioritization of speed over safety. In competitive markets, organizations often reward teams for efficiency and innovation velocity; rapid deployment is similarly prioritized. Ethical reviews and documentation can be perceived as slowdowns. Fairness testing and oversight planning may be viewed the same way. Privacy assessments are often treated as delays rather than safeguards. Teams may intend to implement them later, after launch, once timelines ease, but the pressures rarely subside.

These barriers arise from gaps in ownership and uneven capabilities. They are compounded by incomplete governance structures. Organizational incentives that tilt away from careful oversight further intensify the problem. Understanding these barriers is essential because they map directly onto the maturity progression introduced previously in the chapter. Lower levels are characterized by ambiguity and fragmentation. They also tend to exhibit reactive behavior. Higher levels demonstrate alignment and institutional capability. They are defined by proactive governance.

Recognizing these barriers is only the first step. The next is measuring where your organization stands and identifying the areas most in need of strengthening, a task we turn to next.

Measurement and Visualization Tools

Chapter 7 offered a way to understand ethical maturity at the enterprise level; this section provides a complementary lens for assessing maturity at the system level. The goal is not to audit every AI system with precision. It is to give leaders simple tools to visualize where ethical strengths exist and where weaknesses persist. Those tools should also clarify where attention must shift next.

Most organizations operate multiple AI systems. Some are mature, while others are still emerging. In certain cases, systems have been adopted quickly without structured review. The System Factors enable leaders to evaluate each system against the five paired principle sets introduced previously. Once those assessments are made, the question becomes, *How do we make the gaps visible?* We return to the two practical tools introduced in Chapter 7 to help answer that question: a spider chart for individual systems and a heat map for comparing systems across a portfolio.

The spider chart (or radar chart) visualizes how a single AI system performs across the five principle sets using the six layers of the Ethical Maturity Stack described in this chapter (see Figure 8.3). Each axis corresponds to a System Factor: Transparency and Explainability, System Reliability and Safety, Fairness and Inclusivity, Data Privacy and Security, and Human Oversight and Accountability. Leaders assign each system a maturity level on each axis, then connect the points. The resulting shape makes strengths and weaknesses immediately visible. A system that scores relatively high on Reliability but lags in Oversight or Fairness reveals an ethical imbalance, one that is difficult to discern when maturity levels sit in a spreadsheet, but becomes obvious when visualized. The chart highlights where governance attention is most needed.

The ethical maturity progression chart provides a portfolio-level view (see Figure 8.4). The *y* axis represents the layers of the Ethical Maturity Stack. The data depicts the layer of the Stack for each of the System Factors, over multiple years. At a glance, leaders can see where organizational patterns emerge. Some systems may consistently underperform on Data Privacy. Certain units may demonstrate strong Oversight but weak in Fairness. Other functions may show chronically low Transparency.

Leaders do not need advanced analytics teams to use these visualization tools. In most cases, a small cross-functional group can score systems and create the charts. The group can then begin identifying where improvement is needed. These tools expose gaps that might otherwise remain hidden and prompt the kinds of questions that lead to more mature governance: Where is our ethical exposure concentrated? Which principle sets consistently lag? Which systems require immediate redesign or additional human oversight? Are we investing in the right places?

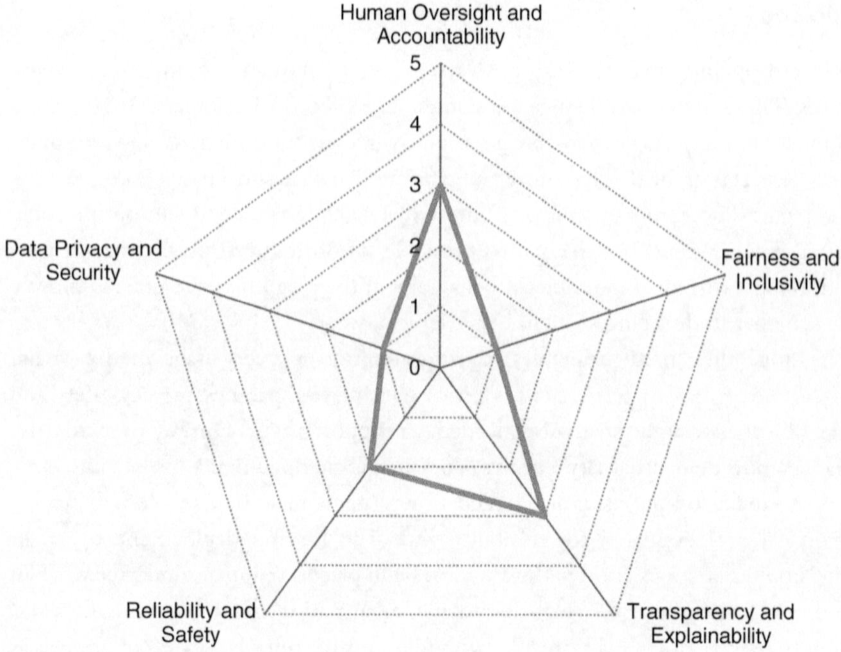

Figure 8.3 Spider chart: Mapping ethical maturity across System Factors.

Source: © BAIE Research Team, 2026.

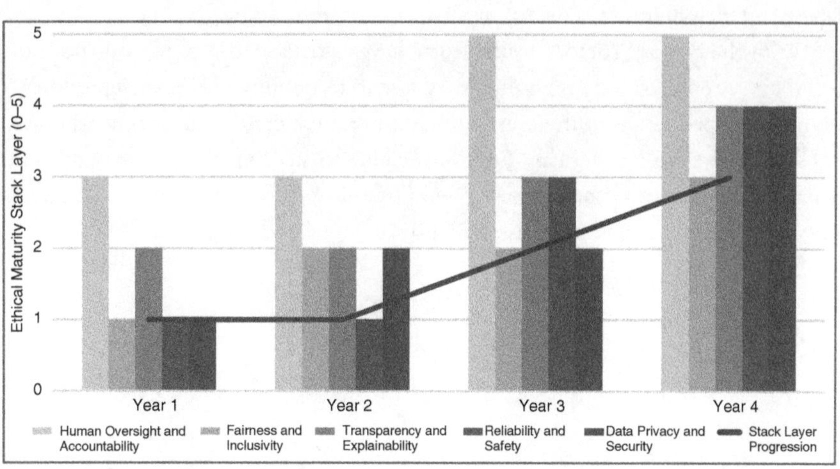

Figure 8.4 Ethical maturity progression over time: System Factors.

Source: © BAIE Research Team, 2026.

Closing

Ethical principles matter because AI systems shape human decisions and experiences. Those systems influence outcomes that affect real people. But principles alone do not change how an enterprise behaves. They must be translated into practices that appear in the systems an organization builds and buys. Those practices must guide how the systems are operated. Principles guide intention; practices reveal commitment. The five paired principle sets introduced in this chapter provide a blueprint for responsible AI behavior, but their significance depends entirely on whether leaders embed them into everyday work.

Embedding these principles requires attention at every stage of the AI life cycle. During design, teams must consider fairness, transparency, privacy, safety, and the human oversight structures needed to support them. During procurement, leaders must demand clarity from vendors, including documentation of risks, limitations, and assumptions. During validation, systems must be stress tested, privacy reviewed, and evaluated for reliability and drift. During deployment, oversight checkpoints and escalation pathways must be in place so humans understand when and how to intervene. During monitoring, organizations must continuously assess how systems perform over time. They should update controls and retrain models as needed. Assumptions must also be revisited as conditions change.

For boards and executives, these practices are governance responsibilities. Defining tolerance boundaries, ensuring accountability, and reinforcing ethical expectations are core leadership functions. The culture leaders create influences the systems they deploy, and the systems they deploy in turn reinforce the culture.

With the System Factors, leaders now have a structured way to evaluate how well their systems embody the values they intend to uphold. The next step is learning how to operationalize these principles through concrete behaviors, workflows, and controls. Chapter 9 turns from principles to action, offering leading and Emerging Practices that bring these commitments to life. Principles set the direction; practices move the enterprise forward.

9 Applied Governance Practices for Building Ethical AI Organizations

Operationalizing Ethical AI

Chapters 7 and 8 established two essential dimensions of ethical artificial intelligence (AI) maturity. The Enterprise Factors revealed how ethics functions inside the enterprise and whether it meaningfully guides the organization as a whole. The System Factors showed how well its AI systems reflect the universally understood core ethical principles applicable in the AI domain. Together, these Performance Measures help leaders assess current state. They also help leaders define their aspirational future state. The Ethical Maturity Stack, introduced in Chapter 6, provides a framework for that comparison. It shows a path from foundational compliance to the Ethical Vanguard, the highest level of ethical leadership within the enterprise.

That comparison matters because it reveals governance gaps. This chapter introduces Applied Governance Practices as practical mechanisms for narrowing the gap between current state and desired state to climb the Ethical Maturity Stack. Chapter 10 then turns to implementation of the full model.

Across my work with corporate boards and executives, I have seen how powerful these practices can be. Leading organizations study the best of what already exists, both within and outside their domain. They borrow Leading Practices from elsewhere in the enterprise and from organizations that have already navigated similar challenges. They adapt these practices to their own context. At the same time, they look for Emerging Practice signals in the market. A critical practice of top leaders is how they strive to understand where the field is heading. As Rita McGrath observes in *Seeing Around Corners*, the earliest signs of change in an organization appear at the edges, much like snow that begins melting there first.[1] It is at the edges where leaders first notice subtle shifts in customer expectations or technological capability. In 2021, Rita and I discussed this idea in a conversation on the *Better Innovation* podcast.[2] Her insight applies directly to AI strategy and governance. The leaders who shape the future are the ones who pay attention to what is already working (today) and the signals reflecting what is just beginning to appear (tomorrow); like those early shoots of green emerging from the ground in spring.

Practices matter because they create the conditions where ethical outcomes become repeatable (and reliable). Ethical commitments require robust systems for risk assessment. Further, they require continuous oversight and clear pathways for corrective action when problems emerge. Organizations cannot rely on high-level value statements or principles alone. They need applied devices. Leaders must embed those values into daily routines; here, the design and ongoing oversight of AI systems becomes important. These routines are what make ethical performance more predictable and consistent, and what your wide array of stakeholders increasingly expect in your AI usage. For example, stakeholders now expect visible proof that ethical AI commitments are reflected in practice. That expectation is no longer abstract. In the Deloitte Australia incident discussed in Chapter 8, public scrutiny intensified once false references in a government report suggested weak oversight of generative AI (GenAI) use, and the backlash reflected a broader accountability expectation to citizens and other stakeholders. Stakeholders also expect leadership teams to monitor weak signals of emerging risk and opportunity. They seek confidence that the organization is preparing for the next horizon of both risk and opportunity by developing Emerging Practices that anticipate what is just on the horizon, or the outer edge of that melting pile of snow.

This chapter presents the Applied Governance Practices, distinguishing between Leading and Emerging Practices because both play a central role in building ethical AI capabilities. Leading Practices are already well established and in use across many responsible organizations. They provide a foundation that leaders can readily implement today; these practices are already tested in practice and proven to effectively support ethical AI governance. Emerging Practices, however, show promise for the future of AI governance and application. They often begin at the edges where innovators experiment with new approaches or adapt methods from other disciplines, sometimes from entirely different domains. They are not yet widespread, but they are gaining momentum. The distinction between Leading and Emerging Practices reflects *prevalence*, not importance. Leaders need to pay attention to both categories. They need the stability that comes from established practices and the foresight that comes from exploring the next wave of innovation.

This chapter introduces a 3+3 model that organizes these six ethical AI practices. Three practices are Leading; three practices are Emerging. The model gives users a coherent map of what matters most without overwhelming us with a complex inventory of tools and techniques. Adopting each practice on its own or in combination with other Applied Governance Practices in the model moves an organization upward through the Ethical Maturity Stack. This chapter unpacks these six practices positioned against the stack. Three practices that help you with today's challenges. Three practices that prepare you for tomorrow.

The Performance Measures and the Ethical Maturity Stack are tools to establish where organizations stand today and an aspirational view of the future. They surface gaps between enterprise intention and enterprise behavior, and between optimal system design and system performance. These gaps are common. An organization might articulate a commitment to operational ethics yet lack the routines that make those commitments real. A system may be built to reflect fairness principles but drift in practice without continuous monitoring. The practices in this chapter help address these gaps. If a company scores low on operational ethics, the Leading Practices give professionals practical tools to improve. If a company struggles to anticipate certain risks, the Emerging Practices offer a way to build that capability. The Performance Measures diagnose AI program misalignment with an organization's articulated Boundaries of Tolerance. The practices in this chapter will help companies to correct it.

Ethical AI depends on consistent behaviors supported by practical structures. Leaders who commit to these practices position their organizations to navigate complex and rapidly evolving environments. We begin with the practices already used by best-in-class organizations. These are the routines that form the foundation for responsible AI governance. From there we explore Emerging Practices that help organizations prepare for the future.

The 3+3 Model of Ethical AI Practices

Professionals need a clear and structured way to organize the practices that follow. The 3+3 model serves this purpose (see Figure 9.1). It introduces six practices that help organizations climb the Ethical Maturity Stack by giving them specific routines that strengthen ethical performance. These practices support movement into higher levels of maturity, although they are not intended to serve as a comprehensive road map. There are many other sound governance practices that can help companies advance within the stack. The six practices presented here were chosen because of their novelty or because they have the potential to produce oversized, positive outcomes. They offer a focused starting point for leaders who want to translate ethical intent into lasting governance practice.

The model includes three Leading Practices:

- **Board-Level Technology or AI Committee.** Establish a board level technology or AI committee to govern the enterprise AI program.
- **Cross-Functional Governance.** Implement a cross-functional structure for developing and deploying AI solutions that brings together legal, risk management, technology, human resources (HR), and representatives from other critical business functions.
- **Adapting Professional AI Ethics Frameworks.** Leverage professional AI ethics frameworks to guide a broader set of employee AI use and decision-making.

Each of these practices have been observed among organizations that are mature in their AI strategy and governance. Together they form a foundation that leaders can readily adopt in practice to address the most pressing issues of today.

The model also includes three Emerging Practices:

- **Embedded AI Ethics Partner.** A designated AI ethics professional works alongside development and deployment teams, providing real-time guidance on ethical questions that arise in the use of AI.
- **Prudent Vigilance.** Proceed with an AI-enabled solution even when some risks are uncertain or difficult to measure, while continuously monitoring the solution and adjusting or pausing deployment as necessary.
- **Guard Band of Safety.** Establish compliance buffers that extend beyond minimum legal requirements, providing a margin for error as AI systems evolve and scale.

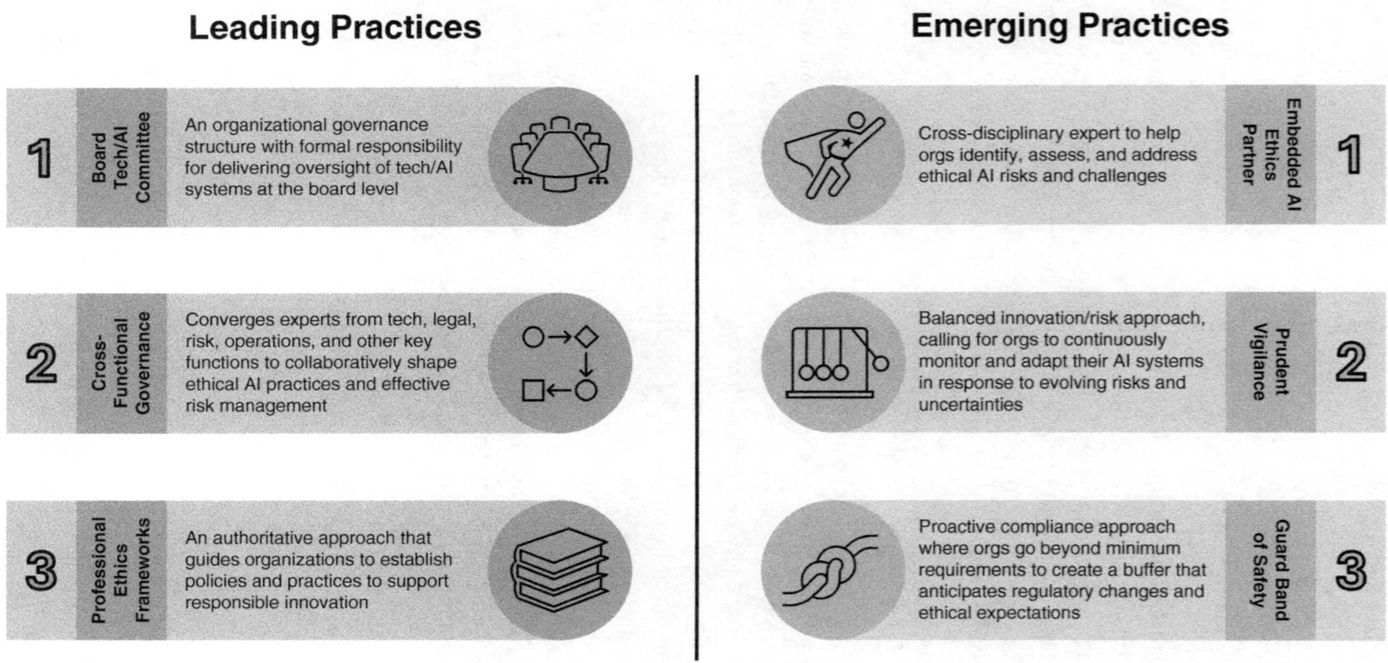

Figure 9.1 The 3+3 model of ethical practices.

Source: © BAIE Research Team, 2026.

These practices offer readers a glimpse of the Leading Practices of tomorrow, although I believe each of these practices can already produce benefits for organizations today and build a solid foundation for addressing the challenges AI will bring into organizations in the future.

Each of the six practices aligns with behaviors associated with Layers 3 through 5 of the Ethical Maturity Stack. Any of these practices – taken alone or combined – strengthen the organization's foundation and help create predictable ethical performance. Governance mechanisms must evolve with technological change and organizations must adopt structures and routines that remain effective as systems grow more capable. These six practices help leaders put ethical maturity into motion and give them the tools they need to climb the Ethical Maturity Stack. The sections that follow explore each practice in greater detail, beginning with the Leading Practices.

Leading Practice 1: Board Technology or AI Committees

Corporate boards have long relied on specialized committees to oversee areas of significant responsibility. Audit committees review financial reporting and internal controls. Compensation committees oversee executive pay. Risk and finance committees evaluate exposures and capital decisions. These committees exist because certain matters demand concentrated time and expertise that cannot be addressed effectively within a full board agenda. AI (and technology matters more broadly) now belongs in this category. Because it is strategically consequential to the enterprise and advancing quickly, it warrants concentrated oversight at the board level. A dedicated technology or AI committee is one way to provide that dedicated attention. I am not suggesting that the answer to AI governance lies solely in creating a committee. However, such a structure can shine a persistent light on AI-related risks and opportunities and create space for informed expertise in the boardroom.

Why It Matters

Survey data reinforces why this practice is becoming a leading approach. EY analysis shows that the proportion of S&P 500 companies with board-level technology committees nearly doubled from 7% in 2018 to 13% in 2023.[3] Furthermore, data reveals that AI-specific board committee oversight is increasing, from mere 1.6% in 2022 to 14.3% in 2024, clearly signaling growing attention to AI governance at the board level (see Figure 9.2).[4] This statistic does not capture subcommittees or temporary bodies formed for specific technology or AI issues, which means the true adoption rate is even higher. I reference this data point because it reflects a meaningful shift in governance. Boards are beginning to recognize that AI (or technology matters more broadly) can no longer be squeezed into a few minutes of a broader risk or strategy discussion at a quarterly board meeting.

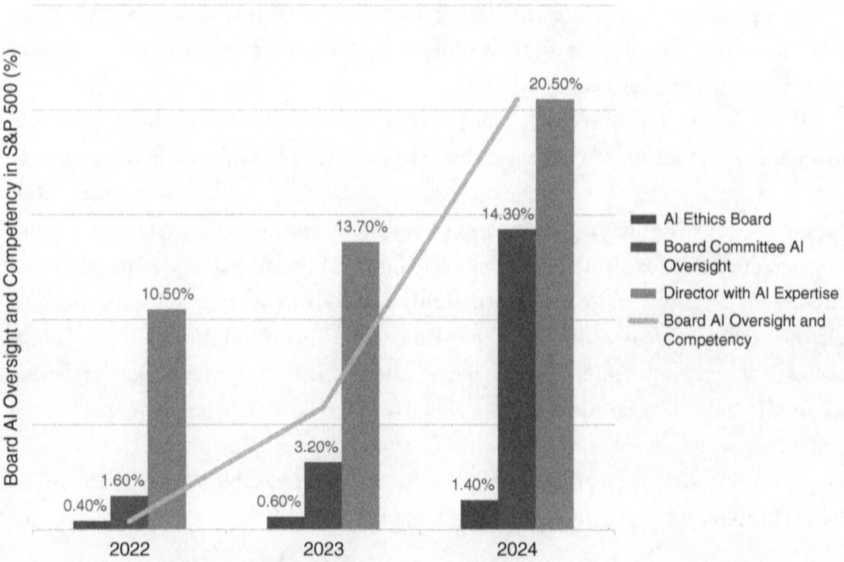

Figure 9.2 Board-level AI oversight (2022–2025).
Source: Rizak and Lomax, 2025 | Chart: BAIE Research Team, 2026.

It is important to distinguish board committees from all other enterprise governance structures within an AI program. A board-level technology or AI committee operates squarely within the board's oversight and fiduciary responsibilities. It evaluates whether AI strategies and actual practices are consistent with the organization's purpose and the level of risk it is prepared to accept. It oversees regulatory exposure and ethical implications. It ensures that management has designed and implemented structures that protect the organization and its stakeholders. Unlike management-level bodies, which are responsible for both system design and execution, a board committee provides independent oversight and sets the strategic frame within which management operates. One focuses on stewardship; the other focuses on implementation.

The establishment of a formal board-level technology or AI committee also carries fiduciary significance. As discussed in Chapter 5, Delaware courts evaluating oversight claims under *Caremark* examine whether boards have implemented reasonable reporting and monitoring systems for mission critical risks. Where technology systems become central to enterprise performance and regulatory exposure, the presence of a dedicated board committee charged with oversight is viewed as evidence that directors have designed a structure capable of surfacing material risk. Courts do not mandate a specific committee format, and other governance mechanisms may satisfy oversight duties. However, judicial commentary has repeatedly treated formal board structures, including specialized committees, as a positive indicator that directors are meeting their obligation to monitor and respond to mission critical risks under *Caremark*.[5]

Board-level committees also help reduce fragmentation at the top of the organization. Based on my observations, AI initiatives are typically divided among legal and cybersecurity teams, engineering and product leadership, and those responsible for talent management and compliance oversight. Consider a company preparing to introduce a new customer-facing AI solution. Management will evaluate design decisions and model limitations. It will also assess privacy exposure and whether the system is ready for deployment. The board committee, by contrast, evaluates whether pursuing this direction aligns with the company's overall risk posture. It must also consider how key decisions reflect stakeholder expectations and whether it advances the company's stated strategic priorities. It connects system-level decisions to enterprise-level commitments established with the aid of the Performance Measures addressed in Chapters 7 and 8.

Implementation

Companies use several board structures to support this work. Some adopt standing technology committees. Others expand the mandate of cyber or risk committees to explicitly include AI oversight. Some create subcommittees dedicated specifically to AI. Others form short-term ad hoc committees to support a particular initiative (see Figure 9.3).

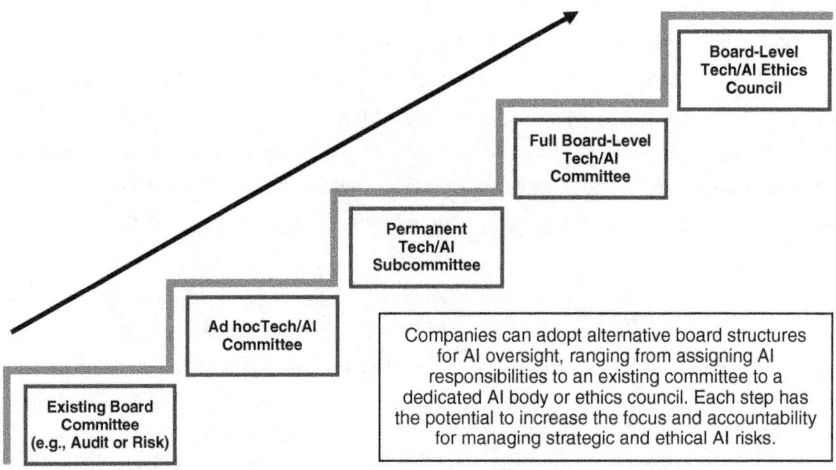

Figure 9.3 Variations of board technology or AI committees.

Source: © BAIE Research Team, 2026.

I observed one novel structure at several companies that has proven effective: a technology-focused subcommittee operating under the audit committee. In this model, the audit committee's governance protocols govern the technology subcommittee's work. Because audit committees are deeply oriented toward risk oversight, their governance standards are typically rigorous. That discipline can strengthen technology risk management. Most audit committees, however, are not designed to oversee innovation or growth initiatives. Companies adopting this structure must ensure the audit committee is appropriately equipped to oversee AI growth initiatives in addition to risk management. The composition of the audit committee also matters. Directors with financial expertise may require supplemental technology literacy to oversee AI effectively. The board may also consider adding a director with technology or AI expertise to the audit committee. This structure signals that technology oversight warrants formal attention and prevents it from being absorbed into an already crowded audit committee agenda. It also avoids establishing a new stand-alone board committee with distinct governance protocols, a sensitive topic for many boards.

Still other companies form advisory groups composed of external experts. Any company, regardless of its size or maturity, can adopt a version of this practice. A large enterprise might need multiple committees. A smaller organization might begin with an ad hoc group that meets regularly. The label is less important than the clarity of purpose and the consistency of oversight.

Ethical Maturity Stack Alignment

A technology or AI board committee aligns closely with the upper layers of the Ethical Maturity Stack. At Layer 3, it creates structured, focused oversight. At Layer 4, such a committee helps ensure operational ethics and appropriate monitoring at the strategic level. At Layer 5, it helps leaders anticipate emerging risks and societal expectations. In addition, companies operating at the highest level of the stack will share their experience with this Leading Practice to influence other organizations. Ethical governance depends on defined bodies empowered to surface issues and take corrective action.

There are challenges to consider. Committees can falter if mandates are unclear or if they rely too heavily on one technical expert. Overlap with audit or risk committees can create confusion if roles are not clearly defined. EY analysis of 2023 trends revealed that many companies were creating new technology committees rather than repurposing existing structures.[6] This suggests that technology, and certainly AI, oversight requires fresh thinking and dedicated governance approaches. Companies should recognize the risk that some directors may actually become *less* engaged in technology oversight if tech responsibility appears confined to a dedicated committee. Boards must reinforce that technology oversight remains a collective responsibility. That expectation should be supported by dedicated time at the full board level to address material technology matters. Committee success depends on persistent leadership commitment and continued learning. It also requires a candid recognition that AI governance must evolve as the technology evolves.

Committee oversight provides structure at the top of the organization, but it is only one part of ethical AI governance. Organizations also need internal systems that oversee AI across its life cycle, from initial design through post-deployment monitoring. The next practice addresses this operational foundation and the program-level governance that supports it.

Leading Practice 2: Cross-Functional Governance

One of the first questions nearly every leadership team asks when beginning its AI journey is deceptively simple: *Where should this initiative live inside the organization?* In my work with dozens of companies across industries, the same uncertainty surfaces almost immediately. This has been a difficult question to address as AI does not fit neatly within any single function, and the struggle to anchor its "enterprise home" reveals how profoundly it cuts across the organization.

For many companies, there is a knee-jerk instinct to place any AI initiative (or any technology-centric initiative for that matter) under the chief technology officer (CTO), treating it as the natural extension of long-running digital transformation efforts. This impulse is understandable. AI often surfaces in connection with cybersecurity initiatives and cloud modernization efforts, and it is frequently tied to data engineering and process automation programs. Other companies anchor AI inside the corporate strategy function, not because of its technical characteristics, but because it is quickly becoming the centerpiece of how the company will compete in the future; from new growth-driven solutions to entirely new business models. A third group of organizations, particularly those wrestling with workforce transformation and automation, places AI within HR or the talent organization, reasoning that AI is, at its core, a tool to work for us, augmenting human capability and reshaping job design.

The diversity of these enterprise home choices signals that AI behaves more like a horizontal capability than an entirely new vertical corporate function. Placing it inside any single enterprise function may narrow its focus and fail to capture the full breadth of this powerful technology. To compensate for this fragmented, siloed approach, most organizations eventually converge around the same solution: a cross-functional AI working group or council that converges professionals from technology, legal, data, security, operations, compliance, HR, and other relevant functions. Cross-functional governance is a formal structure that brings these functions together to oversee decisions across the AI life cycle.

In principle, this cross-functional model represents precisely the kind of interdisciplinary oversight AI requires. Both AI innovation and risk are multifaceted, and no single leader, or corporate function for that matter, can parse strategic growth applications, new AI-enabled business models, algorithmic fairness, privacy obligations, model drift, security vulnerabilities, workforce implications, regulatory exposure, ethical infirmities, and reputational sensitivities alone. A diverse working group promises something more complete: a room of professionals benefiting from the visibility of the entire system.

Why It Matters

Cross-functional governance matters because AI decisions rarely sit within a single domain. A use case may raise technical questions, but it may also create legal exposure. It may affect customers or employees. A cross-functional body ensures these issues are evaluated together, improving coordination across the enterprise and decision quality. It also reduces the risk that material concerns surface too late in the AI development process.

However, as discussed in Chapter 6, cross-functional AI working groups or committees can diffuse ethical responsibility if they are not designed carefully. I explored this topic in a conversation with Reid Blackman on the *Better Innovation* podcast.[7] Blackman describes a familiar dynamic, one I have similarly observed across many companies. When these AI working group members gather, they instinctively emphasize the responsibilities of their day jobs. The privacy leader gravitates to privacy concerns. The general counsel focuses on organizational legal liability issues. The chief information security officer sees cybersecurity threats everywhere (as, of course, they must). The CTO worries about system performance and delivery timelines. The CFO raises questions about cost and investment (along with the expected return on that investment). Each voice is well-intentioned and necessary. But because no one in the room owns AI ethics as their *primary* mandate, ethical considerations never attract the attention they deserve and are subordinate to the other issues aligned to the working group members' day job responsibilities. They become everyone's responsibility and, in practice, no one's.

This phenomenon becomes especially problematic when organizations focus these bodies on the need to develop *responsible* AI systems. The working group name alone creates an expectation of ethical rigor for stakeholders both inside and outside the company. But inside the room, without direct expertise or explicit authority rooted in ethics itself, the working group gradually shifts toward the concerns its members are structurally rewarded to solve: legal defensibility, risk minimization, data governance, financial prudence, and operational efficiency. The more ambiguous, sociotechnical questions – Who is affected? Whose voice is missing? What outcomes are we favoring? What values should guide this system's design? – often receive little to no attention if they are raised at all.

This phenomenon is sometimes referred to as *ethical drift*: the predictable neglect of ethical intention in a governance structure that lacks explicit ownership of ethical responsibility in the AI context. To be clear, ethical drift is almost never the product of bad actors or apathetic leaders. It emerges from a structural misalignment and talent gap. Working groups excel at distributing, well . . . work (and perspective), but they often struggle when responsibility must be concentrated.

I am not suggesting that companies abandon the cross-functional governance model. Quite the opposite. The complexity of AI along with the plethora of corporate functions it affects makes these bodies indispensable. It's the AI working group design and composition that must evolve.

Implementation

Effective cross-functional governance requires a clear mandate. It requires defined decision rights. Without these elements, working groups become forums for discussion rather than mechanisms for governance. In addition, organizations that succeed share a common characteristic: someone at the AI governance table is clearly accountable for AI ethics. That individual or role – perhaps a responsible AI leader, an empowered leader within risk or legal, or a true AI ethicist – ensures that ethical questions do not become subordinate to the more technical or growth-oriented considerations that tend to dominate enterprise AI decision-making. I have seen this need play out in practice. In companies where ethical ownership is diffused, discussions about fairness, explainability, transparency, or stakeholder impact appear late in the development process (if they appear at all), often after solution launch dates are committed to and announced or investments allocated. Some companies have attempted to solve this problem by joining a chief ethics and compliance officer with an AI technical leader. But this model is rarely successful, as these two professionals do not have a shared vocabulary; in fact, they really don't speak the same language at all. This challenge is not insurmountable. It can be addressed through targeted AI literacy efforts and structured cross-functional training. It can also be mitigated by leaders who are able to translate across domains and create a shared language for decision-making.

Ethical Maturity Stack Alignment

Cross-functional governance most naturally aligns with Layer 3: Emerging Ethics on the Ethical Maturity Stack, where organizations formalize governance structures to support responsible AI oversight. When ethical ownership is clearly designated within that structure, the practice can support progression toward Layer 4.

Cross-functional governance is necessary, but insufficient on its own. It provides the breadth of perspective required to govern AI responsibly. Without clearly designated ethical ownership, however, it cannot provide the depth required for sustained ethical decision-making. This structural gap explains why organizations may have active AI working groups in place and still operate at lower maturity levels if ethical responsibility is unassigned or episodic. The Emerging Practice discussed later in this chapter, the Embedded AI Ethics Partner, directly addresses this limitation by placing ethical expertise inside the governance process rather than leaving it diffused across functional leaders.

As AI becomes more deeply embedded in enterprise workflows, organizational roles, and the day-to-day responsibilities of employees, the limitations of working group governance become more pronounced. The friction between speed and oversight intensifies. Technical complexity grows. External expectations from regulators, customers, and investors escalate. Across this landscape, organizations that rely solely on working groups, particularly those that diffuse ethical ownership across many leaders, will find themselves unprepared for the ethical demands of system-level governance.

This realization leads naturally to the next question: *Where should organizations look for guidance when internal governance models fall short?* One answer lies outside the enterprise entirely. Some of the most compelling models for ethical responsibility derive from the regulated professions. In those domains, ethics is formally codified and enforceable. In particular, the legal profession offers a powerful precedent. The American Bar Association (ABA) has developed emerging guidance on AI use that establishes explicit ethical duties for lawyers. The next section turns to this professional standards model and examines how the ABA's provisions can help organizations design clearer ethical expectations.

Leading Practice 3: Adapting Professional AI Ethics Frameworks

As organizations search for practical ways to govern AI responsibly, many look first to regulation or to emerging technical standards. Those tools matter, but they are incomplete; and as stressed throughout this book, it's highly unlikely that we'll see a comprehensive globally consistent set of regulations focused on responsible AI governance anytime soon. Nevertheless, some of the most instructive guidance on

AI ethics is already hiding in plain sight, embedded in the professional ethics frameworks of regulated, trust-based professions. Among them, the ABA offers one of the clearest and most operational (and extendable) examples of how ethical obligations can be adapted to professionals, knowledge workers, and any worker more broadly.

The legal profession is uniquely positioned in this conversation, with an existing model to extend to others. Lawyers operate under formal ethical duties that govern competence, client confidentiality, transparency, supervision (of both people and associated technology tools), and accountability for delegated work. These duties represent enforceable standards that shape daily professional behavior. As a result, the legal profession can serve as an early indicator of how ethical expectations evolve when new technologies alter how human judgment is exercised. In the AI context, this makes the legal profession a useful bellwether for what other knowledge-intensive enterprises, and the people operating within these sectors, will soon face.

The ABA has taken a measured and structured approach to AI. It's important to note that its work did not begin with GenAI, nor did it wait for courts or legislatures to impose new mandates. Instead, the ABA treated AI as a professional ethics issue, one that directly implicates existing duties owed principally to clients, but also to key stakeholders such as the courts and general public.

That leadership began with public policy guidance. In 2019, the ABA House of Delegates adopted Resolution 112, calling for ethical safeguards across AI development and deployment across the legal domain.[8] The resolution emphasized fairness, transparency, explainability, and accountability, principles that now appear in nearly every responsible AI framework. In 2022, Resolution 700 followed, warning explicitly about structural bias in algorithmic systems, particularly those used in criminal justice contexts.[9] In 2023, Resolution 604 expanded the scope further, urging all AI stakeholders, not only lawyers, to preserve meaningful human oversight and document critical decisions, stressing the importance of remaining accountable for harms caused by AI systems.[10]

What distinguishes the ABA's approach is not just the articulation of principles. It is instead the way those principles were translated into professional obligations; a great example of applied ethics. That translation became explicit, and tailored to this GenAI moment, with the issuance of Formal Opinion 512 in July 2024 by the ABA Standing Committee on Ethics and Professional Responsibility.[11]

As a lawyer, I take great pride in being bound by a formal canon of ethics that governs how I exercise judgment in the practice of law. I appreciate that the ABA convened a working group and issued Formal Opinion 512 to provide practical guidance for lawyers navigating GenAI in client service. The opinion reflects a profession willing to confront technological change directly and translate abstract principles into practical working expectations.

Formal Opinion 512 addresses the use of GenAI by lawyers under the existing Model Rules of Professional Conduct.[12] Rather than creating new rules, the opinion clarifies how long-standing professional duties apply when AI tools are used in legal practice. The guidance is practical and specific, providing actionable tools for lawyers (see Figure 9.4). Importantly, lawyers remain fully responsible for work product produced with AI assistance. Confidential information cannot be submitted to AI systems without appropriate safeguards, notably, informed client consent. Lawyers must supervise both human and nonhuman contributors to their work; that is a clarification the ABA stressed in its guidance. And, specific to client service, clients need to be informed when AI materially affects representation and fees must remain reasonable, regardless of efficiency gains achieved through AI-driven automation.

Perhaps most significant is the opinion's forward-looking view of professional *competence*. The committee states that "as [generative] AI tools continue to develop and become more widely available, it is conceivable that lawyers will eventually have to use them to competently complete certain tasks for clients."[13] This is a profound shift in a lawyer's duty of competency. It reframes AI literacy from a technical advantage into an ethical requirement. Failure to understand the tools used in professional judgment becomes a potential breach of that duty.

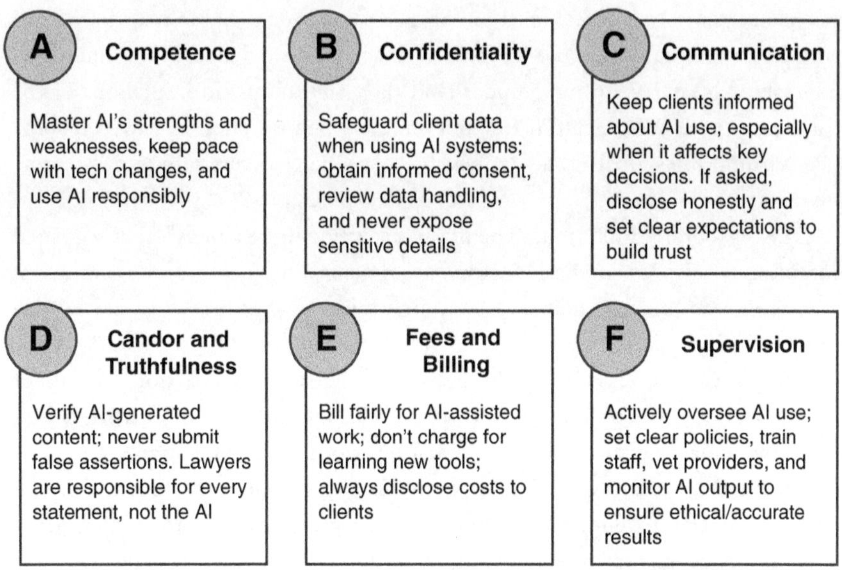

Figure 9.4 ABA Formal Opinion 512: Duties of lawyers in GenAI context.

Source: ABA, 2024 | Chart: BAIE Research Team, 2026.

Why It Matters

Although developed for lawyers, the ABA's framework in its Formal Opinion 512 offers lessons that extend well beyond the legal field. The ethical concerns it addresses are certainly not unique to the law. Enterprises across industries now rely on AI systems in roles that influence judgment and operational outcomes. The effects of those systems extend beyond the enterprise itself. In each case, responsibility still rests with humans.

The ABA AI ethics model reinforces a central insight that many organizations struggle to operationalize. When judgment is informed by technology, the obligation – *human* obligation – to understand, supervise, and take responsibility becomes more important, not less. This is why adapting professional AI ethics frameworks to others outside the profession represents a Leading Practice. Rather than inventing new approaches, organizations can draw from existing AI ethics systems that already integrate expertise with accountability and are designed to maintain stakeholder trust. These systems are designed to function in today's GenAI-influenced world. They assume that professionals will use tools they did not build themselves. They also assume that advanced technology enablement never absolves professional responsibility.

At higher levels of ethical maturity, organizations begin to recognize that AI governance is not only a technical or compliance challenge but also a professional and fiduciary responsibility challenge. Who is accountable for decisions influenced and enabled by AI? Who must understand the application and limitations of the tools being used? Who is ultimately responsible when outputs are flawed or produce harm? Professional ethics frameworks provide structured answers to these questions.

The legal profession is not alone in this evolution. Increasingly other regulated professions – such as medical doctors, accountants, engineers, and government workers – have begun to address AI through the lens of ethical duty, rather than purely technical risk.

On November 12, 2024, the American Medical Association House of Delegates adopted a policy framework on AI in healthcare, emphasizing that physicians remain accountable for clinical decisions, even when those decisions are informed by AI[14] (the AMA refers to AI as augmented intelligence[15]). The AMA stresses transparency with patients and the protection of patient autonomy. When developing new policies, it also continuously emphasizes the need for informed consent when AI tools influence diagnosis or treatment.[16] The AMA's recommendations and policy documents reflect that AI is framed as decision support, not decision replacement. Ethical responsibility remains firmly with the human healthcare professional.

Similarly, the American Institute of Certified Public Accountants (AICPA) has addressed AI through its Code of Professional Conduct and related guidance. The AICPA makes clear that professional judgment must remain intact and that skepticism is required when AI is used in audit and related assurance work, including financial analysis. Practitioners are expected to understand the tools they rely on. They must evaluate the integrity of the underlying data and remain responsible for conclusions drawn from automated (AI) systems.[17]

Across these professions, a common pattern emerges: AI competence is treated as an extension of professional competence. Technology oversight is treated as a continuing obligation. Ethical accountability is not transferred to the tool, it rests solely with the professional.

Implementation

Organizations that adopt this Leading Practice should not attempt to wholly replicate professional licensing regimes. Instead, they should consider adapting the underlying logic and practical guidance offered by the professional governing bodies. These organizations treat AI use as an activity that carries defined responsibilities grounded in ethical obligation. They require clear supervision and expect transparency in how AI tools are used. They embed expectations for responsible AI literacy into leadership roles. Internal policies mirror the professional duties described in this section. Those polices address confidentiality. They also reinforce transparency and ensure accountability for outcomes.

At the enterprise level, this often means referencing external professional ethical standards as governance inputs to the organization's AI program and ethical AI guidelines tailored for the specific organization. As explored in Chapter 8, companies such as Verizon, Pfizer, and IBM have taken a range of steps in this direction: from defining ethical AI principles and publicly committing to them to creating concrete guidelines and developing processes that support the implementation of these principles in practice. As these examples illustrate, it means translating abstract AI principles into concrete expectations for how employees use tools and supervise AI-enabled workflows, and how leaders remain accountable for system-level outcomes. It also means recognizing that ignorance is never bliss, especially in this AI context. In mature organizations, affirmatively *choosing* not to understand how AI influences decisions is itself an ethical risk. Professional ethics frameworks demonstrate that responsibility must remain human even as tools become more powerful. For professionals, the lesson is clear. AI governance is about not only what systems can do but also what leaders must be willing to remain accountable for.

Ethical Maturity Stack Alignment

This practice aligns closely with the upper levels of the Ethical Maturity Stack. At Layer 4, organizations proactively integrate ethical obligations into AI governance by adapting professional standards to the uniqueness of the organization. Ethics becomes operational, a set of applied practices, rather than merely symbolic.

At Layer 5, organizations extend further. They help shape norms and standards within their industries. They treat ethical AI governance as a critical by-product of leadership. They recognize that professional responsibility does not stop at regulated boundaries and that enterprises deploying AI at scale should feel the obligation similar to that of licensed professions.

These Leading Practices provide a strong foundation; we now turn to the three Emerging Practices that round out the Applied Governance Practices and extend ethical oversight further into the enterprise.

Emerging Practice 1: The Embedded AI Ethics Partner

As organizations move from defining and pledging allegiance to ethical AI principles, to operationalizing them, a persistent challenge emerges. Legal, risk, compliance, technology, and business teams each should own part of the mandate, but for most companies no single role (or person) is accountable for translating ethical intent into consistent practice. The Embedded AI Ethics Partner has emerged as a promising response to this gap.

This role also addresses the ethical drift described in the cross-functional working group discussion. By holding clear ownership of ethics for the AI program (issue discovery and resolution), the Embedded AI Ethics Partner ensures *someone* in the organization is accountable for AI ethics.

Sometimes such a position is described as a *fractional AI ethicist*. However, it is more appropriately understood as an embedded ethical governance partner; I believe this distinction matters. The value of the role lies not in occasional consultation, but instead in close proximity to critical decision-making and continuity across the AI life cycle. The Embedded AI Ethics Partner operates alongside leadership and cross-functional teams within the enterprise AI program to ensure that ethical considerations are not treated as an afterthought, but as an integral component of AI program strategy.

Why It Matters

The Embedded AI Ethics Partner is a senior, cross-disciplinary expert who combines technical fluency in AI systems with grounding in ethics. The role also requires a working command of relevant legal frameworks and an understanding of enterprise governance structures. AI introduces ethical questions that demand familiarity with technical system design as well as fluency in normative ethical frameworks. It also requires an understanding of the potential impact of AI systems on society at large. Most enterprises do not have this unique blend of expertise in-house, nor should they be expected to develop it overnight. In fact, there is a dearth of professionals on the planet with this expertise.

At the same time, fiduciary expectations are rising. As we addressed in Chapter 5, pursuant to *Caremark* and related corporate governance doctrines, boards are expected to engage appropriate expertise when overseeing complex, mission critical risks. AI increasingly meets that threshold. The Embedded AI Ethics Partner helps satisfy this expectation by providing the unique blend of expertise discussed previously and continuity across initiatives that would otherwise be fragmented at best and many times entirely nonexistent.

Implementation

In practice, organizations can deploy this role in several ways, depending on scale and maturity. In an embedded model, the AI ethics partner works closely with internal teams over an extended period. This may include participation in internal governance forums, AI use case reviews, and leadership briefings, serving as a key liaison between management and AI solution teams.

In a part-time or advisory model, the Embedded AI Ethics Partner supports defined initiatives within the enterprise. This may include developing AI governance policies and providing education to both leadership and employees. It may also include the evaluation of proposed AI deployments. A hybrid model balances these approaches. Organizations maintain ongoing access to AI ethics expertise while reserving deeper involvement for periods of heightened activity or risk. This mirrors other accepted governance arrangements, such as part-time data privacy officers or external cybersecurity advisors.

An additional advantage of the fractional model lies in the breadth of experience it can bring. Just as a fractional CFO often draws insight from issues addressed across multiple companies and sectors, an Embedded AI Ethics Partner working across several enterprises can identify recurring governance blind spots and common implementation pitfalls before they escalate into crises.

A defining feature of the Embedded AI Ethics Partner role is responsibility for implementation, not merely advice. In organizations adopting the Boundaries of Tolerance model, this role can serve as the principal steward of the model. At the enterprise level, the Embedded AI Ethics Partner can lead the application of the Performance Measure's Enterprise Factors. This includes evaluating how leadership commitment, stakeholder accountability, operational ethics, and related factors are reflected in governance structures and decision-making practices. From an AI systems perspective, the ethics partner can support application of the System Factors to AI use cases and deployments. This enables the organization to assess whether ethical principles are meaningfully embedded in the systems themselves.

Across both dimensions, the Embedded AI Ethics Partner can facilitate structured assessments of both current and future state on the Ethical Maturity Stack. This involves helping leadership align on where the organization stands today, where it intends to be tomorrow, and what ethical posture it is willing to defend publicly. Crucially, the role also extends to closing the gap between those states. The Embedded AI Ethics Partner can help design and prioritize a remediation plan that translates assessment results into action. These plans may involve changes to governance structures and targeted training initiatives. They may also introduce continuous monitoring mechanisms and support implementation of the Applied Governance Practices discussed in this chapter. Executives overseeing AI strategy and governance have expressed strong interest in formalizing this capability within their organizations.

In this way, the Embedded AI Ethics Partner becomes the connective tissue within the enterprise. It links ethical aspiration to execution and strategy to operations. Consider the opportunity for such a partner to lead or participate in implementation of the Boundaries of Tolerance model, described more fully in Chapter 10.

Despite its promise, this practice is Emerging today rather than Leading. Very few organizations have institutionalized such a role at scale. There are no widely accepted professional standards or certification pathways, and role definitions vary significantly across enterprises and sectors. There is also a real risk of ambiguity. Without a clear mandate or authority, the Embedded AI Ethics Partner can be marginalized or treated as symbolic. In other cases, organizations may be tempted to outsource ethical responsibility rather than embed it directly within the enterprise. Said another way, this critical need should not be met through a consulting project. These limitations explain why the practice has not yet reached Leading status. The model is still being refined and adapted across industries.

When implemented thoughtfully, the Embedded AI Ethics Partner offers clear advantages. Organizations gain access to senior-level ethical expertise without committing to a full-time role. The perspective is often broader and more candid than a mix of professionals across various corporate functions can provide. The presence of a dedicated AI ethics partner can also strengthen credibility with regulators and external stakeholders.

At the same time, there are certain risks to consider. Overreliance on a lone individual can weaken institutional capability. Poorly scoped and novel roles that are not present at the majority of companies can lead to confusion across the many corporate functions that touch an enterprise AI program.

Ethical Maturity Stack Alignment

The embedded ethics partner aligns most naturally with Layers 3 and 4 of the Ethical Maturity Stack. At these stages, organizations are moving beyond Core Compliance and beginning to systematically integrate ethics into governance and decision-making processes. With strong leadership commitment, the role can also support progression toward Layer 5. At that level, organizations begin shaping emerging norms and influencing peer behavior. They may also contribute to the development of broader ethical standards within their sector and, in some cases, beyond it. That potential, however, depends on how seriously the role is embedded and supported by both leadership and the broader employee base.

As AI adoption accelerates and its applications grow in complexity, access to AI-specific ethical expertise will become less optional. The Embedded AI Ethics Partner represents one plausible path forward. Over time, this role may evolve into teams within the enterprise, and networks or ecosystems of trusted experts, shared across organizations and governed by common standards. For now, it remains an Emerging Practice.

Emerging Practice 2: Prudent Vigilance as a Governance Mindset

As organizations expand the use of AI across core business functions and customer-facing applications, they face a persistent governance dilemma. How should leaders act when risks are real (but incomplete) or only partially understood. This challenge is not unique to AI, but AI certainly magnifies it. Systems learn and interact with humans in ways that often defy advance prediction. In this context, Prudent Vigilance offers a rational governance mindset well suited to the ethical realities of AI deployment.

Prudent Vigilance originated in the field of bioethics, where policymakers and scientists confronted similar questions about emerging technologies whose benefits were promising but whose risks were uncertain. The concept was articulated by the U.S. Presidential Commission for the Study of Bioethical Issues in 2010 as a response to technologies that demanded neither risk-fearing paralysis nor innovation-at-all-costs permissiveness. Instead, it permitted the advancement of new ideas and solutions but called for an ongoing duty to continuously learn and adapt as knowledge evolves.[18]

I was first introduced to Prudent Vigilance in 2023 through the work of Danielle Allen and her coauthors in their writing on the ethics of decentralized social technologies.[19] Danielle was leading the Edmond and Lily Safra Center for Ethics at Harvard University when I began my appointment there to study business AI ethics for senior leaders. What struck me immediately about Prudent Vigilance was its practical application (and wisdom). Having spent many years in corporate innovation leadership roles, I had often struggled to find a practical approach that allowed new solution teams to advance their innovative ideas while simultaneously respecting their responsibility to manage risk thoughtfully. This innovation/risk paradigm doesn't have to be so binary; we need a middle ground. Notions of Prudent Vigilance respect this delicate balance in a way that feels both ethically grounded and operationally realistic (see Figure 9.5).

Governance frameworks for emerging technologies often fall at one of two extremes. The Precautionary Principle calls for restraint, sometimes even inaction, until risks are fully understood. This approach prioritizes harm avoidance, but it can slow innovation and leave organizations unprepared for competitive or societal shifts. At the opposite end of the spectrum, the Proactionary Principle encourages experimentation and rapid adoption, based on the belief that innovation itself reduces long-term risk. This posture favors progress, but it can often underestimate downstream harms.[20]

Prudent Vigilance occupies a deliberate middle ground. It accepts that uncertainty is unavoidable, but it refuses to treat uncertainty as an excuse for either inaction or idea abandonment. Rather than asking leaders to decide once and for all whether a technology is acceptable, it imposes an ongoing obligation to continuously pay attention, to reassess, and to respond as conditions change. Amy Gutmann, who was appointed by President Barack Obama to chair the Presidential Commission for the Study of Bioethical Issues, captured this concept clearly: "Prudent vigilance does not demand extreme aversion to all risks. Not all safety and security questions can be definitively answered before projects begin, but prudent vigilance does call for ongoing evaluation of risks along with benefits. The iterative nature of this review is a key feature of responsible stewardship. It recognizes that future developments demand that decisions be revisited and amended as warranted by additional information about risks and potential benefits."[21]

Precautionary Principle *Conservative*	Prudent Vigilance *Middle Ground*	Proactionary Principle *Aggressive*
Do not introduce new products (or processes) unless you know and can appropriately manage the risks If the ultimate effects (risks) are disputed or unknown, then *do not proceed*	Move forward with innovations but have *ongoing assessments* as the risk developments Proceed, but with considerable safeguards	Freedom to innovate technologically is critical to the enterprise (and humanity) and should be protected Measure the cost of restrictions; favor ones that are proportionate to the probability and magnitude of negative impacts
Innovation: 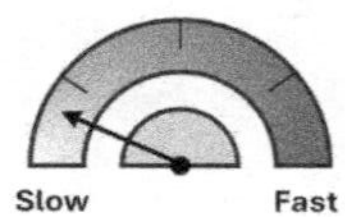 **Risk:** 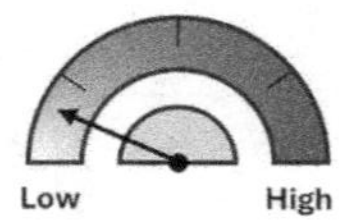	**Innovation:** 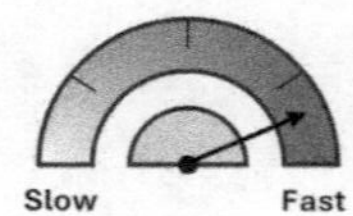 **Risk:** 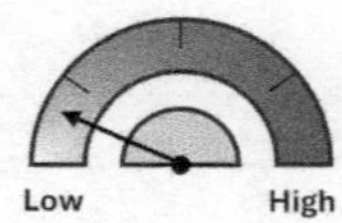	**Innovation:** 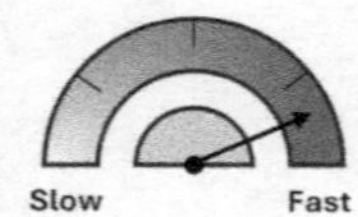 **Risk:** 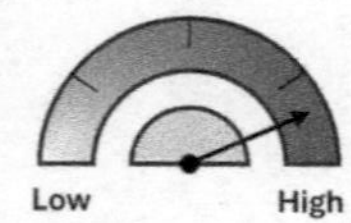

Figure 9.5 A measured approach to risk tolerance: Prudent Vigilance.

Source: © BAIE Research Team, 2026.

Why It Matters

This principle is particularly relevant in the AI context. Most organizations recognize that AI introduces meaningful risks, including the myriad risks discussed in Chapter 4. What remains unclear is how these risks will manifest over time, particularly as systems scale and begin interacting with users.

Traditional governance approaches are often front-loaded. Risk assessments are conducted before launch and controls are documented. Responsibility is then assigned across the enterprise. While these steps are necessary, they are largely insufficient for AI. Many ethical failures occur not before or at the moment of deployment, but months later. Systems may begin to behave differently than expected or be applied in ways not originally intended. Over time, their effects can accumulate in ways that were not anticipated.

Prudent Vigilance reframes governance as a continuous process. It enables organizations to move forward with AI development and deployment while maintaining an obligation to examine outcomes and intervene when systems begin to drift beyond acceptable ethical boundaries.

Implementation

In practice, Prudent Vigilance depends on two foundational capabilities. First, organizations must develop a working understanding of known AI risks, informed by internal experience and the external stories that are now coming to light. (A few of these stories are outlined in this book, especially in Chapters 7 and 8). This understanding does not need to be perfect, but it must be honest and current. Second, organizations must invest in monitoring mechanisms that enable them to continuously observe how AI systems behave over time and escalate concerns when necessary. Without these capabilities, governance efforts tend to slide toward complacency or overconfidence. Prudent Vigilance counters this tendency by treating ethical alignment as something that must be continuously maintained over time.

Within the Boundaries of Tolerance model, vigilant monitoring plays a critical role. It helps ensure that AI systems remain within the ethical boundaries an organization has articulated, even as business conditions and societal expectations change. In this sense, Prudent Vigilance is not separate from ethical governance. It is what keeps ethical commitments alive after deployment.

Despite its appeal, Prudent Vigilance is still an Emerging Practice in enterprise AI governance. Many organizations continue to rely on static risk assessments and compliance-oriented controls. Few have built governance systems designed explicitly for ongoing ethical recalibration. Adopting Prudent Vigilance requires more than new processes. It requires a cultural shift toward learning and responsiveness.

This should help explain why Prudent Vigilance has not yet reached Leading Practice status.

Ethical Maturity Stack Alignment

Prudent Vigilance aligns most clearly with Layer 5 of the Ethical Maturity Stack. Leaders recognize that ethical responsibility does not end with compliance or initial system approval. It continues as long as systems operate and influence human outcomes.

Layer 5: Ethical Vanguard organizations treat uncertainty as a condition to be managed, not avoided. They design governance structures that support ongoing evaluation and adjustment through test-and-learn cycles. Prudent Vigilance is a hallmark of this posture. In fast-moving AI environments, the temptation is to choose between speed and safety. Prudent Vigilance rejects that false choice. It offers leaders a way to move forward responsibly, without pretending that uncertainty can be eliminated. Organizations that adopt this mindset signal both ethical seriousness and strategic maturity. They recognize that trust in AI systems is built by sustained ethical stewardship as technology and context evolve.

Emerging Practice 3: Building a Guard Band of Safety

As AI becomes more deeply embedded in enterprise decision-making, many organizations continue to anchor their governance efforts in formal compliance requirements. This approach is necessary, but insufficient. In fast-evolving domains like AI, where legal frameworks lag technological change and ethical expectations shift quickly, resilience requires a more anticipatory posture. The Guard Band of Safety offers one such approach.

The concept of a Guard Band of Safety borrows from engineering and legal strategy. It refers to the intentional creation of a margin above minimum compliance requirements. Rather than operating at the edge of what is legally permissible, organizations adopt standards and controls that exceed baseline compliance obligations. The objective is not perfection; it is protection against foreseeable risk in environments where rules are still forming and the stakes of getting it wrong are quite high.

Why It Matters

AI governance presents a distinct challenge for compliance-driven organizations. Regulatory regimes are fragmented across jurisdictions and continue to evolve. In many cases, AI-specific laws do not yet exist, while older legal frameworks continue to apply only indirectly. These include rules governing data protection and consumer protection, as well as doctrines related to product liability and nondiscrimination. In many cases, AI-specific laws do not yet exist, while older legal frameworks continue to apply only indirectly. These include rules governing data protection and consumer protection, as well as doctrines related to product liability and nondiscrimination. As a result, many AI risks emerge in gray areas rather than through clear regulatory frameworks.

History suggests that ethical failures often surface before legal ones. Reputational damage and regulatory scrutiny frequently arise when stakeholders perceive harm, even if existing legal obligations have technically been satisfied. An AI system that complies with current rules can still produce outcomes that appear unfair or irresponsible once deployed broadly. Guard bands address this gap. By building proactive compliance margins, organizations reduce their exposure to shifting standards and unanticipated consequences.

Traditional compliance programs often emphasize minimum compliance. The focus is on meeting explicit legal requirements at a specific point in time. While efficient, this approach carries risk. Operating close to the boundary of legality leaves little room for error when expectations change or when new interpretations emerge.

Guard band thinking takes a different view. It assumes that thresholds will move and that acceptable practices today may be questioned tomorrow. By exceeding current requirements in high-risk or high-impact areas, organizations create buffers that protect against enforcement actions and reputational harm.

The shortcomings of minimum compliance are well documented. The Ford Pinto case, in which during the 1970s Ford Motor Company rushed into production a compact car that had a tendency in rear-end collisions to leak fuel and explode – resulting in more than two dozen injuries or fatalities before the company issued a recall – remains a cautionary example of how narrow legal reasoning can fail to account for foreseeable harm.[22] While the context differs, the lesson carries forward. Decisions that satisfy the letter of the law may still violate broader societal expectations.

The origin of guard band thinking derives from Intel's response to antitrust scrutiny in the early 2000s. Rather than limiting its actions to what the law required at the time, Intel adopted internal policies and communication protocols that went well beyond baseline obligations (see Figure 9.6).[23] These measures were designed to reduce future risk and signal a commitment to responsible conduct. It is worth noting that Intel ultimately faced antitrust penalties in Europe.[24] Even so, the guard band concept remains viable. Without such measures, the outcome could have been far more severe. This Guard Band of Safety approach has been recognized by legal commentators as an important compliance strategy that has preserved its relevance in modern legal practice, including in efforts to ensure compliance with *Caremark* standards.[25]

1. Learn the Rules

- Master the law's complexities: educate your team and stay informed
- Spot and navigate gray areas with confidence
- Anticipate how legal changes will affect your business as company grows

2. Make Compliance Instinctive

- Pamphlets and lectures aren't enough
- Build the right habits through repeated training, role-playing, and drills
- Instill an instinct to do the right thing

3. Sweat the Small Stuff

- 80-20 rule doesn't apply; catch even the smallest details
- Toe the line every single time
- Remember: just a few errors can have devastating legal consequences

Figure 9.6 Guard Band of Safety: Keys to success – three must-dos.
Source: Yoffe and Kwak, 2001 | Chart: BAIE Research Team, 2026.

In my own work advising companies on AI governance, I repeatedly heard a similar concern from senior leaders. They were less worried about technical failure than about a public AI incident that could damage enterprise reputation and possibly even trigger financial loss. As high-profile AI failures were increasingly reaching mainstream media, many expressed interest in governance practices that would reduce the likelihood of such a misstep. The logic of Intel's deliberate superconservatism in an area of extreme legal sensitivity translates directly to AI systems deployed at scale, where reputational harm often moves faster than regulatory enforcement.

Implementation

In an AI context, guard bands might include stronger documentation practices, more robust human oversight, clearer disclosure to affected stakeholders, or stricter internal review processes than regulations demand. The goal is to anticipate regulatory and other scrutiny rather than wait for it. This approach reflects strategic discipline.

Organizations must identify AI use cases where legal ambiguity or ethical risk is highest. These often include scaled systems that affect individual rights or shape access to opportunities, or operate at a significant scale. Once identified, governance controls are designed to exceed minimum standards. This may involve more frequent reviews with stronger escalation paths, or higher thresholds for deployment approval. Importantly, these expectations must be embedded into daily operations.

Guard bands fail when they exist only on paper. Leadership commitment is essential. When teams are rewarded solely for speed or efficiency, guard bands erode. When leaders model precision and accountability, guard bands become part of Organizational Culture.

Despite its advantages, the Guard Band of Safety remains an Emerging Practice. Many organizations continue to optimize for minimum compliance, particularly when resources are constrained. The benefits of guard bands are often invisible. They manifest as risks avoided rather than returns generated.

Implementing guard bands also requires discipline and patience. It demands that leaders invest ahead of enforcement and accept short-term friction in exchange for long-term resilience. These qualities are unevenly distributed across enterprises, which helps explain why guard bands are not yet common practice.

Ethical Maturity Stack Alignment

The Guard Band of Safety aligns most clearly with Layer 3: Emerging Ethics of the Ethical Maturity Stack. At this level, organizations are beginning to move beyond compliance as a defensive posture and embrace some ethical practices within their governance protocols. Layer 3 organizations do not ask only whether an action is legal; they seek to go further. Guard bands signal that leaders show an appreciation of the ethical issues that could emanate from their AI systems. Within the Boundaries of Tolerance model, guard bands serve as a stabilizing force. They help ensure that organizations remain within their declared ethical boundaries even as external expectations evolve. By aligning legal risk posture with ethical aspiration, guard bands create space for innovation without ethical drift.

As AI technologies become increasingly central to enterprise strategy, the ability to anticipate rather than react will distinguish resilient organizations from vulnerable ones. Building a Guard Band of Safety is one way leaders can demonstrate readiness for that responsibility.

Closing

Ethical AI organizations are not defined by intention alone. They are defined by practice. Throughout this chapter, we have shifted from abstract principles to the concrete Applied Governance Practices that determine how AI is actually governed inside modern enterprises. The central insight is clear: ethical maturity is built through reinforced structures and leadership choices that endure under pressure.

The six practices introduced here provide a practical tool for advancing along the Ethical Maturity Stack. Together, they show how organizations move from fragmented or reactive governance toward integrated, adaptive oversight. The Leading

Practices establish the foundations of accountability and structure. The Emerging Practices point toward a future in which AI governance becomes continuous and resilient in the face of uncertainty.

These practices are intentionally modular. Organizations do not need to adopt all of them at once, nor must they wait for ideal conditions to begin. Any single practice can be implemented immediately. A board can formalize AI oversight through committee structures. Leadership can adopt Prudent Vigilance as a governing mindset. Enterprises can introduce a Guard Band of Safety in high-risk AI domains.

What distinguishes organizations operating at higher levels of ethical maturity is their commitment to the cause. Layer 5 organizations understand that ethical AI governance is not a destination. It is an ongoing responsibility that evolves alongside technology regulation and societal expectations. They design governance systems that can learn and course correct over time, rather than relying on static controls or one-time assessments.

This chapter has focused on what strong ethical AI governance looks like in practice. Chapter 10 focuses on how to make it real. Having established the practices that support ethical maturity, we now turn to implementation. Chapter 10 provides a step-by-step approach for operationalizing the Boundaries of Tolerance model inside existing enterprise governance systems. It is where assessment leads to action, aspiration becomes execution, and ethical intent is translated into enduring, defensible practice.

10 Implementing the Boundaries of Tolerance Model

Execution Framework

The Boundaries of Tolerance model was designed as an operating discipline that helps organizations translate ethical intent into enduring governance execution. This chapter focuses on implementation of the model because ethical artificial intelligence (AI) governance shapes how systems are actually deployed and how leaders respond when challenges arise.

Implementation in this regard follows a structured sequence that mirrors how responsible organizations manage complex change, especially in the digital environment (see Figure 10.1). The process begins with Assess. It then moves to Plan. It concludes with Execute. These stages are sequential because ethical maturity cannot be meaningfully advanced without first understanding current conditions. This opening establishes the logic of implementation before moving into detailed protocols. The Boundaries of Tolerance model depends on appropriate accountability, a clear division of responsibility across the enterprise. Management owns execution. Boards own oversight. These roles are connected through information flow and escalation discipline, but they are not interchangeable.

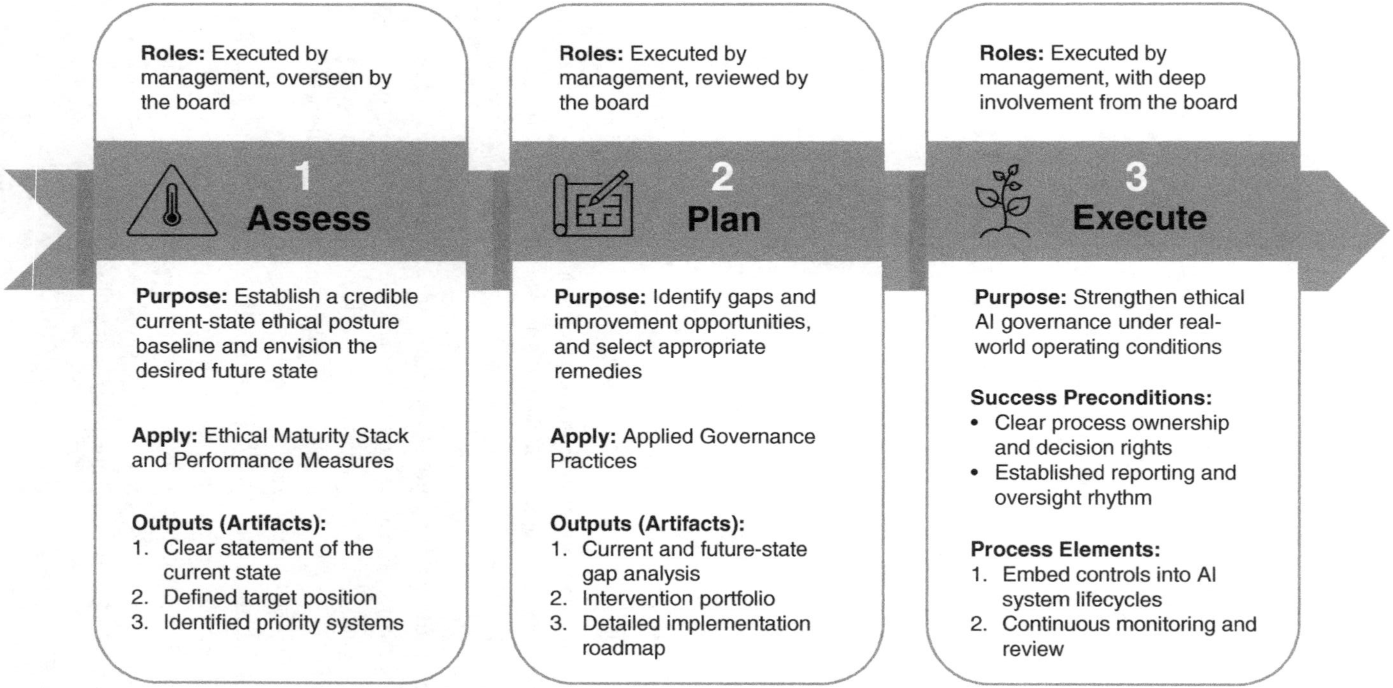

Figure 10.1 Boundaries of Tolerance model execution framework.

Source: © BAIE Research Team, 2026.

Management is responsible for bringing the model to life inside the organization. This responsibility includes applying the Performance Measures aligned with the Ethical Maturity Stack. It includes selecting the Applied Governance Practices that match the organization's risk profile and ethical ambition. It also includes designing and executing the action plan that turns governance intent into operational reality. And when systems drift or fail, it's management that owns remediation.

Boards are responsible for creating the conditions that make responsible execution possible. This responsibility includes ensuring that expectations for ethical AI governance are explicit; it includes verifying that monitoring systems are designed to surface material risk in time to act. And it includes resisting the tendency to treat ethical governance as a side effort that recedes when commercial pressure increases.

Defining the future state requires ambition. Executive leadership and boards should treat this stage as an opportunity to envision what ethical AI governance could look like if it were fully integrated into the enterprise. Some improvements will require consistent effort over several years. The purpose of the exercise is to define an ambitious direction of travel. Leaders should challenge the organization to reach Layer 5: Ethical Vanguard. Shoot for the moon for the benefit of the planet.

The implementation model relies on the three core tools introduced earlier in Chapters 6–9. Each tool plays a distinct role in execution. Together, they create a common language that supports disciplined decision making.

The first tool is the Ethical Maturity Stack. It provides a structured way to describe how deeply ethics is integrated into AI governance and the enterprise more broadly. The stack enables leaders to distinguish between compliance oriented posture and ethical capabilities. It creates shared reference points for discussing ethical maturity progress.

The second tool is the set of Performance Measures. Chapter 6 introduces the two measures, and their factor sets, while Chapters 7 and 8 examine each factor in detail. In this chapter, our focus is on execution.

The third tool is the Applied Governance Practices. These practices represent some of the mechanisms through which gaps between the current and desired state are closed. The Leading Practices are already visible in more mature organizations. The Emerging Practices, based on our research, are in response to AI systems that are more autonomous and difficult to govern through traditional controls. Together, they provide practical levers for enterprise transformation.

This chapter is written primarily for management teams, and more specifically for cross-functional AI program teams (and the Embedded AI Ethics Partner, if such a role exists in the organization), because they are principally responsible for the design of AI programs and integrating governance protocols into daily operations. At the same time, board directors cannot treat implementation as something to receive passively at their quarterly meetings. AI systems increasingly operate inside mission critical processes. When that is true, oversight expectations rise. Boards must ensure that monitoring systems are reasonably designed to surface risk and escalation pathways function well when challenges arise. As such, the implementation approach in this chapter integrates established expectations for oversight in high-risk domains. These expectations shape how the Boundaries of Tolerance model is operationalized. The implementation model therefore integrates management execution with board oversight discipline.

Over the past several years, I have discussed the Boundaries of Tolerance model with senior leaders across industries through board sessions, executive education, and most recently in my MIT Sloan School of Management classrooms. These leaders are craving guidance in implementing the model. Several students in my MIT executive MBA course have indicated that they plan to adopt the Boundaries of Tolerance model inside their organizations as they refine AI oversight.

This book is being published before formal pilots of the model can be completed. We considered delaying until after one or a few pilots. We ultimately chose to publish now because the demand for practical execution guidance is immediate. The core elements of the model have been shaped through direct engagement with organizations and already provide practical governance approaches that can be applied today. In our experience, applying the model helps organizations better understand their current and desired future state of ethical maturity and begin adopting both Leading and Emerging Practices. Conducting formal pilots of the model with organizations is the next step. Readers who are interested in adopting the model in practice are encouraged to reach out.

Stage 1: Assess

Implementation begins with a disciplined assessment. Many organizations believe they understand their ethical posture with respect to AI; few have tested that belief against observable conditions inside the enterprise and within their deployed systems. Assumptions about ethical maturity often rest on policy statements and anecdotal episodes rather than direct evidence. The purpose of the Assess stage is to accomplish two objectives:

- Establish a credible current-state baseline.
- Envision the desired future state.

This stage is executed by management (a cross-functional working group if such a body exists) and overseen by the board.

Apply the Performance Measures to Establish the Current State Baseline

The Assess stage begins with the disciplined application of the Performance Measures to establish the current state of affairs. These measures are designed to evaluate how ethical governance practices actually operate inside the organization, not how they are described in policy and leadership statements (if such documents even exist). We focus in this stage on observable behavior and examine how decisions are made when trade-offs arise. They also test how responsibility is exercised when systems behave unexpectedly or when commercial pressure intensifies.

The structure of the Performance Measures is summarized in Chapter 6 and examined in detail in Chapters 7 and 8. This chapter focuses instead on how those measures are actually applied in practice to establish a credible baseline and implementation plan.

The *Performance Measures* operate across two distinct but interdependent dimensions. One set evaluates enterprise conditions, the other evaluates system behavior. Both are required to establish a credible baseline. Ethical maturity can only be understood when these perspectives are examined together. Assessment at this stage is not an audit or compliance review. Its credibility depends on grounding conclusions in evidence tied to corporate functions and AI systems that carry real operational or fiduciary consequence.

Before applying the Performance Measures, organizations must define what is actually being assessed. Ethical maturity cannot be evaluated in the abstract; it must be anchored to AI systems that influence meaningful outcomes. This stage begins with an inventory of AI systems that are in production or active deployment. From that inventory, organizations then identify the material systems that affect revenue decisions and regulatory exposure, as well as those that shape stakeholder risk more broadly. Systems that have wide operational reach or with meaningful autonomy require particular attention. Low-impact or exploratory tools may be excluded if it can be demonstrated that failure would not produce material harm or fiduciary exposure. Systems whose failure would require executive or board explanation must be included. The output is a documented definition of assessment scope, including the rationale for inclusion or exclusion. Once the scope is set, the team responsible for implementation proceeds with this Stage 1 assessment using the two Performance Measures.

This analysis begins with the Enterprise Factors described in Chapter 6 and examined in detail in Chapter 7. The objective at this stage is to collect evidence. The Stage 1 Assess team conducts structured interviews with responsible parties within the organization and reviews internal artifacts such as governance charters, meeting records, escalation documentation, and retrospective reviews of important AI-related decisions. For each Enterprise Factor, the team reviews supporting evidence and assigns a qualitative maturity characterization aligned with the Ethical Maturity Stack. The emphasis throughout is on how the organization actually operates rather than how it merely describes itself. For each Enterprise Factor, the Assess team documents observed behavior and supporting evidence; importantly, it also includes a qualitative maturity characterization aligned to the Ethical Maturity Stack (as described in the following section).

System-level assessment evaluates how AI systems operate in practice using the System Factors described in Chapter 6 and further examined in Chapter 8. Evidence should be drawn from technical and operational sources, including system monitoring outputs and incident documentation. Where evidence is incomplete or unavailable, that absence is documented explicitly. Further, where third-party systems are involved, the Assess team must also review vendor documentation together with internal controls that demonstrate how accountability is retained. For each System Factor, the Assess team produces a concise finding grounded in evidence and assigns a qualitative maturity characterization aligned with the Ethical Maturity Stack.

Boards have a defined oversight role during the Assess stage. Directors do not conduct the assessment, but instead ensure that the assessment is sufficiently rigorous. Boards confirm that mission critical AI systems are included in scope, particularly those that affect stakeholder safety or materially influence core business decisions. Boards also confirm that a clear pathway exists for assessment findings to reach them in a usable form. This oversight function aligns with *Caremark* expectations. The board's responsibility is to ensure that management has built a monitoring process capable of surfacing material risk in time to act.

As discussed, once the Performance Measures have been applied, the Assess team must translate the findings into placement on the Ethical Maturity Stack. This step requires judgment grounded in the evidence collected during the assessment. The stack is not a quantitative scoring tool; it is a shared language for describing how deeply ethics is integrated into enterprise AI governance and its AI systems as it operates in practice.

Placement on the stack must reflect the material exposures identified by applying the Performance Measures. A single weak point in a high-impact system can outweigh stronger practices elsewhere. For that reason, placement should be heavily influenced by where governance fails under pressure rather than where it performs well under ideal conditions. Most organizations exhibit uneven ethical maturity. Some business units operate with stronger governance discipline than others. Some AI use cases receive sustained oversight while others are managed more lightly. The Assess team should strive to surface this unevenness. Attempts to smooth differences into a single composite view obscure material risk and undermine credibility.

The Assess team must document the rationale for placement on the Stack. That rationale should reference direct evidence gathered during assessment. It should explain how controls operate in real decision-making rather than how they are designed on paper. It should also reflect observed system behavior during normal operation, including how issues are detected and addressed.

Importantly, when evidence is mixed or incomplete, placement should default *downward*. Higher placement requires a stronger burden of proof. Ambiguity is treated as a signal of exposure. This discipline protects against optimism bias and reinforces the purpose of the stack as a critical governance tool. This step is intentionally conservative. Overstating maturity weakens oversight and increases the likelihood of surprise when systems drift or fail.

Boards play a critical validation role at this stage. The role of directors is to challenge whether management's conclusions are supported by direct evidence. Boards should demand clarity on what drives the current placement on the stack. Evidence matters more than mere policy language. Operational controls matter more than stated intent. Observed behavior matters more than declared values. Directors should probe whether claims of maturity are grounded in how decisions are actually made and how systems are actually governed.

Boards should also push back on what appears to be "paper maturity." Policies without operational proof create the appearance of governance without substance. This challenge function is central to effective oversight and directly supports its *Caremark* obligations. At this stage, the board's role is to ensure that management's articulation of current ethical maturity is reasonable to support responsible planning and execution.

Envision the Desired Future

This section marks the transition from the current state determination described previously to the aspirational state. The objective of defining the future state is to decide where deeper ethical integration is required across the enterprise. These decisions must reflect the ethical boundaries of what the organization will tolerate, and where failure would produce unacceptable consequences. The desired future state is defined by selecting a target position on the Ethical Maturity Stack. That position reflects how deeply ethical considerations are expected to shape the enterprise and its AI systems.

Management begins this work by articulating why a particular target state is appropriate. Strategic priorities matter because they determine which AI-enabled activities are essential to business performance. Risk appetite matters because it shapes how conservative governance must be when outcomes are uncertain. Stakeholder exposure matters because it clarifies where failure would erode trust or legitimacy.

These rationales must be explicit; when the reasoning (and boundary setting) behind the target state is well-documented, later trade-offs become easier to navigate. Without this clarity, ethical ambition tends to soften when commercial pressure increases.

The future state must then be defined using the same Performance Measures, and the specific factors that support them, applied at the outset of the Assess stage. At the enterprise level, the future state should describe how Leadership Priorities will change so that ethical considerations shape strategic discussion. Operational ethics must be reflected in clear decision guidance that teams can apply under time pressure. Stakeholder accountability must extend beyond identification and meaningfully influence how systems are actually designed and deployed.

Expectations for ecosystem partners must also be addressed directly. Ethical responsibility does not disappear when AI capability is sourced externally. The future state should therefore define how governance expectations extend across vendors and partners, including how accountability is retained when third-party systems influence outcomes. Cultural expectations must also be stated plainly. The future state should describe how challenge is expected to occur and how escalation is treated in practice.

System-level expectations require equal specificity. The future state should define who (a real human) is accountable for AI outcomes and when intervention is required. It should clarify how fairness is evaluated and how findings influence deployment decisions. Further, it should explain what transparency means in practice for both internal users and affected stakeholders. It must also define how reliability is monitored over time and how data is protected across the system life cycle. A future state that lacks this level of specificity cannot guide detailed governance design.

The desired future state must embed oversight capabilities that align with fiduciary expectations. These capabilities are operating requirements of responsible AI governance. Management must explicitly identify which AI applications are mission critical since these systems warrant heightened scrutiny when failure would affect compliance or core enterprise operations.

Board-level oversight of AI risk must be clearly assigned within the future state. Oversight may reside with a committee or with the full board, but responsibility must be explicit. Continuous monitoring procedures must also be defined. These procedures should specify what information is collected and how often it is reviewed. They must also make clear the escalation pathway when predefined thresholds are crossed.

Access to AI oversight expertise must be ensured as part of the future state design. Boards and executives must be able to draw on informed judgment at the point of decision rather than after issues emerge. Monitoring systems should surface emerging risk without waiting for incidents to force attention.

The future state must also reflect how AI risk is discussed at the board level. Regular agenda time reinforces accountability and creates an evidentiary record of oversight (and, as it was addressed in Chapter 5, has been specifically highlighted by the Delaware courts as a positive governance measure). Organization-wide AI education must support these structures. Monitoring fails when employees cannot recognize ethical concerns or simply do not know how to elevate them. Embedding these capabilities into the desired future state ensures that ethical ambition is supported by oversight capacity.

Assessment Outputs and Deliverables

The Assess stage produces a defined set of outputs that anchor the remainder of the implementation process. These outputs are decision tools designed to support action and real accountability. If assessment outputs are vague or difficult to use, the entire implementation effort weakens before planning even begins.

The first output is a clear statement of current placement on the Ethical Maturity Stack. This statement should be concise and defensible, reflecting the evidence gathered during assessment. Its purpose is to establish a shared understanding of where the organization actually operates today with respect to ethical AI governance and practices. This output should include a short maturity narrative that explains the placement on the stack. This narrative should describe where governance practices are holding and where they are fragile. It should surface areas of relative strength (without overstating them). It should also describe areas of exposure with enough specificity to support informed discussion and remediation. Most importantly, it should identify where ethical risk appears across the enterprise.

The second output is the result of the future state determination. It is a clear description of the governance environment the organization intends to build. This output includes a defined target position on the Ethical Maturity Stack, specific expectations aligned to the Enterprise and System Factors.

The third output is a focused identification of priority systems. This includes AI systems whose impact is high enough to warrant executive or board scrutiny.

These outputs must be designed for actual use to promote real change in the organization. Long narrative reports tend to obscure responsibility and dilute oversight. Effective outputs take the form of structured summaries that support discussion and, importantly, real decision-making. Well-designed dashboards are often more useful than exhaustive documentation, especially when paired with concise briefing materials prepared for focused board discussion.

Board oversight at this stage focuses on whether the outputs support informed decision-making. Directors should assess whether the outputs enable meaningful action. They should confirm that the artifacts described previously are the product of a fair and honest assessment by management. They should also ensure that these artifacts can be revisited over time to track progress. This oversight aligns directly with the board's *Caremark* obligations. A monitoring system is only effective if it produces information that directors can actually use; Stage 1 assessment outputs are the foundation of that system.

Stage 2: Plan

Stage 2 identifies the gaps between current conditions and the desired future state. Organizations assess where governance does not meet expectations and determine which gaps require attention. The focus is on defining where change is needed.

Identify Gaps and Improvement Opportunities

Planning begins with a gap analysis that compares the current baseline established in Stage 1 with the desired future state. Not all gaps carry the same consequence. Some gaps increase the likelihood of direct stakeholder harm. Other gaps heighten regulatory or fiduciary exposure. Still others undermine trust by creating distance between stated values and observed behavior. There are also gaps that introduce fragility into systems the organization depends on for its core operations.

Gaps should be described in clear operational terms. Each gap should be tied to observed conditions documented during the Assess stage and be linked to a plausible consequence if left unaddressed. When consequences cannot be clearly articulated, the gap may not warrant immediate attention. Some gaps can be addressed through staged investment as ethical maturity increases. Other gaps demand immediate action because delay compounds risk or narrows response options. The primary goal of this step is to determine where governance must be strengthened now to protect the organization and its stakeholders.

Boards review prioritized gaps through a fiduciary lens. Directors should test whether management's prioritization reflects material exposure. They should press for clarity on which gaps are intolerable given the organization's risk profile. They should also explore where sequencing is appropriate and where delay would expose the organization to unacceptable consequence. This open board and management dialogue reinforces the connection between ethical governance and enterprise resilience. It also ensures that planning decisions are grounded in a shared understanding. By the end of this Plan stage, the organization should have a focused set of improvement opportunities that justify investment and prepare for selecting governance interventions.

Select Applied Governance Practices and Design Other Initiatives to Close the Gap

Once priority gaps have been identified, planning turns to selecting governance practices (beginning with the Applied Governance Practices) and other initiatives that will close them. This step demands a certain degree of restraint. Attempting to deploy too many practices at once dilutes accountability and slows progress. Effective planning requires choosing a limited set of practices that directly address the weaknesses that matter most. It is important to note that the Applied Governance Practices alone will not close the gap articulated at the conclusion of assessment. Other initiatives should be identified outside of the Applied Governance Practices, aligned with that gap assessment.

Selection begins by matching practices to the actual gaps identified. Some practices formalize oversight in areas where authority is unclear. Others adopt professional ethics standards as a proxy applicable to all workers. Still others improve coordination where responsibility has been fragmented across corporate functions. Emerging Practices become relevant when AI systems are more adaptive and harder to govern through legacy controls.

For each selected practice, strategic alignment must be established first. The practice should support strategic objectives that the organization depends on for performance. It must reflect the organization's tolerance for uncertainty and consequence. It must also advance the enterprise to its desired position on the Ethical Maturity Stack. Practices that are misaligned create friction and invite quiet resistance during execution. Once alignment is clear, business outcomes must be defined. Outcomes describe, for example, how decision-making or oversight will change in practice. Timelines must be realistic enough to survive operating pressure. An action plan then translates selected practices into concrete initiatives. Each initiative should be tied to a specific gap identified during the Assess stage.

Planning Outputs and Deliverables

The Plan stage produces a defined set of artifacts that translate assessment findings and selected interventions into an executable program. These artifacts must reflect the full scope of planning work, including gap analysis and remediation plan, selection of relevant Applied Governance Practices, and the design of supporting initiatives.

The first output is a prioritized current and future state gap analysis and intervention register. This register should link each material gap identified to the specific governance practice or initiative selected to address it. It should also describe the intended outcome and the consequence if the gap remains unresolved.

The second output is a defined intervention portfolio. This output should document the relevant set of Applied Governance Practices and other initiatives selected during planning. For each intervention, it should clearly state scope, ownership, and the governance capability it is intended to strengthen.

The third output is a detailed implementation road map, which should translate the selected portfolio into sequenced workstreams with assigned owners and realistic timing. It should identify dependencies and required resources. It should also define key decision points where escalation or board visibility is required.

The outputs produced thus far can also be translated into visual decision tools. Spider (Radar) charts and maturity progression charts, introduced in Chapter 7, help management and the board interpret assessment findings across both the Enterprise and System Factors. A radar chart (see Figures 7.4 and 8.3) displays relative maturity across factors, making uneven governance capability visible across the organization or across different AI systems. An ethical maturity progression chart (see Figures 7.5 and 8.4) highlights where ethical exposure is concentrated and where governance gaps require priority attention. Used together, these visualizations enable leaders to see patterns that may not be obvious in narrative findings alone. They help management focus improvement efforts and support board discussion about where intervention is most necessary.

Boards review the selected practices through a focused oversight lens. Directors should confirm that the practices strengthen monitoring capability in areas of material exposure. They should also confirm that the practices improve readiness to respond when issues surface rather than after harm occurs. Accountability must be assigned to individuals with sufficient authority rather than diffused across structures or committees. This validation step ensures that planning decisions support execution and oversight at the same time.

Stage 3: Execute

Stage 3 focuses on executing against the prioritized gaps identified in Stage 2. Organizations implement governance practices and initiatives designed to close those gaps. The emphasis is on translating planning into sustained action.

Execute the Action Plan

This stage is when ethical AI governance and practices become an operating discipline. The work here often proves difficult because it requires sustained attention after initial enthusiasm fades. Execution is owned by management because it involves day-to-day decisions that shape how AI systems and business functions actually operate. Boards remain deeply involved because execution quality determines whether oversight obligations are actually met in practice.

Ethical AI practices cannot endure if monitoring weakens once systems are deployed. Stage 3 therefore focuses on strengthening governance under real operating conditions, especially when commercial pressure intensifies or system behavior begins to shift. Execution begins with authority. Management must assign responsibility and accountability for executing this plan to a named role (and actual leader) with decision rights that match the scope of risk. This leader must be empowered to influence priorities and to intervene when ethical thresholds are approached.

Most enterprises have already built change muscle through past digital transformation initiatives. The mechanics of execution are familiar: clear ownership, defined milestones, disciplined program governance, and feedback loops that surface risks early. Learnings from these digital transformation initiatives will help inform execution of the Boundaries of Tolerance model as outlined in this chapter.

Execution also requires a defined reporting and oversight rhythm. Ethical AI oversight cannot rely on merely ad hoc updates or informal conversations. Management should define a regular process for reporting that reflects how quickly systems change and how material their impact has become. Execution also requires discipline in how information flows. Reports must be structured to support professional judgment. Leaders must be able to see when systems are operating within their acceptable tolerance levels and when they are approaching established boundaries.

Boards play a vital verification role at this stage. Directors should test whether the accountable leader controls sufficient budget to act and whether escalation pathways function well. They should also confirm that leadership has the ability to pause or redirect high-risk use cases when ethical concerns arise. This verification is essential. Oversight expectations are satisfied when governance systems function under pressure and when authority can be exercised in a timely manner.

Embed Controls into AI System Life Cycles

Execution requires that governance controls be embedded directly into how AI systems are built and operated. Controls that sit outside development workflows are often bypassed when timelines compress or priorities shift. Ethical oversight must therefore become part of the system life cycle itself rather than an external review step applied after decisions have already been made. Embedding begins at system design. Management must ensure that ethical considerations are addressed when objectives are set and system architectures are chosen. Accountability for outcomes should be clearly defined at this stage. Expectations for testing must also be established early so that ethical performance is treated as a design requirement rather than a post hoc concern.

As systems move into development, controls must shape how models are trained and evaluated. When ethical requirements are integrated into development workflows, they become an established part of how teams define quality. When systems are prepared for deployment, governance controls must guide release decisions. Management should ensure that *ethical* readiness is assessed alongside *technical* readiness. Communication with users and affected stakeholders should reflect defined transparency expectations. Decisions to delay or stage deployment should be treated as legitimate governance outcomes. Embedding controls into AI system life cycles is therefore a core requirement of responsible execution.

Boards focus on whether this embedding is real rather than nominal. Directors should examine whether monitoring occurs as a routine part of operations or only after incidents draw attention. They should assess whether oversight information is produced systematically rather than assembled reactively. This focus aligns directly with fiduciary expectations for system monitoring.

Continuous Monitoring

Execution does not end with AI solution deployment. AI systems change as data shifts and operating conditions evolve, often in ways that expand system usage beyond original expectations; governance practices must change with them. Monitoring is therefore an ongoing responsibility rather than a periodic review conducted to satisfy enterprise risk management expectations. Intervention mechanisms must be available and exercised when performance approaches defined boundaries. For high-impact systems, continuous oversight must be treated as nonnegotiable.

Effective monitoring focuses on how systems behave against defined ethical expectations. Management should track performance signals that indicate stability as well as signals that suggest drift. When incidents occur, they should be treated as governance data rather than as isolated failures. Each incident provides insight into whether controls are functioning and whether escalation pathways are being used. It also reveals whether accountability is clearly assigned and exercised in practice.

Governance practices must adapt based on what monitoring reveals. Some controls may prove insufficient as systems scale or contexts change. Other controls may introduce friction without meaningfully reducing risk. Adaptation in response to evidence is a sign of responsible execution.

Boards require visibility into patterns rather than anecdotes. Directors should look for recurring issues that point to structural weakness. They should watch for persistent control failures that suggest flaws in design or authority and pay attention to repeated exceptions that signal erosion of discipline over time. Pattern recognition enables boards to distinguish between isolated errors and systemic problems.

Trend visibility supports informed oversight. It enables directors to ask better questions and to intervene earlier. It also reinforces accountability by making it harder for issues to remain hidden within operational noise. This stage ensures that plans developed earlier translate into operating reality.

Respond to Red Flags

Even the strongest governance systems will encounter failure. Ethical AI governance is therefore judged not only by how well risks are anticipated but also by how leaders actually respond when warning signals appear. This section defines how escalation and response must function when AI systems behave in unexpected or harmful ways. Red flags can surface through many channels, including monitoring outputs, employee concerns, audit findings, or external scrutiny. What matters most is not the source of the signal, but the quality of the response that follows. When response is delayed or responsibility becomes diffused, ethical credibility erodes and fiduciary responsibility weakens.

Not all signals arrive with the clarity of a red flag. Many begin as weaker indicators of emerging opportunities or risk. In Chapter 3, drawing on Rita McGrath's work, we described these as weak signals. In the risk context, they often appear as early anomalies or patterns that do not yet rise to the level of failure producing a red flag. Organizations that respond only to red flags are reacting late. Effective governance requires attention to these earlier signals, when intervention will likely be less costly and more effective.

Management owns the initial response when a red flag appears. Once acknowledged, investigation must begin promptly, with scope defined clearly enough to determine cause and impact. Management must ensure that corrective actions are implemented in practice rather than discussed in theory. Remediation must be tracked until resolution is confirmed through direct evidence.

Preparedness is a critical component of responsible execution. During the pandemic, our *Better Innovation* podcast ran a special series on innovating in a crisis. The number one priority shared by the leaders we interviewed was to ensure they were prepared well before the crisis materialized. Organizations should develop and maintain response plans for AI-related crises *well before* incidents occur. These plans clarify decision authority so that escalation does not stall at moments of uncertainty. They also define communication pathways so that information flows through the enterprise. Criteria for pausing or withdrawing systems should be established in advance. Preparation reduces confusion when stakes escalate quickly and supports timely action when public trust is threatened or when regulatory or operational stability is at risk.

Boards have a distinct responsibility once red flags surface. Oversight shifts from monitoring to response. As explored in Chapter 5, pursuant to its *Caremark* obligations, directors must ensure that issues are elevated to the board when material risk is present rather than remaining confined to management channels. Board-level discussion is essential at this stage. Directors should engage directly with management on the nature of the risk and the scope of the investigation. They must also assess whether the proposed response is adequate under the circumstances. Passive awareness does not satisfy *Caremark* obligations.

Boards must also confirm that investigations actually occur and that they are not prematurely closed. Corrective actions should be tracked to completion with evidence that identified changes have taken effect. Directors should confirm that crisis playbooks exist before incidents arise. Advance planning demonstrates that risk was treated as foreseeable (rather than hypothetical) and reinforces accountability when response is required.

Caremark's second prong centers on action. Knowledge of a problem without response exposes organizations to legal risk and ethical failure. Effective boards understand this distinction and insist on disciplined follow-through. Response to red flags is where ethical governance is tested most clearly. Systems may fail despite good intentions, but leadership response determines whether failure remains contained or becomes systemic. When escalation works and response is timely, organizations preserve trust and reinforce the credibility of their governance model.

Change Management and Cultural Reinforcement

Ethical AI governance cannot be sustained through structure alone. Even well-designed controls weaken over time if they are not reinforced through leadership behavior and shared norms. This section focuses on the change management work required to sustain ethical vigilance in environments where AI systems evolve quickly and competitive pressure remains constant.

Change management begins with alignment across functions. AI governance often fails when responsibility is fragmented between legal and technical teams, or when business leadership operates without a shared operating model. Ethical considerations must travel with decisions as they move across the organization. Governance roles must be understood broadly rather than confined to a small group of specialists. Alignment becomes stronger when ethical expectations are embedded into existing decision forums. Ethical considerations should appear within AI system reviews as part of normal deliberation. They should also be present in risk discussions that shape operating priorities. Investment decisions should reflect ethical implications alongside performance considerations.

Leadership education plays a central role in sustaining this alignment. Education should not be limited to technical briefings or one-time training events. It must focus on judgment under uncertainty and on how leaders are expected to act when ethical signals are ambiguous. Board education and executive education serve distinct purposes, but both must reinforce shared expectations about responsibility and consequence.

Boards require education that supports effective oversight, aligned with the leading corporate governance judicial opinions discussed in Chapter 5. Directors must understand how AI systems operate at a level sufficient to evaluate whether monitoring and response mechanisms are credible. They do not need extensive technical depth; they do need fluency in how risk travels through systems and where governance can fail.

Executive education should focus on execution. Senior leaders must understand how ethical expectations translate into operating decisions under their control. And they must understand their own accountability when systems produce harm. Education that treats ethics as abstract principles rarely changes behavior; education that connects ethics to authority and consequence does.

Cultural reinforcement depends on norms that shape behavior when trade-offs arise. One critical norm centers on escalation. Employees must believe that raising ethical concerns is expected rather than discouraged. Escalation should be framed as a critical contribution to organizational resilience rather than a disruption to delivery: see something, say something.

Another essential norm is ethical challenge. Teams should feel permitted to question assumptions and surface uncertainty. Transparency within the enterprise reinforces both escalation and challenge. When decisions and outcomes are visible within the organization, accountability follows more naturally. Transparency does not require public disclosure of *every* detail. It requires internal clarity about why decisions were made and how risks were addressed.

Continuing these norms requires attention long after initial implementation. Many governance programs launch with energy and then fade as priorities shift. This pattern is especially common in fast-moving technology environments. Preventing governance fade requires deliberate reinforcement. Regular review cycles help maintain attention over time. Education must be refreshed as systems evolve; practices must be revisited as new use cases emerge. Boards play a critical role in preventing fade. Continued inquiry signals that ethical oversight remains a priority.

Cultural reinforcement moves more slowly than structural change. It is also more lasting. When ethical vigilance becomes part of how decisions are made, governance and operations adapt as technology changes. This is what enables organizations to sustain responsible AI practices in high-velocity environments.

Closing

The Boundaries of Tolerance model becomes real when it changes how decisions are made when outcomes will materially affect the business. Frameworks matter only when they shape decisions that affect financial outcomes or expose the organization to risk. This chapter has focused on implementation for that reason.

Performance Measures provide the starting point for that movement. They focus attention on how AI systems and business processes actually function rather than how they are described. The Ethical Maturity Stack provides this direction by defining where boundaries must be enforced. When leaders use the stack to decide where higher maturity is desired (or required), they replace vague commitment with deliberate design choices. The stack helps organizations decide where values must be enforced through governance. Applied Governance Practices complete the translation from intent to action. Practices matter when they are embedded in daily workflows.

Operationalizing ethical AI governance requires a distinct focus on execution. Management is responsible for building systems that function day-to-day. That responsibility includes assigning clear authority and embedding controls directly into operations. It also requires adjusting practices as operating conditions change. And ethical AI governance requires vigilance. Boards play a central role by ensuring that monitoring systems remain effective and escalation pathways function when needed. Response discipline is the final test. Red flags reveal whether governance is performative or real. When issues arise, leaders must act. Investigation must lead to correction. Correction must be tracked to completion.

Taken together, these elements transform the Boundaries of Tolerance model from a tool into an operating discipline. Ethical AI governance is sustained through consistent execution and active oversight. It depends on a credible response when systems fail or begin to drift. Organizations that treat the Boundaries of Tolerance model as a living operating system rather than a static framework are better prepared for uncertainty. They are also better positioned to earn trust as AI becomes more deeply embedded in decisions that shape individual lives and institutional outcomes.

Conclusion: Defining Your Boundaries of Tolerance in the Age of AI

Let's return to the boardroom moment described at the outset of this book, shared with me during our Harvard Business School forum. The bank director described the company's struggle with a bias issue emerging from a new artificial intelligence (AI) system developed by the bank. The AI team building the system confronted the issue first. Management then intervened. The board was eventually drawn into the discussion. The question raised at the outset was simple. Why were these teams struggling with how to deal with an AI ethics issue? These teams were struggling not because the technology was too complex or because the ethical questions were impossible to manage. My hypothesis is that they were struggling because the organization had not done the foundational work of determining the ethical outcomes they will and will not tolerate in their AI systems, their *boundaries of tolerance*. That is the core challenge. Without that clarity, even very capable teams can reach different conclusions about how to respond, introducing risk for the enterprise and for society. This book has addressed that very challenge.

The leaders in that boardroom were thrust into a moment that is becoming common across industries. AI systems are no longer experimental tools operating at the edge of the enterprise. These systems increasingly shape how organizations allocate resources and prioritize investments. And they influence how organizations engage with customers. Decisions that once relied entirely on human judgment are now informed by systems capable of producing recommendations at unprecedented speed and scale (and effectiveness).

Many AI experts recognize the significance of this shift, even if its full implications are still unfolding. AI changes how organizations learn and how they make decisions. When AI systems operate without clearly defined ethical limits, the consequences can ripple through the organization before leaders even recognize that a boundary has been crossed.

But the speed of technological progress is outpacing the development of governance practices capable of guiding its use. Leaders often discover ethical questions only after a system has already influenced real outcomes. Customers have already been affected. Employees have already relied on the system's recommendations. The organization then finds itself responding to consequences that might have been avoided with clearer ethical boundaries at the outset.

A key insight from that boardroom moment told to us at Harvard is that this generation of AI systems introduces governance challenges that traditional frameworks were never designed to manage. Companies throughout the economy are embarking on a new wave of technology-enabled innovation unlike anything they have experienced in other digital transformations. This is in part due to the ubiquity of generative AI capabilities across organizations. This technology is widely accessible. Even free versions can produce impressive results. But the governance challenges also exist because of the strong capabilities of generative AI intersecting with agentic systems. Organizations worldwide are already generating value from these systems. At the same time, new forms of enterprise risk and societal risk are emerging.

An additional complexity arises when companies license AI tools or partner with a technology company to develop and ultimately deploy AI systems. In those buy or partner decisions, governance can be especially challenging. Leaders must determine who is accountable when harm occurs. They must determine how partnering organizations align their governance decisions. In every scenario, leaders must ensure a *human* is responsible for outcomes. The AI community is realizing that traditional compliance frameworks are not sufficient for governing today's AI behavior; a fresh governance approach is needed. The governance gap exists because leaders lacked a structured way to define acceptable conduct for AI systems.

The governance challenge described previously is not limited to one industry. It appears in financial services when lending algorithms influence access to credit. It appears in healthcare when decision systems shape treatment recommendations. It appears in hiring systems when algorithms filter applicants before a human ever reviews a résumé. Across these settings the same question emerges: Who is responsible for the outcomes produced by systems that increasingly shape human decisions? The answer cannot be the technology itself. Responsibility remains with the organizations that deploy these systems and with the leaders who authorize their use.

The Boundaries of Tolerance model is an attempt to address this governance vacuum and is the principal contribution of this work. The framework places ethics at the center of AI decision-making. As outlined in Part III of this book, the model includes three structural components. First, the Ethical Maturity Stack provides a reference point that enables organizations to assess their ethical posture today and define the level of maturity they aspire to reach. Second, the Performance Measures, the Enterprise Factors and System Factors, provide a structured way to evaluate how ethical commitments appear across the organization and inside the systems it deploys. Third, the Applied Governance Practices highlight Leading Practices that can help organizations close their ethical maturity gap today. They also introduce Emerging Practices that are already shaping the next generation of AI governance. The Boundaries of Tolerance model serves as a practical governance tool, ready for adoption by companies today.

The model was designed to give leaders a practical starting point. It does not attempt to resolve every ethical question raised by AI. No single framework could accomplish that task. *Instead, the Boundaries of Tolerance model provides a structure that enables organizations to examine their own values and determine how those values should appear in the systems they build or deploy*. Once those boundaries are defined, governance becomes far more manageable. Leaders are no longer reacting to ethical surprises. They are applying principles that the organization has already chosen to uphold.

AI governance has emerged as the defining leadership discipline of our time. Leaders must ensure that the enterprise benefits from this powerful technology responsibly. Leadership teams within organizations developing or deploying AI systems should consider adopting the Boundaries of Tolerance model and its core elements. The model helps them determine their current state of ethical maturity, define an aspirational future state, and assess the resulting gap. I hope leaders come away from this book with a clear road map to adopt this model within their own organizations to ultimately determine the enterprise boundaries of ethical tolerance. This leadership obligation begins with the board of directors and extends throughout the enterprise. Senior executives must embed these boundaries into business strategy and enterprise risk management. AI governance and implementation teams must apply these boundaries in system design and monitoring. Each of these teams carry AI governance obligations that can be strengthened by this model. In this regard, governance becomes a core, strategic leadership responsibility rather than a mere compliance exercise.

History offers many examples of technologies that advanced more quickly than the governance structures surrounding them. AI may prove to be the most consequential example. The decisions leaders make today will influence how this technology shapes organizations and society for decades to come.

This responsibility ultimately rests with *human* leadership. AI systems may assist decision-making and surface patterns that humans would struggle to detect. They may operate at speeds that no human organization could replicate. These systems remain tools created and deployed by *people*. Because of this reality, the ethical posture of an organization will always reflect the decisions of its leaders. Technology may amplify those decisions. It cannot replace them.

What will you do differently in your organization tomorrow as a result of the principles serving as the foundation for this book? Where must human judgment remain central? How will you know when an AI system has crossed an ethical boundary? What outcomes would your organization refuse to tolerate from an AI system? What boundaries should the enterprise establish as a result? It has been wonderful to hear many stories from students in my executive education courses and from leaders within organizations applying these ideas. These professionals are passionate about convening teams within their organizations to address these issues head-on and engage the enterprise in the principles underlying the model.

My aim is that the concepts presented throughout this book influence how organizations interact with the communities they serve. They influence whether customers trust the systems that increasingly affect their daily lives. They influence whether employees feel empowered to question automated recommendations when they appear inconsistent with the organization's values.

In each of these moments, the ethical boundaries established by leadership will determine how the organization responds. Organizations that have defined those boundaries respond with clarity. Organizations that have not often find themselves debating fundamental ethical (and therefore, enterprise risk) questions in the midst of operational crises. The difference between those outcomes is preparation.

The pace of AI development suggests that these governance challenges will only intensify in the years ahead. More powerful AI systems will emerge. Capabilities that appear extraordinary today will soon become routine. Organizations will rely on increasingly complex systems that operate across both internal operations and customer engagement. The need for thoughtful governance will grow alongside these capabilities. Leaders who invest in ethical clarity today will be far better prepared to manage the systems of tomorrow.

The ideas in this book emerged from research conducted at the Harvard Edmond & Lily Safra Center for Ethics and from my direct engagement with organizations confronting real AI governance challenges. This work will now continue through teaching and executive education at MIT Sloan and Open Learning, where these ideas will be refined with leaders responsible for deploying AI systems. In parallel, I will continue to develop practical materials to support application of the model inside organizations, helping translate these ideas from the page into daily decision-making. The Boundaries of Tolerance model will evolve as organizations apply it in practice and as those field applications generate insights that strengthen its usefulness and credibility.

I recognize the need to continue this work, because in many ways we are still in the early stages of AI adoption. The technology is advancing quickly, from generative systems to agentic capabilities, with potential that is difficult to fully anticipate. The Leading and Emerging Practices introduced in this book will also continue to develop, and new practices will need to be identified as AI becomes more deeply integrated into enterprise operations.

The next stage of this work will extend the governance principles addressed in this book beyond organizations and into the personal choices individuals make when interacting with AI systems. This governance analysis is essential at the organizational level, but ethics is deeply personal. My aim is to help individuals determine their own boundaries of tolerance in relation to AI systems. I am excited to explore this next phase in the evolution of the Boundaries of Tolerance model. There is therefore a clear need to continue refining the model and the other concepts developed in this book. That is what comes next. To this end, I would welcome hearing from readers interested in applying the ideas in this book.

Let's return one last time to the boardroom (and leadership) moment at Harvard Business School forum described at the beginning of the book. Senior leaders gathered to discuss the opportunities and risks created by rapidly advancing AI systems. The conversation revealed both excitement and uncertainty. Executives understood that AI would transform their organizations. They also sensed that existing governance approaches were not sufficient to manage the ethical and operational consequences of these systems.

I ask you to empathize with the leader protagonists at the heart of that story. With the new knowledge and principles from this book, do you now see that moment differently? The leaders in that room were not struggling because the technology was too complex. They were struggling because they had not articulated the ethical boundaries within which their AI systems should operate.

Assume your organization had already done the hard foundational work of defining its ethical boundaries and then faced the bias issue described by the bank director. How would that preparation have changed the discussion? How would it have helped the organization respond in a way that better protected the stakeholders negatively affected?

These questions point directly to the central contribution of this book. Readers may now see the challenge of AI governance with greater clarity and appreciate the need for an approach like the Boundaries of Tolerance model, with ethics at the center. The model provides leaders with a structured way to define those boundaries and govern how AI systems behave within their organizations. That work matters because ethical failures in AI are never only technical failures. They reach people. They restrict opportunities, sometimes causing harm that is difficult to reverse. The more deeply AI systems enter everyday life, the more urgent it becomes for leaders to decide what their institutions will stand for when those systems are placed in positions of influence.

The impact of these decisions extend beyond the organizations that deploy AI systems. These intelligent systems increasingly influence how people access information and products/services. When these systems operate responsibly they can expand personal opportunities. When they operate without ethical boundaries they can reinforce inequities or erode trust in institutions.

Every major technological transformation forces societies to decide what kinds of outcomes they are willing to accept and what kinds they are not. AI simply brings that decision into sharper focus. Organizations cannot outsource responsibility for AI behavior. Leaders must define the boundaries within which AI innovation operates. Ethical AI governance begins when leaders decide what their organizations will and will not tolerate from the systems they deploy. Those decisions will shape not only the future of their organizations but also how people experience technology in their daily lives. My hope is that this book serves you well in that work and that the principles outlined here help you lead with clarity as you define and uphold those boundaries within your organization. The responsibility is significant. So is the opportunity.

Appendix: Categorization of AI Stakeholders

This Appendix provides a structured categorization of stakeholders affected by artificial intelligence (AI) systems. It extends the stakeholder lens developed throughout the book by organizing individuals and institutions based on how they interact with AI systems or are affected by their outcomes. The intent is to support more complete governance by ensuring that stakeholder considerations remain central to oversight decisions.

Internal Stakeholders

These are individuals and teams within the enterprise who build or manage AI systems, along with those who are affected by how those systems are designed or deployed.

- **Employees and workforce.** Workers are often the first group to feel AI's effects, whether through automation or algorithmic management. Monitoring systems can also influence productivity and privacy. Any stakeholder analysis must include clear provisions that address how AI systems affect the workforce, the lifeblood of the enterprise.

- **Board of directors.** Boards face fiduciary responsibility for AI risk and must ensure oversight aligns with stakeholder interests. Further, boards establish the critical tone at the top, vitally important for ethical AI governance.
- **Management and executives.** Senior leaders depend on AI-driven analytics to make strategic decisions while bearing accountability for their ethical use.
- **Data scientists and engineers.** Those designing models face ethical trade-offs in data collection and model selection. Decisions about deployment timing introduce additional risk that must be governed deliberately.
- **Legal and compliance teams, including ethics functions.** These teams interpret emerging laws and ensure that governance processes keep pace with technological change.
- **Labor unions and work councils.** These work groups are increasingly active in negotiating algorithmic management practices and workforce retraining.

Direct External Stakeholders

These groups interact directly with a company's AI systems or outputs.

- **Customers and end users.** These groups experience algorithmic decisions through personalization and pricing. Automated recommendations also shape those interactions. Their trust depends on fairness and transparency. They must also receive explanations that enable them to understand how decisions are made.
- **Suppliers and vendors.** These providers are subject to AI-driven procurement scoring or quality evaluation. Predictive logistics systems can also shape how they are assessed and selected.
- **Business partners and distributors.** These business groups share responsibility for ethical deployment across joint ventures and supply networks.
- **Developers of third-party AI tools.** Foundation models and application programming interfaces embedded in enterprise workflows create shared accountability for outcomes.
- **Investors and shareholders.** These groups increasingly link capital to responsible AI adoption and disclosure practices.
- **Auditors and assurance professionals.** These audit groups evaluate governance controls and verify the integrity of AI-related reporting.

Indirect or Downstream Stakeholders

These stakeholders are affected indirectly through the secondary impacts of AI deployment.

- **Communities and local economies.** Automation can alter employment patterns and economic stability.
- **Individuals represented in training data.** These individuals may face privacy risks or reputational harm when data are misused or biased.
- **Competitors.** Competitors are influenced by market norms established through AI-driven practices, such as dynamic pricing or recommendation algorithms.
- **Media and civil society organizations.** These organizations shape public trust and hold enterprises accountable for AI misuse or misinformation.
- **Academic and research partners.** These partners depend on transparency and data sharing to advance responsible innovation.

Regulatory and Governance Stakeholders

These are the institutions that shape or enforce the ethical boundaries of AI use.

- **Regulators and supervisory authorities.** These groups enforce privacy and safety laws that apply to AI systems. They also oversee compliance with consumer protection requirements.
- **Legislators and policymakers.** These actors observe corporate behavior to guide new AI policy frameworks.
- **Judiciary.** The judiciary interprets legal standards as they apply to algorithmic decision systems and establishes precedent that shapes how AI is governed across sectors.
- **Standards bodies (ISO, IEEE, NIST).** These organizations translate high-level principles into operational guidelines.
- **Professional associations.** These associations set ethical norms for practitioners (for example, the American Bar Association's guidance on generative AI use).

Societal and Global Stakeholders

Finally, AI systems exert influence well beyond the enterprise or industry, shaping broader human and planetary outcomes.

- **Consumers at large.** Consumers are affected by AI-generated content or digital manipulation enabled through automated systems.
- **Marginalized or vulnerable populations.** These groups are disproportionately harmed by bias or exclusion in algorithmic systems.
- **Future generations.** The next generations will inherit the labor structures created today and the ethical precedents set by current AI deployment. Environmental consequences will also shape the conditions they face.
- **Planetary environment.** AI's energy demands contribute to emissions and resource consumption; sustainable AI practices mitigate this impact.
- **Global institutions and ethical forums.** Bodies such as the United Nations and the OECD help establish shared principles for AI stewardship.

Notes

Chapter 1: This Is the AI Moment

1. QuantumBlack AI by McKinsey, "The State of AI in 2025: Agents, Innovation, and Transformation," November 5, 2025, 3, https://www.mckinsey.com/capabilities/quantumblack/our-insights/the-state-of-ai.
2. Ibid., 7.
3. Stanford Graduate School of Business, "Leading in a Time of Change: Jamie Dimon, Chairman and CEO, JP Morgan Chase," *YouTube* video, 56:08, March 7, 2025, https://www.youtube.com/watch?v=PdzMvk66wao, at 27:39.
4. World Bank, "Digital Progress and Trends Report 2025: Strengthening AI Foundations," 2025, 1, 17, https://doi.org/10.1596/978-1-4648-2264-3.
5. Microsoft and LinkedIn, "2024 Work Trend Index Annual Report: AI at Work Is Here. Now Comes the Hard Part," *Microsoft WorkLab,* May 8, 2024, https://www.microsoft.com/en-us/worklab/work-trend-index/ai-at-work-is-here-now-comes-the-hard-part.
6. World Economic Forum, "AI at Work: From Productivity Hacks to Organizational Transformation," Community Paper, 2026, 5, https://reports.weforum.org/docs/WEF_AI_at_Work_from_Productivity_Hacks_to_Organizational_Transformation_2026.pdf.
7. Rita McGrath, *Seeing Around Corners: How to Spot Inflection Points in Business Before They Happen – The First Hands-On Guide to Strategic Advantage and Market Leadership* (Mariner Books, 2021), 1.
8. Nicole Gillespie, Steven Lockey, Tabi Ward, Alexandria Macdade, and Gerard Hassed, "*Trust, Attitudes and Use of Artificial Intelligence: A Global Study 2025*," The University of Melbourne and KPMG, 2025, 69, https://doi.org/10.26188/28822919.

9. International Energy Agency, "*Energy and AI: World Energy Outlook Special Report*," April 10, 2025, 25, https://www.iea.org/reports/energy-and-ai.
10. Alan M. Turing, "Computing Machinery and Intelligence," *Mind* 59, no. 236 (October 1950): 433–460, https://www.hec.edu/sites/default/files/documents/Computing%20Machinery%20and%20Intelligence%20by%20Alan%20Turing.pdf.
11. Dartmouth College, "Artificial Intelligence (AI) Coined at Dartmouth," 1956, accessed March 11, 2026, https://home.dartmouth.edu/about/artificial-intelligence-ai-coined-dartmouth.
12. Frank Rosenblatt, "*The Perceptron: A Perceiving and Recognizing Automaton*," Project PARA Report No. 85-460-1, Cornell Aeronautical Laboratory, January 1957, https://bpb-us-e2.wpmucdn.com/websites.umass.edu/dist/a/27637/files/2016/03/rosenblatt-1957.pdf.
13. Joseph Weizenbaum, "ELIZA—A Computer Program for the Study of Natural Language Communication Between Man and Machine," *Communications of the ACM* 9, no. 1 (January 1966): 36–45, https://web.stanford.edu/class/cs124/p36-weizenabaum.pdf.
14. A. Jay Goldstein, Leon D. Harmon, and Ann B. Lesk, "Man-Machine Interaction in Human-Face Identification," *Bell System Technical Journal* 51, no. 2 (February 1972): 399–427, https://ieeexplore.ieee.org/document/6774125.
15. James Lighthill, "Artificial Intelligence: A General Survey," in *Artificial Intelligence: A Paper Symposium*, ed. James Lighthill, Stuart Sutherland, Roger Needham, Hugh Christopher Longuet-Higgins, and Donald Michie (Science Research Council, 1973), https://rodsmith.nz/wp-content/uploads/Lighthill_1973_Report.pdf.
16. Janosch Delcker, "The Man Who Invented the Self-Driving Car (in 1986)," *Politico*, July 19, 2018, https://www.politico.eu/article/delf-driving-car-born-1986-ernst-dickmanns-mercedes/.
17. IBM, "Deep Blue," *IBM Heritage*, n.d., accessed March 11, 2026, https://www.ibm.com/history/deep-blue.
18. Jia Deng, Wei Dong, Richard Socher, Li-Jia Li, Kai Li, and Li Fei-Fei, "ImageNet: A Large-Scale Hierarchical Image Database," in *Proceedings of the IEEE Conference on Computer Vision and Pattern Recognition (CVPR)* (IEEE, 2009), 248–255, https://image-net.org/static_files/papers/imagenet_cvpr09.pdf.
19. Rebecca Orner, "Siri (Computer Program)," *EBSCO Research Starters*, 2024, https://www.ebsco.com/research-starters/computer-science/siri-computer-program.

20. IBM, "Watson, 'Jeopardy!' Champion," *IBM Heritage*, n.d., accessed March 11, 2026, https://www.ibm.com/history/watson-jeopardy.

21. Alex Krizhevsky, Ilya Sutskever, and Geoffrey E. Hinton, "ImageNet Classification with Deep Convolutional Neural Networks," in *Advances in Neural Information Processing Systems 25 (NIPS 2012)*, ed. F. Pereira, C. J. C. Burges, L. Bottou, and K. Q. Weinberger (Curran Associates, 2012), 1097–1105.

22. Google DeepMind, "*AlphaGo*," n.d., accessed March 11, 2026, https://deepmind.google/research/alphago/.

23. Google DeepMind, "AlphaFold: A Solution to a 50-Year-Old Grand Challenge in Biology," *Google DeepMind Blog*, November 30, 2020, https://deepmind.google/blog/alphafold-a-solution-to-a-50-year-old-grand-challenge-in-biology/.

24. IBM, "History of Artificial Intelligence," *IBM Think*, n.d., accessed March 22, 2026, https://www.ibm.com/think/topics/history-of-artificial-intelligence.

25. McKinsey & Company, "AI Bank of the Future: Can Banks Meet the AI Challenge?," September 2020, 3–4, https://www.mckinsey.de/~/media/McKinsey/Industries/Financial%20Services/Our%20Insights/AI%20bank%20of%20the%20future%20Can%20banks%20meet%20the%20AI%20challenge/AI-bank-of-the-future-Can-banks-meet-the-AI-challenge.pdf.

26. Visa Inc., "Visa Announces Improved Payment Card Fraud Detection," October 2, 2013, https://investor.visa.com/news/news-details/2013/Visa-Announces-Improved-Payment-Card-Fraud-Detection/default.aspx.

27. AI Action Summit, "International AI Safety Report: The International Scientific Report on the Safety of Advanced AI," January 2025, 49, https://internationalaisafetyreport.org/sites/default/files/2025-10/international_ai_safety_report_2025_english.pdf.

28. OpenAI, "ChatGPT," *OpenAI*, n.d., accessed February 25, 2026, https://openai.com/index/chatgpt/.

29. Le Ngoc Luyen and Marie-Hélène Abel, "How Well Do LLMs Predict Prerequisite Skills? Zero-Shot Comparison to Expert-Defined Concepts," *ResearchGate*, July 2025, https://www.researchgate.net/publication/393983430_How_Well_Do_LLMs_Predict_Prerequisite_Skills_Zero-Shot_Comparison_to_Expert-Defined_Concepts.

30. Microsoft and LinkedIn, "2024 Work Trend Index Annual Report: AI at Work Is Here."

31. Nefi Alarcon, "OpenAI Presents GPT-3, a 175 Billion Parameters Language Model," *NVIDIA Developer Technical Blog,* July 7, 2020, https://developer.nvidia.com/blog/openai-presents-gpt-3-a-175-billion-parameters-language-model/.

32. Tesla, "Full Self-Driving (Supervised)," n.d., accessed March 17, 2026, https://www.tesla.com/fsd.

33. OpenAI, "DALL·E: Creating Images from Text," January 5, 2021, https://openai.com/index/dall-e/.

34. OpenAI, "Introducing ChatGPT," November 30, 2022, https://openai.com/index/chatgpt/.

35. Rebecca Bellan, "Sam Altman Says ChatGPT Has Hit 800M Weekly Active Users," *TechCrunch*, October 6, 2025, https://techcrunch.com/2025/10/06/sam-altman-says-chatgpt-has-hit-800m-weekly-active-users/.

36. Meta AI, "Introducing LLaMA: A Foundational, 65-Billion-Parameter Large Language Model," February 24, 2023, https://ai.meta.com/blog/large-language-model-llama-meta-ai/.

37. OpenAI, "GPT-4," March 14, 2023, https://openai.com/index/gpt-4-research/.

38. Yusef Mehdi, "Announcing Microsoft Copilot, Your Everyday AI Companion," *Microsoft Blog*, September 21, 2023, https://blogs.microsoft.com/blog/2023/09/21/announcing-microsoft-copilot-your-everyday-ai-companion/.

39. Jared Spataro, "Announcing Microsoft Copilot Studio: Customize Copilot for Microsoft 365 and Build Your Own Standalone Copilots," *Microsoft 365 Blog*, November 15, 2023, https://www.microsoft.com/en-us/microsoft-365/blog/2023/11/15/announcing-microsoft-copilot-studio-customize-copilot-for-microsoft-365-and-build-your-own-standalone-copilots/.

40. Sundar Pichai and Demis Hassabis, "Introducing Our Next-Generation Model: Gemini 1.5," *Google*, February 15, 2024, https://blog.google/innovation-and-ai/products/google-gemini-next-generation-model-february-2024/.

41. OpenAI, "Sora: Creating Video from Text," February 15, 2024, https://openai.com/index/sora/.

42. IBM, "Granite," n.d., accessed March 17, 2026, https://www.ibm.com/granite.

43. Apple "Introducing Apple Intelligence, The Personal Intelligence System That Puts Powerful Generative Models at the Core of iPhone, iPad, and Mac" *Apple Newsroom*, June 10, 2024, https://www.apple.com/newsroom/2024/06/introducing-apple-intelligence-for-iphone-ipad-and-mac/.

44. DeepSeek, "DeepSeek-R1 Release," *DeepSeek API Docs*, January 20, 2025, https://api-docs.deepseek.com/news/news250120.

45. OpenAI, "Introducing GPT-5," August 7, 2025, https://openai.com/index/introducing-gpt-5/.

46. Matt O'Brien, "Hyundai and Boston Dynamics Unveil Humanoid Robot Atlas at CES," *AP News*, January 5, 2026, https://apnews.com/article/ces-humanoid-robots-atlas-hyundai-boston-dynamics-8de7b2470c23f5f22441ad1ad7555136.

47. Microsoft, "Microsoft Propels Retail Forward with Agentic AI Capabilities That Power Intelligent Automation for Every Retail Function," *Microsoft News*, January 8, 2026, https://news.microsoft.com/source/2026/01/08/microsoft-propels-retail-forward-with-agentic-ai-capabilities-that-power-intelligent-automation-for-every-retail-function/.

48. Yoshua Bengio et al., "International AI Safety Report 2026," February 2026, 44, https://internationalaisafetyreport.org/sites/default/files/2026-02/international-ai-safety-report-2026_1.pdf.

49. Marc Zao-Sanders, "How People Are Really Using Gen AI in 2025," *Harvard Business Review*, April 9, 2025, https://hbr.org/2025/04/how-people-are-really-using-gen-ai-in-2025.

50. Microsoft AI Economy Institute, "Global AI Adoption in 2025, A Widening Digital Divide," January 2026, 5, https://www.microsoft.com/en-us/research/wp-content/uploads/2026/01/Microsoft-AI-Diffusion-Report-2025-H2.pdf.

51. Christof Ebert and Panos Louridas, "Generative AI for Software Practitioners," *IEEE Software* 40, no. 4 (July 2023): 30–38, https://www.researchgate.net/publication/372212988_Generative_AI_for_Software_Practitioners.

52. World Bank, "*Digital Progress and Trends Report 2025*," 2025, 15–16, https://www.worldbank.org/en/publication/dptr2025-ai-foundations.

53. Ibid., 14.

54. Nestor Maslej et al., "*Artificial Intelligence Index Report 2025*," AI Index Steering Committee, Stanford Institute for Human-Centered Artificial Intelligence, April 2025, 265, https://hai.stanford.edu/ai-index/2025-ai-index-report.

55. Ibid., 243.

56. World Bank, "*Digital Progress and Trends Report 2025*," 17.

57. Organisation for Economic Co-operation and Development (OECD), *Governing with Artificial Intelligence: The State of Play and Way Forward in Core Government Functions* (OECD Publishing, 2025), 85–87, 91, https://www.oecd.org/content/dam/oecd/en/publications/reports/2025/06/governing-with-artificial-intelligence_398fa287/795de142-en.pdf.

58. World Bank, "*Digital Progress and Trends Report 2025*," 81.

59. International Energy Agency, "*Energy and AI*," 24.

60. OECD, "*AI Adoption by Small and Medium-Sized Enterprises*," 2025, 10–11, https://www.oecd.org/content/dam/oecd/en/publications/reports/2025/12/ai-adoption-by-small-and-medium-sized-enterprises_9c48eae6/426399c1-en.pdf.

61. Microsoft AI Economy Institute, "Global AI Adoption in 2025, A Widening Digital Divide," January 2026, 3, https://www.microsoft.com/en-us/research/wp-content/uploads/2026/01/Microsoft-AI-Diffusion-Report-2025-H2.pdf.

62. World Bank, "*Digital Progress and Trends Report 2025*," 20–21.

63. Gillespie, Lockey, Ward, Macdade, and Hassed, "*Trust, Attitudes and Use of Artificial Intelligence*," 4, 80.

64. Sean McGregor, "Funding the AIID – Part I," *AI Incident Database Blog*, January 25, 2026, https://incidentdatabase.ai/blog/funding-the-aiid-part-1/.

65. Sha Sajadieh et al., "Artificial Intelligence Index Report 2026," AI Index Steering Committee, Stanford Institute for Human-Centered Artificial Intelligence, April 2026), 132, https://hai.stanford.edu/ai-index/2026-ai-index-report.

66. Gillespie, Lockey, Ward, Macdade, and Hassed, "*Trust, Attitudes and Use of Artificial Intelligence*," 22, 25, 29.

67. Ibid, 31–32.

68. Ibid, 41.

69. Ibid, 77.

70. Qualtrics XM Institute, Global Study: Global Consumer and Employee Attitudes Toward AI, November 2023, 20, https://www.qualtrics.com/m/www.xminstitute.com/wp-content/uploads/2023/11/XMI_RR_DS_GlobalConsumerEmployeeAttitudeTowardAI-1.pdf.

71. Sajadieh et al., "*Artificial Intelligence Index Report 2026*," 16–17.

72. International Energy Agency, "*Energy and AI*," 14.

73. UNESCO, "*Smarter, Smaller, Stronger: Resource-Efficient Generative AI & the Future of Digital Transformation*," 2025, 6–7, https://unesdoc.unesco.org/ark:/48223/pf0000394521.

74. Ibid., 6–7, 9–10.

75. Organisation for Economic Co-operation and Development (OECD), "*OECD Digital Economy Outlook 2024 (Volume 2): Strengthening Connectivity, Innovation and Trust*," 2024, 90, https://www.oecd.org/content/dam/oecd/en/publications/reports/2024/11/oecd-digital-economy-outlook-2024-volume-2_9b2801fc/3adf705b-en.pdf.

76. World Bank, "*Digital Progress and Trends Report 2025*," 20.

77. Gartner, "Top 10 Strategic Technology Trends for 2026," October 2025, https://www.gartner.com/en/articles/top-technology-trends-2026.
78. OECD, "*Explanatory Memorandum on the Updated OECD Definition of an AI System*," 2024, 4, https://www.oecd.org/content/dam/oecd/en/publications/reports/2024/03/explanatory-memorandum-on-the-updated-oecd-definition-of-an-ai-system_3c815e51/623da898-en.pdf.
79. OECD, "*AI Language Models: Technological, Socio-economic, and Policy Considerations*," 2023, 25, https://www.oecd.org/content/dam/oecd/en/publications/reports/2023/04/ai-language-models_46d9d9b4/13d38f92-en.pdf.
80. Cole Stryker, "What is agentic AI?," *IBM Think*, n.d., accessed March 23, 2026, https://www.ibm.com/think/topics/agentic-ai.
81. OECD, "Artificial Intelligence and Competitive Dynamics in Downstream Markets – Background Note," December 2025, 9, https://one.oecd.org/document/DAF/COMP/GF(2025)4/en/pdf.
82. Ibid.
83. Ibid.

Chapter 2: Global Public Policy and Regulation

1. Nestor Maslej et al., "*Artificial Intelligence Index Report 2025*," AI Index Steering Committee, Stanford Institute for Human-Centered Artificial Intelligence, April 2025, 337–338, https://hai.stanford.edu/assets/files/hai_ai_index_report_2025.pdf.
2. National Institute of Standards and Technology, "*Artificial Intelligence Risk Management Framework (AI RMF 1.0)*, NIST AI 100-1," U.S. Department of Commerce, January 2023, https://nvlpubs.nist.gov/nistpubs/ai/nist.ai.100-1.pdf.
3. National Institute of Standards and Technology, "*Artificial Intelligence Risk Management Framework: Generative Artificial Intelligence Profile*," NIST AI 600-1, U.S. Department of Commerce, July 2024, https://nvlpubs.nist.gov/nistpubs/ai/NIST.AI.600-1.pdf.
4. Public Services and Procurement Canada, "Supplier Diversity Action Plan," Government of Canada, last modified May 8, 2025, https://www.canada.ca/en/public-services-procurement/services/acquisitions/social-procurement/supplier-divsersity-action-plan.html.
5. Jefferey Saviano, "What Was the Obama Administration's Artificial Intelligence Legacy?" *Better Innovation,* podcast audio, April 16, 2018, https://podcasts.apple.com/us/podcast/what-was-the-obama-administrations-artificial/id1313870002?i=1000409006566.

6. Massachusetts Department of Revenue, "830 CMR 63.38M.1: Massachusetts Research Credit," October 2, 1998, https://www.mass.gov/regulations/830-CMR-6338m1-massachusetts-research-credit.
7. HM Revenue & Customs, "Use The Patent Box to Reduce Your Corporation Tax on Profits," GOV.UK, updated March 7, 2020, https://www.gov.uk/guidance/corporation-tax-the-patent-box.
8. Organisation for Economic Co-operation and Development, "AI Principles," accessed February 16, 2026, https://www.oecd.org/en/topics/ai-principles.html.
9. United Nations Educational, Scientific and Cultural Organization, "*Recommendation on the Ethics of Artificial Intelligence*," SHS/BIO/REC-AIETHICS/2021, November 23, 2021, https://unesdoc.unesco.org/ark:/48223/pf0000380455.
10. Council of Europe, "Recommendation CM/Rec(2020)1 of the Committee of Ministers to Member States on The Human Rights Impacts of Algorithmic Systems," adopted April 8, 2020, https://search.coe.int/cm?i=09000016809e1154.
11. Organisation for Economic Co-operation and Development, "Global Partnership on Artificial Intelligence," accessed February 16, 2026, https://www.oecd.org/en/about/programmes/global-partnership-on-artificial-intelligence.html.
12. World Health Organization, "*Ethics and Governance of Artificial Intelligence for Health: WHO Guidance*," 2021, https://iris.who.int/server/api/core/bitstreams/f780d926-4ae3-42ce-a6d6-e898a5562621/content.
13. International Organization of Securities Commissions, "The Use of Artificial Intelligence and Machine Learning by Market Intermediaries and Asset Managers," FR06/2021, September 2021, https://www.iosco.org/library/pubdocs/pdf/IOSCOPD684.pdf.
14. Ministry of Foreign Affairs of Japan, "*Hiroshima Process International Guiding Principles for Organizations Developing Advanced AI Systems*, 2023, https://www.mofa.go.jp/files/100573471.pdf; Group of Seven (G7), "G7 Leaders' Statement on the Hiroshima AI Process," October 30, 2023, https://www.mofa.go.jp/files/100573466.pdf.
15. International Organization for Standardization/International Electrotechnical Commission, "ISO/IEC JTC 1/SC 42: Artificial Intelligence," accessed February 16, 2026, https://www.iso.org/committee/6794475.html.
16. International Organization for Standardization/International Electrotechnical Commission, "*ISO/IEC 42001:2023 — Information Technology — Artificial Intelligence — Management System*," 2023, https://www.iso.org/standard/42001.

17. Institute of Electrical and Electronics Engineers, "*IEEE Standard 7000-2021: Model Process for Addressing Ethical Concerns During System Design*," September 15, 2021, https://standards.ieee.org/ieee/7000/6781/.

18. Association of Southeast Asian Nations (ASEAN), "*ASEAN Guide on AI Governance and Ethics*," February 2024, https://www.asean.org/wp-content/uploads/2024/02/ASEAN-Guide-on-AI-Governance-and-Ethics_beautified_201223_v2.pdf.

19. Association of Southeast Asian Nations (ASEAN), "*Expanded ASEAN Guide on AI Governance and Ethics – Generative AI*," 2025, https://asean.org/wp-content/uploads/2025/01/Expanded-ASEAN-Guide-on-AI-Governance-and-Ethics-Generative-AI.pdf.

20. United Nations General Assembly, "Resolution A/RES/78/265: Seizing the Opportunities of Safe, Secure and Trustworthy Artificial Intelligence Systems for Sustainable Development," adopted March 21, 2024, 6, https://docs.un.org/en/A/res/78/265.

21. African Union, "Continental Artificial Intelligence Strategy," July 2024, https://au.int/sites/default/files/documents/44004-doc-EN-_Continental_AI_Strategy_July_2024.pdf.

22. Council of Europe, "Framework Convention on Artificial Intelligence, Human Rights, Democracy and the Rule of Law," CETS No. 225, adopted September 5, 2024, https://rm.coe.int/1680afae3c.

23. Council of Europe, "Signatures and Ratifications of the Framework Convention on AI," The Framework Convention on Artificial Intelligence, Council of Europe, accessed March 24, 2026, https://www.coe.int/en/web/artificial-intelligence/the-framework-convention-on-artificial-intelligence#implementation.

24. European Commission High-Level Expert Group on Artificial Intelligence, "*Ethics Guidelines for Trustworthy AI*," 2019, https://digital-strategy.ec.europa.eu/en/library/ethics-guidelines-trustworthy-ai.

25. Pope Leo XIV, *Magnifica Humanitas*, encyclical letter, May 15, 2026, §5 and §9, https://www.vatican.va/content/leo-xiv/en/encyclicals/documents/20260515-magnifica-humanitas.html.

26. Civil Rights Act of 1964, Pub. L. No. 88-352, Title II, § 201(a), 78 Stat. 241; Title VII, § 703(a), 78 Stat. 241.

27. Fair Housing Act, Pub. L. No. 90-284, Title VIII, 82 Stat. 81 (1968).

28. *Mobley v. Workday, Inc.*, No. 3:23-cv-00770-RFL, N.D. Cal., filed February 16, 2023; U.S. Equal Employment Opportunity Commission, "Select Issues: Assessing Adverse Impact in Software, Algorithms, and Artificial Intelligence Used in Employment Selection Procedures Under Title VII of the Civil Rights

Act of 1964," May 18, 2023, https://data.aclum.org/storage/2025/01/EOCC_www_eeoc_gov_laws_guidance_select-issues-assessing-adverse-impact-software-algorithms-and-artificial.pdf.

29. Donald J. Trump, "Maintaining American Leadership in Artificial Intelligence," February 14, 2019, https://www.federalregister.gov/documents/2019/02/14/2019-02544/maintaining-american-leadership-in-artificial-intelligence.

30. Joseph R. Biden Jr., "Safe, Secure, and Trustworthy Development and Use of Artificial Intelligence," November 1, 2023, https://www.federalregister.gov/documents/2023/11/01/2023-24283/safe-secure-and-trustworthy-development-and-use-of-artificial-intelligence.

31. National Institute of Standards and Technology, Artificial Intelligence Risk Management Framework (AI RMF 1.0)," NIST AI 100-1, U.S. Department of Commerce, January 2023, https://nvlpubs.nist.gov/nistpubs/ai/NIST.AI.100-1.pdf.

32. U.S. Department of Commerce, "At the Direction of President Biden, Department of Commerce to Establish U.S. Artificial Intelligence Safety Institute to Lead Efforts on AI Safety," November 1, 2023, https://www.commerce.gov/news/press-releases/2023/11/direction-president-biden-department-commerce-establish-us-artificial.

33. Donald J. Trump, "Removing Barriers to American Leadership in Artificial Intelligence," January 23, 2025, https://www.federalregister.gov/documents/2025/01/31/2025-02172/removing-barriers-to-american-leadership-in-artificial-intelligence.

34. Office of the President of the United States, "Winning the AI Race: America's AI Action Plan," July 23, 2025, https://www.whitehouse.gov/wp-content/uploads/2025/07/Americas-AI-Action-Plan.pdf.

35. Donald J. Trump, "Ensuring a National Policy Framework for Artificial Intelligence," December 11, 2025, https://www.govinfo.gov/app/details/DCPD-202501186.

36. The White House, "Legislative Recommendations: A National Policy Framework for Artificial Intelligence," March 2026, https://www.whitehouse.gov/wp-content/uploads/2026/03/03.20.26-National-Policy-Framework-for-Artificial-Intelligence-Legislative-Recommendations.pdf.

37. Donald J. Trump, "Promoting Advanced Artificial Intelligence Innovation and Security," June 2, 2026, https://www.whitehouse.gov/presidential-actions/2026/06/promoting-advanced-artificial-intelligence-innovation-and-security/.

38. Maggie Eastland, Oma Seddiq and Courtney Subramanian, "Trump Set to Sign AI Cybersecurity Executive Order," Government Technology, May 21, 2026, https://www.govtech.com/artificial-intelligence/trump-set-to-sign-ai-cybersecurity-executive-order; Collin Binkley and Matt O'Brien, "Trump Calls Off AI Executive Order over Concern It Could Weaken US Tech Edge," *AP News*, May 21, 2026, https://apnews.com/article/trump-ai-executive-order-ee318f35acc8a2c43e47f3ebf26cb459.

39. Federal Food, Drug, and Cosmetic Act, 21 U.S.C. §§ 301–399i, https://www.law.cornell.edu/uscode/text/21/chapter-9.

40. Sha Sajadjeh et al., "*Artificial Intelligence Index Report 2026*," AI Index Steering Committee, Stanford Institute for Human-Centered Artificial Intelligence, April 2026, 344, https://hai.stanford.edu/ai-index/2026-ai-index-report.

41. Colorado General Assembly, "Consumer Protections for Artificial Intelligence," SB 24-205, enacted May 17, 2024, codified at Colorado Revised Statutes §§ 6-1-1701 et seq., https://leg.colorado.gov/bills/sb24-205.

42. California Consumer Privacy Act of 2018, Cal. Civ. Code §§ 1798.100–1798.199.100, https://leginfo.legislature.ca.gov/faces/codes_displayText.xhtml?division=3.&part=4.&lawCode=CIV&title=1.81.5.

43. California Privacy Rights Act, Cal. Civ. Code §§ 1798.100–1798.199.100, https://thecpra.org/.

44. California Legislature, "Transparency in Frontier Artificial Intelligence Act (SB 53)," 2025 Cal. Stat. ch. 138.

45. New York City Council, Local Law No. 144, "Automated Employment Decision Tools," codified in N.Y.C. Admin. Code §§ 20-870–20-874 (2021).

46. Utah Artificial Intelligence Policy Act (SB 149), Utah Code Ann. §§ 13-72-101–13-72-404 (2024).

47. Illinois Biometric Information Privacy Act, 740 Ill. Comp. Stat. 14/1 et seq. (2008).

48. European Union, "Regulation (EU) 2024/1689 of the European Parliament and of the Council of 13 June 2024 Laying Down Harmonised Rules on Artificial Intelligence and Amending Regulations (EC) No 300/2008, (EU) No 167/2013, (EU) No 168/2013, (EU) 2018/858, (EU) 2018/1139 and (EU) 2019/2144 and Directives 2014/90/EU, (EU) 2016/797 and (EU) 2020/1828 (Artificial Intelligence Act)," OJ L 206, July 12, 2024, 1–144, http://data.europa.eu/eli/reg/2024/1689/oj.

49. European Commission, "Proposal for a Regulation of the European Parliament and of the Council Amending Regulations (EU) 2024/1689 and (EU) 2018/1139 as Regards the Simplification of the Implementation of Harmonised Rules on Artificial Intelligence (Digital Omnibus on AI)," COM(2025) 836 final, November 19, 2025, https://eur-lex.europa.eu/legal-content/EN/TXT/?uri=CELEX:52025PC0836.

50. EU Agrees to Simplify AI Rules to Boost Innovation and Ban "Nudification" Apps to Protect Citizens, European Commission, May 6, 2026, https://ec.europa.eu/commission/presscorner/detail/en/ip_26_1024.

51. Mario Draghi, "*The Future of European Competitiveness*," 2024, https://commission.europa.eu/document/download/97e481fd-2dc3-412d-be4c-f152a8232961_en?filename=The%20future%20of%20European%20competitiveness%20_%20A%20competitiveness%20strategy%20for%20Europe.pdf.

52. European Commission, "*Competitiveness Compass for the EU*," 2024, https://commission.europa.eu/document/download/10017eb1-4722-4333-add2-e0ed18105a34_en?filename=Communication_1.pdf.

53. European Commission, "EU Launches InvestAI Initiative to Mobilise €200 Billion of Investment in Artificial Intelligence," press release, February 11, 2025, *Shaping Europe's Digital Future*, https://digital-strategy.ec.europa.eu/en/news/eu-launches-investai-initiative-mobilise-eu200-billion-investment-artificial-intelligence.

54. European Commission, "AI Pact," *Shaping Europe's Digital Future*, last modified February 26, 2026, https://digital-strategy.ec.europa.eu/en/policies/ai-pact.

55. Graham Webster, Rogier Creemers, Elsa Kania, and Paul Triolo, "Full Translation: China's 'New Generation Artificial Intelligence Development Plan (2017).'" *DigiChina*, Stanford Cyber Policy Center, August 1, 2017. https://digichina.stanford.edu/work/full-translation-chinas-new-generation-artificial-intelligence-development-plan-2017/.

56. Tracy Qu, "China's DeepSeek Unveils New AI Model That Could Halve Usage Cost," *The Wall Street Journal*, September 30, 2025, https://www.wsj.com/tech/ai/chinas-deepseek-unveils-new-ai-model-that-could-halve-usage-cost-785facc2?mod=Searchresults&pos=4&page=1.

57. China Aerospace Studies Institute, trans. Josh Baughman, "Interim Measures for the Management of Generative Artificial Intelligence Services," Cyberspace Administration of China et al. July 13, 2023, effective August 15, 2023, translation dated August 7, 2023, https://www.airuniversity.af.edu/Portals/10/CASI/documents/Translations/2023-08-07%20ITOW%20Interim%20Measures%20for%20the%20Management%20of%20Generative%20Artificial%20Intelligence%20Services.pdf.

58. Rogier Creemers and Graham Webster, "Translation: Personal Information Protection Law of the People's Republic of China – Effective Nov. 1, 2021," *DigiChina*, Stanford Cyber Policy Center, September 7, 2021, https://digichina.stanford.edu/work/translation-personal-information-protection-law-of-the-peoples-republic-of-china-effective-nov-1-2021/.

59. United Kingdom, Department for Science, Innovation and Technology, "A Pro-Innovation Approach to AI Regulation," 2023, https://www.gov.uk/government/publications/ai-regulation-a-pro-innovation-approach/white-paper.

60. United Kingdom, Department for Science, Innovation and Technology, "AI Opportunities Action Plan," January 13, 2025, https://www.gov.uk/government/publications/ai-opportunities-action-plan/ai-opportunities-action-plan.

61. United Kingdom, Government Digital Service, "Artificial Intelligence Playbook for the UK Government," February 10, 2025, https://www.gov.uk/government/publications/ai-playbook-for-the-uk-government.

62. Japan, Cabinet Office, AI Strategic Council and AI Institutional Study Group, "Interim Report," February 4, 2025, https://www8.cao.go.jp/cstp/ai/interim_report_en.pdf.

63. Government of Japan, "Artificial Intelligence Basic Plan — 'Japan Rebooted' Through 'Trustworthy AI,'" December 23, 2025, https://www8.cao.go.jp/cstp/ai/ai_plan/aiplan_eng_20260312.pdf.

64. Government of India, Press Information Bureau, "India's Digital Public Infrastructure: Setting a Global Benchmark for Population-Scale DPI," March 6, 2026, https://www.pib.gov.in/PressReleasePage.aspx?PRID=2235812&reg=3&lang=1.

65. NITI Aayog, "*Responsible AI for All: Strategy for India*, Government of India, February 2021, 7, https://www.niti.gov.in/sites/default/files/2021-02/Responsible-AI-22022021.pdf.

Chapter 3: Strategic Deployment

1. "How Adobe Design Is Shaping the Firefly Generative AI Experience. A Look at the Design Thinking and Strategy Behind the New Technology," *Adobe Design*, March 22, 2023, https://adobe.design/stories/leading-design/how-adobe-design-is-shaping-the-firefly-gen-ai-experience.

2. Shantanu Narayen, "Adobe's CEO on Making Big Bets on Innovation," *Harvard Business Review*, November–December 2023, https://hbr.org/2023/11/adobes-ceo-on-making-big-bets-on-innovation.

3. Nestor Maslej et al., "*Artificial Intelligence Index Report 2025*," Stanford Institute for Human-Centered Artificial Intelligence, April 2025, 247, https://hai.stanford.edu/ai-index/2025-ai-index-report.
4. QuantumBlack, AI by McKinsey, "The State of AI in 2025: Agents, Innovation, and Transformation," November 10, 2025, https://www.mckinsey.com/capabilities/quantumblack/our-insights/the-state-of-ai#/.
5. Alex Tamkin and Peter McCrory, "Estimating AI Productivity Gains from Claude Conversations," *Anthropic*, November 5, 2025, https://www-cdn.anthropic.com/e5645986a7ce8fbcc48fa6d2fc67753c87642c30.pdf.
6. QuantumBlack. AI by McKinsey, "The State of AI in 2025," 8.
7. Aditya Challapally et al., "The GenAI Divide. State of AI in Business 2025," MIT NANDA, July 2025, 2, https://mlq.ai/media/quarterly_decks/v0.1_State_of_AI_in_Business_2025_Report.pdf.
8. QuantumBlack. AI by McKinsey, "The State of AI in 2025," 10–11.
9. "Get AI Ready: What IT Leaders Need to Know and Do," Gartner, accessed February 24, 2026, https://www.gartner.com/en/information-technology/topics/ai-readiness. GARTNER is a trademark of Gartner, Inc. and/or its affiliates.
10. Ivarov I. Bojinov et al., "JPMorgan Chase: Leadership in the Age of GenAI," Harvard Business School Case 325-066, April 3–4, 2025, https://www.hbs.edu/faculty/Pages/item.aspx?num=67230.
11. "Evident AI Index. 2025 Edition," Evident Insights, accessed February 17, 2026, https://evidentinsights.com/ai-index/?utm_source=hubspot&utm_medium=brief&utm_campaign=v42.
12. "Open Box in Case of an Idea," Kickbox Foundation, accessed February 26, 2026, https://kickbox.org/.
13. David Burkus, "Inside Adobe's Innovation Kit," *Harvard Business Review*, February 23, 2015, https://hbr.org/2015/02/inside-adobes-innovation-kit.
14. "Fending Off 'Pilotitis' in Global Tech," Digital Impact Alliance, May 23, 2016, https://dial.global/fending-off-pilotitis-in-global-tech/; "Practical Insights on Pilotitis," ICTworks, accessed April 20, 2026, https://www.ictworks.org/tag/pilotitis/#:~:text=Pilotitis%20in%20the%20context%20of,impact%20due%20to%20various%20constraints.
15. Microsoft and LinkedIn, "2024 Work Trend Index Annual Report: AI at Work Is Here. Now Comes the Hard Part," *Microsoft WorkLab*, May 8, 2024, https://www.microsoft.com/en-us/worklab/work-trend-index/ai-at-work-is-here-now-comes-the-hard-part.

16. QuantumBlack.AI by McKinsey, "The State of AI in 2025," 17.
17. Konstantinos Trantopoulos et al., "Will Your Gen AI Strategy Shape Your Future or Derail It?" *Harvard Business Review*, July 25, 2025, https://hbr.org/2025/07/will-your-gen-ai-strategy-shape-your-future-or-derail-it.
18. Loran Nordgren and David Schonthal, *The Human Element: Overcoming the Resistance That Awaits New Ideas* (Wiley, 2022), 34.
19. Rita McGrath, *Seeing Around Corners: How to Spot Inflection Points in Business Before They Happen – The First Hands-On Guide to Strategic Advantage and Market Leadership* (Mariner Books, 2021), 38.
20. Xinyang Sun, "Two Decades and More: Evolution of Netflix's Business Models and Outlook of Future," *SHS Web of Conferences* 148, 03032 (2022), 2–5, https://doi.org/10.1051/shsconf/202214803032.

Chapter 4: Risk Exposure

1. "Targeted Compliance Framework Assurance Review – Final Report," Australian Government, Department of Employment and Workplace Relations, accessed February 21, 2026, https://www.dewr.gov.au/assuring-integrity-targeted-compliance-framework/resources/targeted-compliance-framework-assurance-review-final-report.
2. Krishani Dhanji, "Deloitte to Pay Money Back to Albanese Government After Using AI in $440,000 Report," *The Guardian*, October 6, 2025, https://www.theguardian.com/australia-news/2025/oct/06/deloitte-to-pay-money-back-to-albanese-government-after-using-ai-in-440000-report.
3. "AIM: AI Incidents and Hazards Monitor," OECD AI Policy Observatory, accessed March 20, 2026, https://oecd.ai/en/incidents.
4. ACA, "2025 AI Benchmarking Report. Survey Results," 2025, 9, https://web.acaglobal.com/hubfs/2025%20AI%20Benchmarking%20Survey/ACA%20Group_AI%20Benchmarking%20Report.pdf; NSCP, ACA, "2024 AI Benchmarking Survey. Full Report of Findings," 2024, 39, https://web.acaglobal.com/hubfs/Survey%20Results/NSCP%20-%20ACA%202024%20AI%20Benchmarking%20Survey.pdf.
5. QuantumBlack.AI by McKinsey, "The State of AI in 2025: Agents, Innovation, and Transformation," November 2025, 26, https://www.mckinsey.com/capabilities/quantumblack/our-insights/the-state-of-ai#/.

6. National Institute of Standards and Technology, "Artificial Intelligence Risk Management Framework (AI RMF 1.0)," January 2023, 4–5, https://nvlpubs.nist.gov/nistpubs/ai/NIST.AI.100-1.pdf.
7. Spencer Stuart, "2025 U.S. Spencer Stuart Board Index," 2025, 20, https://www.spencerstuart.com/-/media/2025/10/ssbi2025/2025-us-board-index.pdf.
8. National Institute of Standards and Technology (NIST), "Artificial Intelligence Risk Management Framework (AI RMF 1.0)," January 2023, 38, https://nvlpubs.nist.gov/nistpubs/ai/NIST.AI.100-1.pdf.
9. Simon Mylius et al., "Mapping the AI Governance Landscape. Pilot Test and Update," MIT AI Risk Initiative, October 2025, 2, https://cdn.prod.website-files.com/669550d38372f33552d2516e/68eec3108ecc30bf1c98cc1d_e337afdab4fcdee6dbaa48dcd136e221_Mapping%20the%20AI%20Governance%20Landscape.pdf.
10. National Institute of Standards and Technology (NIST), "Artificial Intelligence Risk Management Framework (AI RMF 1.0)," 25.
11. "Incident 1179: McDonald's McHire AI Recruitment Platform Reportedly Exposed Date of 64 Million Applicants via Default Login and API Vulnerability," AI Incident Database, accessed February 21, 2026, https://incidentdatabase.ai/cite/1179.
12. Ian Carroll and Sam Curry, "Would You Like an IDOR with That? Leaking 64 Million McDonald's Job Applications," accessed February 21, 2026, https://ian.sh/mcdonalds.
13. Andy Greennberg, "McDonald's AI Hiring Bot Exposed Millions of Applicants' Data to Hackers Who Tried the Password '123456,'" *Wired*, July 9, 2025, https://www.wired.com/story/mcdonalds-ai-hiring-chat-bot-paradoxai/.
14. "AIM: AI Incidents and Hazards Monitor," OECD.AI Policy Observatory, accessed February 21, 2026, https://oecd.ai/en/incidents/2025-10-05-be45.
15. Carroll and Curry, "Would You Like an IDOR with That?"
16. National Institute of Standards and Technology (NIST), "Artificial Intelligence Risk Management Framework," 3.
17. Yoshua Bengio et al., "International AI Safety Report 2026," February 2026, 71, https://internationalaisafetyreport.org/sites/default/files/2026-02/international-ai-safety-report-2026_0.pdf.
18. SailPoint, "AI Agents: The New Attack Surface. A Global Survey of Security and IT Professionals and Executives," 2025, 7, https://docs.sailpoint.com/pdf/en/special-report/SailPoint-The-Rising-Risk-of-AI-Agents-Expanding-the-Attack-Surface-report-SP2648%20.pdf.
19. Bengio et al., "International AI Safety Report 2026," 45.

20. Anthropic, "Threat Intelligence Report: August 2025," August 2025, 4, https://www-cdn.anthropic.com/b2a76c6f6992465c09a6f2fce282f6c0cea8c200.pdf.

Chapter 5: Fiduciary Oversight

1. JPMorgan Chase & Co., "Investor Day 2024. Asset & Wealth Management," 2024, 14, https://www.jpmorganchase.com/content/dam/jpmc/jpmorgan-chase-and-co/investor-relations/documents/events/2024/jpmc-2024-investor-day/asset-wealth-management.pdf.
2. JPMorgan Chase & Co., "Resolute Annual Report 2024," 2025, 160, https://www.jpmorganchase.com/content/dam/jpmc/jpmorgan-chase-and-co/investor-relations/documents/annualreport-2024.pdf.
3. Stanford Graduate School of Business, "Leading in a Time of Change: Jamie Dimon, Chairman and CEO, JP Morgan Chase," *YouTube* video, 56:08, March 7, 2025, https://www.youtube.com/watch?v=PdzMvk66wao, at 27:39.
4. JPMorgan Chase & Co., "Resolute Annual Report 2024," 160.
5. "Evident AI Index. 2025 Edition," Evident Insights, accessed February 17, 2026, https://evidentinsights.com/ai-index/?utm_source=hubspot&utm_medium=brief&utm_campaign=v42.
6. JPMorgan Chase & Co., "Investor Day 2024: Asset & Wealth Management, 14, 2024, https://www.jpmorganchase.com/content/dam/jpmc/jpmorgan-chase-and-co/investor-relations/documents/events/2024/jpmc-2024-investor-day/asset-wealth-management.pdf.
7. JPMorgan Chase & Co., Annual Report on Form 10-K for the Fiscal Year Ended December 31, 2025, filed February 13, 2026, Part I, Item 1A, pp. 20–27, U.S. Securities and Exchange Commission, https://www.sec.gov/Archives/edgar/data/19617/000162828026008131/jpm-20251231.htm.
8. Ivarov I. Bojinov et al., "JPMorgan Chase: Leadership in the Age of GenAI," Harvard Business School Case 325-066, April 2025, 4, https://www.hbs.edu/faculty/Pages/item.aspx?num=67230.
9. *In re Caremark International Inc. Derivative Litigation*, 698 A.2d 959, 970–971 (Del. Ch. 1996).
10. Ibid., 971.
11. Ibid.
12. Ibid.
13. *Stone v. Ritter*, 911 A.2d 362, 370 (Del. 2006).
14. *Marchand v. Barnhill*, 212 A.3d 805, 822, 824 (Del. 2019).
15. *In re Clovis Oncology, Inc.*, CONSOLIDATED C.A. No. 2017-0222-JRS, 44 (Del. Ch. Oct. 1, 2019).

16. *In re The Boeing Co. Derivative Litig.*, C.A. 2019-0907-MTZ, 91 (Del. Ch. Sep. 7, 2021).
17. Ibid., 74–89.
18. Ibid., 94–96.
19. *In re McDonald's Corp. Stockholder Derivative Litig.*, 289 A.3d 343, 358 (Del. Ch. 2023).
20. Ibid., 378–379.
21. *Constr. Indus. Laborers Pension Fund v. Bingle*, C. A. 2021-0940-SG, 20-21 (Del. Ch. Sep. 6, 2022).
22. Elizabeth Gaydou, "Seven People Die After Taking Cyanide-Laced Tylenol," *EBSCO Knowledge Advantage*, 2023, https://www.ebsco.com/research-starters/history/seven-people-die-after-taking-cyanide-laced-tylenol.
23. Johnson & Johnson, "Notice of Annual Meeting & Proxy Statement," March 12, 2025, 26, 36, https://www.sec.gov/Archives/edgar/data/200406/000020040625000099/jnj-20250311.htm.
24. *In re The Boeing Co. Derivative Litig.*, C. A. 2019-0907-MTZ, 77 (Del. Ch. Sep. 7, 2021); *Hughes ex rel. Kandi Tech. Grp. v. Xiaoming Hu*, C.A. No. 2019-0112-JTL, 42–45 (Del. Ch. Apr. 27, 2020).

Chapter 6: Introducing the Boundaries of Tolerance Model

1. Lindsey Stewart, "Investor Views on AI Oversight: What Do Proxy Votes Tell Us?," *Harvard Law School Forum on Corporate Governance*, May 30, 2025, https://corpgov.law.harvard.edu/2025/05/30/investor-views-on-ai-oversight-what-do-proxy-votes-tell-us/.
2. "Incident 608: UnitedHealth Accused of Deploying Allegedly Flawed AI to Deny Medical Coverage," AI Incident Database, accessed February 10, 2026, https://incidentdatabase.ai/cite/608/.
3. *Estate of Gene B. Lokken, The et al v. UnitedHealth Group, Inc. et al*, Docket Information, Bloomberg Law, accessed March 21, 2026, https://www.bloomberglaw.com/public/desktop/document/EstateofGeneBLokkenTheetalvUnitedHealthGroupIncetalDocketNo023cv0?doc_id=X1Q6OKVPB982.
4. *The Estate of Gene B. Lokken, et al. v. UnitedHealth Group, Inc.*, UnitedHealthcare, Inc., and naviHealth, Inc., No. 0:23-cv-03514 (D. Minn. Nov. 14, 2023) (complaint), para. 3.

5. "Incident 267: Clearview AI Algorithm Built on Photos Scraped from Social Media Profiles Without Consent," AI Incident Database, accessed February 10, 2026, https://incidentdatabase.ai/cite/267/.

6. "Facial Recognition: Italian SA Fines Clearview AI Eur 20 Million Bans Use of Biometric Data and Monitoring of Italian Data Subjects," Grante Per La Protezione Dei Dati Personali, accessed February 10, 2026, https://www.garanteprivacy.it/web/guest/home/docweb/-/docweb-display/docweb/9751323#english; "French Regulator Fines US Face Recognition Firm Clearview AI €20 Million," *Le Monde*, accessed February 10, 2026, https://www.lemonde.fr/en/pixels/article/2022/10/20/french-regulator-fines-us-face-recognition-firm-clearview-ai-20-million_6001116_13.html.

7. Ella Fincken, "Clearview AI USD 51.75 Million Class Action Settlement Approved," *ICLG*, March 24, 2025, https://iclg.com/news/22418-clearview-ai-usd-51-75-million-class-action-settlement-approved.

8. "Facial Recognition: Italian SA Fines Clearview AI Eur 20 Million Bans Use of Biometric Data and Monitoring of Italian Data Subjects."

9. "Case Number: 1:24-bk-11007 - Joonko Diversity Inc. - Delaware Bankruptcy Court," inforuptcy, accessed March 21, 2026, https://www.inforuptcy.com/browse-filings/delaware-bankruptcy-court/1%3A24-bk-11007/bankruptcy-case-joonko-diversity-inc.

10. "SEC Charges Founder of AI Hiring Startup Joonko with Fraud," U.S. Securities and Exchange Commission, accessed February 10, 2026, https://www.sec.gov/newsroom/press-releases/2024-70.

11. Jeffrey Saviano, host, *Better Innovation*, season 7, episode 10, "Demystifying AI Ethics with Reid Blackman," Apple Podcasts, July 22, 2024, 1 hour 23 min., https://podcasts.apple.com/us/podcast/demystifying-ai-ethics-with-reid-blackman/id1313870002?i=1000663020952.

12. Barton Edgerton and Cigdem Oktem. "Four Ways Boards Can Support the Effective Use of AI," EY, April 24, 2024, https://www.ey.com/en_us/board-matters/four-ways-boards-can-support-the-effective-use-of-ai; Jeffrey Saviano, "Politicians and Nonprofits Will Struggle to Keep AI in Check – But Corporate Boards Can't Afford to Fail," *Fortune*, May 8, 2024, accessed February 10, 2026, https://fortune.com/2024/05/08/ai-corporate-boards-ethics-tech-leadership/.

13. "Six Approaches to Making Ethical Decisions in Cases of Uncertainty and Risk," Markkula Center for Applied Ethics, Santa Clara University, accessed February

10, 2026. https://www.scu.edu/ethics/focus-areas/technology-ethics/resources/six-approaches-to-making-ethical-decisions-in-cases-of-uncertainty-and-risk/.

14. David B. Yoffie and Mary Kwak, "Playing by the Rules: How Intel Avoids AntitrustLitigation," *Harvard Business Review*, June 2001, 119–122.

Chapter 7: Enterprise Factors

1. U.S. Environmental Protection Agency, "Notice of Violation to Volkswagen Regarding Clean Air Act Violations," September 18, 2015, accessed February 28, 2026, https://www.epa.gov/sites/default/files/2015-10/documents/vw-nov-caa-09-18-15.pdf.
2. "EPA, California Notify Volkswagen of Clean Air Act Violations," California Air Resources Board, September 18, 2015, https://ww2.arb.ca.gov/news/epa-california-notify-volkswagen-clean-air-act-violations.
3. Andreas Cremer, "Volkswagen Says 11 MLN Cars Hit by Scandal, Probes Multiply," Reuters, September 23, 2015, https://www.reuters.com/article/markets/commodities/volkswagen-says-11-mln-cars-hit-by-scandal-probes-multiply-idUSL5N11S052/.
4. "Learn About Volkswagen Violations," Environmental Protection Agency, accessed February 28, 2026, https://www.epa.gov/vw/learn-about-volkswagen-violations.
5. *United States v. Volkswagen AG*, Rule 11 Plea Agreement, No. 16-CR-20394 (E.D. Mich. Jan. 11, 2017), U.S. Department of Justice, 12–13, https://www.justice.gov/archives/opa/press-release/file/924436/dl?inline.
6. Edward Taylor, "Volkswagen Says Diesel Scandal Has Cost It 31.3 Billion Euros," Reuters, March 17, 2020, https://www.reuters.com/article/business/volkswagen-says-diesel-scandal-has-cost-it-313-billion-euros-idUSKBN2141JA/.
7. "Volkswagen Senior Manager Sentenced to 84 Months in Prison for Role in Conspiracy to Cheat U.S. Emissions Tests," Archives, U.S. Department of Justice, December 6, 2017, https://www.justice.gov/archives/opa/pr/volkswagen-senior-manager-sentenced-84-months-prison-role-conspiracy-cheat-us-emissions-tests; "Former CEO of Volkswagen AG Charged with Conspiracy and Wire Fraud in Diesel Emissions Scandal," Archives, U.S. Department of Justice, May 3, 2018, https://www.justice.gov/archives/opa/pr/former-ceo-volkswagen-ag-charged-conspiracy-and-wire-fraud-diesel-emissions-scandal; "Four Former Volkswagen Managers Convicted of Fraud in 'Dieselgate' Trial," *The Guardian*, May 26, 2025, https://www.

theguardian.com/business/2025/may/26/germany-former-volkswagen-managers-convicted-fraud-dieselgate.

8. "Statement by Prof. Dr. Winterkorn," VW US Media Site, September 23, 2015, https://media.vw.com/releases/575.

9. "Factbox: Response from National Regulators on Volkswagen Emissions Tests," Reuters, September 22, 2015, https://www.reuters.com/article/business/factbox-response-from-national-regulators-on-volkswagen-emissions-tests-idUSKCN0RM1V3/.

10. "Dieselgate," European Commission, accessed March 1, 2026, https://commission.europa.eu/live-work-travel-eu/consumer-rights-and-complaints/enforcement-consumer-protection/coordinated-actions/dieselgate_en.

11. "EPA, California Notify Volkswagen of Clean Air Act Violations," *California Air Resources Board.*

12. "Volkswagen Group Is Officially Reinstated as a Participant of the UN Global Compact," Volkswagen Group, February 25, 2021, https://www.volkswagen-group.com/en/press-releases/volkswagen-group-is-officially-reinstated-as-a-participant-of-the-un-global-compact-16743.html.

13. Unilever, "Unilever Sustainable Living Plan," 2010, 5, 19, https://www.unilever.com/files/origin/9752ff2d82b8afabb507eb92c47b5dad795801d5.pdf/unilever-sustainable-living-plan.pdf.

14. Unilever, "Unilever Sustainable Living Plan," Progress Report 2012, 44–45, https://www.unilever.com/files/origin/c9eee4b1879b6af98a4b7464d8f2d0b14e201a59.pdf/uslp-progress-report-2012-fi.pdf.

15. Unilever, "Annual Report and Accounts 2014," Strategic Report, 1, https://www.unilever.com/files/origin/39bbabc7955fe755dac8f5b0d4cbe674a2fcc340.pdf/ir_Strategic_Report_AR14.pdf.

16. Unilever, "Unilever Sustainable Living Plan 2010 to 2020: Summary of 10 Years' Progress," March 2021, 4, 24, https://www.unilever.com/files/92ui5egz/production/16cb778e4d31b81509dc5937001559f1f5c863ab.pdf.

17. University of Cambridge Institute for Sustainability Leadership (CISL), "Unilever: Aligning Purpose and Strategy with Net Zero," 2020, p. 1, https://www.cisl.cam.ac.uk/sites/default/files/unilever.pdf; Unilever, "Unilever Annual Report and Accounts 2020," *Purpose-led, future-fit*, 6-7, https://www.unilever.com/files/196bb9f6-5fbf-4424-ab92-949db305ba4f/annual-report-and-accounts-2020.pdf.

18. Unilever, "Unilever Annual Report and Accounts 2018," *Making Sustainable Living Commonplace*, 1, https://www.unilever.com/files/origin/9fbb2cb4402c390d78734e74baa53603223abd8c.pdf/Unilever-Annual-Report-and-Accounts-2018.pdf.

19. Paul Millerd, "Edgar Schein's Anxiety & Assumptions: Powerful Ideas on Culture," November 1, 2019, https://pmillerd.com/edgar-scheins-anxiety-assumptions-powerful-ideas-on-culture/.

20. Harvard Business Review Editorial Staff, "Our Favorite Management Tips on Building Trust on Your Team," *Harvard Business Review*, February 25, 2026, https://hbr.org/2026/02/our-favorite-management-tips-on-building-trust-on-your-team.

21. Michael D. Watkins, "What Is Organizational Culture? And Why Should We Care?" *Harvard Business Review*, May 15, 2013, https://hbr.org/2013/05/what-is-organizational-culture.

22. Amy Gallo, "What Is Psychological Safety?" *Harvard Business Review*, February 15, 2023, https://hbr.org/2023/02/what-is-psychological-safety.

23. Microsoft, "2025 Responsible AI Transparency Report. How We Build, Support Our Customers, and Grow," 7–8, 12–13, https://cdn-dynmedia-1.microsoft.com/is/content/microsoftcorp/microsoft/msc/documents/presentations/CSR/Responsible-AI-Transparency-Report-2025.pdf.

24. Microsoft, "Microsoft Responsible AI Standard, v2. General Requirements," June 2022, 4, 7–8, 11, https://msblogs.thesourcemediaassets.com/sites/5/2022/06/Microsoft-Responsible-AI-Standard-v2-General-Requirements-3.pdf.

25. Nick Lichtenberg, "Satya Nadella on the 'Enigma of Success' in the Age of AI: A Thriving Business, But 15,000+ Layoffs," *Fortune*, July 24, 2025, https://fortune.com/2025/07/24/satya-nadella-memo-microsoft-layoffs-enigma-of-success-artificial-intelligence/.

26. Satya Nadella, "AI Is the Defining Technology of Our Time," LinkedIn, accessed March 1, 2026, https://www.linkedin.com/posts/satyanadella_ai-is-the-defining-technology-of-our-time-activity-7369432203736305666-Nf9O/.

27. Brad Smith, "How Do We Best Govern AI?" *Microsoft on the Issues*, May 25, 2023, https://blogs.microsoft.com/on-the-issues/2023/05/25/how-do-we-best-govern-ai/.

28. Jeffrey Dastin, "Insight: Amazon Scraps Secret AI Recruiting Tool That Showed Bias Against Women," Reuters, October 11, 2018, https://www.reuters.com/article/world/insight-amazon-scraps-secret-ai-recruiting-tool-that-showed-bias-against-women-idUSKCN1MK0AG/.

29. Sriram Vasudevan and Krishnaram Kenthapadi, "LiFT: A Scalable Framework for Measuring Fairness in ML Applications," *CIKM '20: Proceedings of the*

29th ACM International Conference on Information & Knowledge Management, October 19, 2020, https://arxiv.org/pdf/2008.07433.

30. LinkedIn, "LiFT," GitHub, accessed February 28, 2026, https://github.com/linkedin/LiFT.

31. "The LinkedIn Fairness Toolkit (LiFT)," OECD.AI Public Observatory. *Catalogue of Tools & Metrics for Trustworthy AI*, September 15, 2022, https://oecd.ai/en/catalogue/tools/the-linkedin-fairness-toolkit-lift.

32. Heloise Logan et al., "A Closer Look at How LinkedIn Integrates Fairness into Its AI Products," *LinkedIn Engineering Blog*, January 13, 2022, https://www.linkedin.com/blog/engineering/fairness/a-closer-look-at-how-linkedin-integrates-fairness-into-its-ai-pr.

33. Blake Lawit and Ya Xu, "Sharing LinkedIn's Responsible AI Principles," *LinkedIn Official Blog*, February 22, 2023, https://www.linkedin.com/blog/member/trust-and-safety/responsible-ai-principles.; Osonde Ope Osoba et al., "Responsible AI Update: Testing How We Measure Bias in the U.S.," *LinkedIn Engineering Blog*, May 9, 2024, https://www.linkedin.com/blog/engineering/responsible-ai/responsible-ai-update-testing-how-we-measure-bias-in-the-us.

34. Taylor Telford, "Apple Card Algorithm Sparks Gender Bias Allegations Against Goldman Sachs," *The Washington Post*, November 11, 2019, https://www.washingtonpost.com/business/2019/11/11/apple-card-algorithm-sparks-gender-bias-allegations-against-goldman-sachs/.

35. New York State Department of Financial Services," *Report on the Apple Card Investigation*," March 2021, 4, 7–8, 14–16, https://www.dfs.ny.gov/system/files/documents/2021/03/rpt_202103_apple_card_investigation.pdf.

36. Ibid., 2.

37. World Economic Forum, "Responsible Use of Technology: The Salesforce Case Study." White Paper, September 2022, 9, https://www3.weforum.org/docs/WEF_Responsible_Use_of_Technology_Salesforce_Case_Study_2022.pdf.

38. Alex Hern, "'Partnership on AI' Formed by Google, Facebook, Amazon, IBM and Microsoft," *The Guardian*, September 28, 2016, https://www.theguardian.com/technology/2016/sep/28/google-facebook-amazon-ibm-microsoft-partnership-on-ai-tech-firms.

39. Jeffrey Heer, "Partnership on AI," *AI Matters* 4, no. 3 (2018): 25, https://dl.acm.org/doi/epdf/10.1145/3284751.3284760.

40. "Our Partners," Partnership on AI, accessed March 1, 2026, https://partnershiponai.org/partners/.

41. Partnership on AI, *Annual Report 2025*, accessed March 1, 2026, https://partnershiponai.org/annual-report-2025/.
42. Partnership on AI, "PAI's Responsible Practices for Synthetic Media. A Framework for Collective Action," February 27, 2023, https://partnershiponai.org/wp-content/uploads/2023/02/PAI_synthetic_media_framework.pdf.
43. Partnership on AI, "Guidelines for AI and Shared Prosperity: Tools for Improving AI's Impact on Jobs," June 2023, accessed March 1, 2026, https://partnershiponai.org/wp-content/uploads/dlm_uploads/2023/06/pai_guidelines_shared_prosperity-1.pdf.

Chapter 8: System Factors

1. Marisa Gracia, "What Air Canada Lost in 'Remarkable' Lying AI Chatbot Case," *Forbes*, February 19, 2024, https://www.forbes.com/sites/marisagarcia/2024/02/19/what-air-canada-lost-in-remarkable-lying-ai-chatbot-case/.
2. *Moffatt v. Air Canada*, Civil Resolution Tribunal Decision SC-2023-005609 (British Columbia Civil Resolution Tribunal, February 14, 2024), https://decisions.civilresolutionbc.ca/crt/crtd/en/item/525448/index.do?q=SC-2023-005609.
3. Ashley Belanger, "Air Canada Has to Honor a Refund Policy Its Chatbot Made Up," *Wired*, February 17, 2024, https://www.wired.com/story/air-canada-chatbot-refund-policy/.
4. "AIM: AI Incidents and Hazards Monitor," OECD.AI Policy Observatory, accessed March 25, 2026, https://oecd.ai/en/incidents?search_terms=%5B%7B%22type%22:%22KEYWORD%22,%22value%22:%22air%20canada%22%7D%5D&and_condition=false&from_date=2014-01-01&to_date=2025-07-11&properties_config=%7B%22principles%22:%5B%5D,%22industries%22:%5B%5D,%22harm_types%22:%5B%5D,%22harm_levels%22:%5B%5D,%22harmed_entities%22:%5B%5D,%22languages%22:%5B%5D%7D&order_by=date&num_results=20.
5. "Air Canada Ordered to Compensate Passenger Mislead by Chatbot's Incorrect Fare Advice," OECD.AI Policy Observatory, accessed March 3, 2026, https://oecd.ai/en/incidents/2024-02-15-7d63.
6. IBM, "IBM's Principles for Trust and Transparency," 2018, 1, https://www.ibm.com/downloads/documents/us-en/10c31775c3d40dd8.

7. Christina Montgomery and Francesca Rossi, "A Look into IBM's AI Ethics Governance Framework," IBM, accessed March 4, 2026, https://www.ibm.com/think/insights/a-look-into-ibms-ai-ethics-governance-framework.
8. Lucy Buchholz, "IBM: If AI Deployment Is Done Right, the Future of Work Is HR Leaders' Biggest Opportunity Yet," Unleash, November 26, 2025, https://www.unleash.ai/artificial-intelligence/ibm-if-ai-deployment-is-done-right-the-future-of-work-is-hr-leaders-biggest-opportunity-yet/.
9. "Foundations of Trustworthy AI: Trusted AI for the Workforce," IBM, accessed March 4, 2026, https://www.ibm.com/think/insights/trustworthy-ai-for-employee-experience.
10. Kiran Rao, "IBM AI HR: Transforming Human Resources with Artificial Intelligence," August 24, 2024, https://www.hr-analytics-trends.com/blog/ibm-ai-hr-transforming-human-resources-with-artificial-intelligence.
11. Color of Change, "Response to NIST Request for Information on the Artificial Intelligence Risk Management Framework (AI RMF)," submitted to the National Institute of Standards and Technology, September 2021, https://www.nist.gov/system/files/documents/2021/09/17/ai-rmf-rfi-0094.pdf.
12. Emmanuel Martinez and Lauren Kirchner, "The Secret Bias Hidden in Mortgage-Approval Algorithms," August 25, 2021, https://themarkup.org/denied/2021/08/25/the-secret-bias-hidden-in-mortgage-approval-algorithms.
13. Jenifer Tsai, "Jordan Crowley Would Be in Line for a Kidney – if He Were Deemed White Enough," Slate, June 27, 2021, https://slate.com/technology/2021/06/kidney-transplant-dialysis-race-adjustment.html.
14. Verizon Communications and Institute for Experiential AI at Northeastern University, "Experiential AI for the Largest Wireless Carrier in the United States," n.d., 2, https://assets-global.website-files.com/657141b092d019b05ff57885/660d7dda830e56ceddf94c1c_Verizon_Communications_EAI_Case_%20Study.pdf.
15. Randy Bean, "How Verizon Uses Data, Analytics, and AI to Deliver Responsible AI That Drives Innovation," *Forbes*, October 14, 2024, https://www.forbes.com/sites/randybean/2024/10/14/how-verizon-uses-data-analytics-and-ai-to-deliver-responsible-ai-that-drives-innovation/.
16. Verizon Communications and Institute for Experiential AI at Northeastern University, "Experiential AI for the Largest Wireless Carrier in the United States,"4–6.
17. "Responsible Artificial Intelligence,"Verizon, accessed March 7, 2026, https://www.verizon.com/about/investors/responsible-ai-program.

18. Verizon Business, "A Smarter Path to AI," 2025, 6, https://www.verizon.com/business/resources/articles/3-steps-to-scale-enterprise-ai.pdf.
19. "Targeted Compliance Framework Assurance Review – Final Report," Australian Government, Department of Employment and Workplace Relations, accessed February 21, 2026, https://www.dewr.gov.au/assuring-integrity-targeted-compliance-framework/resources/targeted-compliance-framework-assurance-review-final-report.
20. Krishani Dhanji, "Deloitte to Pay Money Back to Albanese Government After Using AI in $440,000 Report," *The Guardian*, October 6, 2025, https://www.theguardian.com/australia-news/2025/oct/06/deloitte-to-pay-money-back-to-albanese-government-after-using-ai-in-440000-report.
21. "Deloitte Refunds Australia After AI-Generated Report Errors," OECD.AI Public Observatory, accessed March 7, 2026, https://oecd.ai/en/incidents/2025-10-05-be45.
22. Evident Insights, "Evident AI Index: Banks: Key Findings Report," October 2025, 1.
23. Evident Insights, "Evident AI Index. 2025 Edition," October 2025, https://evidentinsights.com/ai-index/?utm_source=hubspot&utm_medium=brief&utm_campaign=v42.
24. Evident Insights, "Evident AI Index: Banks," 5.
25. Ibid., 45.
26. JPMorgan Chase & Co., "Resolute Annual Report 2024," 2025, 160, https://www.jpmorganchase.com/content/dam/jpmc/jpmorgan-chase-and-co/investor-relations/documents/annualreport-2024.pdf.
27. Ivarov I. Bojinov et al., "JPMorgan Chase: Leadership in the Age of GenAI," Harvard Business School Case 325-066, April 2025, 3–4, https://www.hbs.edu/faculty/Pages/item.aspx?num=67230.
28. JPMorganChase, "Artificial Intelligence Research," accessed March 8, 2026, https://www.jpmorganchase.com/about/technology/research/ai.
29. JPMorganChase, "Trustworthy AI Center of Excellence," accessed March 8, 2026, https://www.jpmorganchase.com/about/technology/research/ai/trustai.
30. Tim McLauglin and Laila Kearney, "Los Angeles Wildfires Were 10 Times Bigger Than Utility's AI Forecast," Reuters, June 9, 2026, https://www.reuters.com/business/environment/los-angeles-wildfires-were-10-times-bigger-than-utilitys-ai-forecast-2025-06-09/.
31. Reuters, "Southern California Edison Faces Lawsuits over Los Angeles Wildfires," January 14, 2025, https://www.reuters.com/world/us/edison-utility-sued-over-role-equipment-la-wildfires-bloomberg-news-says-2025-01-13/.

32. "Los Angeles County Sues Utility Edison over Deadly Wildfire," *Insurance Journal*, March 5, 2025, https://www.insurancejournal.com/news/west/2025/03/05/814405.htm.

33. "United States Sues Southern California Edison Co., Seeking Tens of Millions of Dollars in Damages for Eaton and Fairview Fires," United States Attorney's Office, Central District of California, September 4, 2025, https://www.justice.gov/usao-cdca/pr/united-states-sues-southern-california-edison-co-seeking-tens-millions-dollars-damages.

34. McLauglin and Kearney, "Los Angeles Wildfires Were 10 Times Bigger Than Utility's AI Forecast."

35. Ibid.

36. Southern California Edison, "2026–2028 Wildfire Mitigation Plan," May 16, 2025, 1, https://wildfire.pnnl.gov/mitigationPlans/pages/documents?selectedPlan=ef3b34ce-227b-4f29-a067-a455a4254776&stateAndUtility=California-Southern+California+Edison.

37. Ibid., 80–81.

38. "Core Views on AI Safety: When, Why, What, and How," Anthropic, March 8, 2023, https://www.anthropic.com/news/core-views-on-ai-safety.

39. "Building Safeguards for Claude," Anthropic, August 12, 2025, https://www.anthropic.com/news/building-safeguards-for-claude.

40. Anthropic, "Threat Intelligence Report: August 2025," August 27, 2025, https://www-cdn.anthropic.com/b2a76c6f6992465c09a6f2fce282f6c0cea8c200.pdf.

41. "Research," Anthropic, accessed March 8, 2026, https://www.anthropic.com/research.

42. "Samsung Bans Staff's AI Use After Spotting ChatGPT Data Leak," *The Peninsula*, May 2, 2023, https://thepeninsulaqatar.com/article/02/05/2023/samsung-bans-staffs-ai-use-after-spotting-chatgpt-data-leak.

43. Siladitya Ray, "Samsung Bans ChatGPT Among Employees After Sensitive Code Leak," *Forbes*, May 2, 2023, https://www.forbes.com/sites/siladityaray/2023/05/02/samsung-bans-chatgpt-and-other-chatbots-for-employees-after-sensitive-code-leak/.

44. "Implementing our AI Ethics Principles," Samsung, last updated August 9, 2024, https://www.samsung.com/global/sustainability/popup/popup_doc/AYUqlrQ6CusAIx_C/.

45. "Three Principles of Responsibility for Artificial Intelligence (AI) in Healthcare," Pfizer, accessed March 8, 2025, https://www.pfizer.com/news/articles/three_principles_of_responsibility_for_artificial_intelligence_ai_in_healthcare.

46. Pfizer, "Policy Position on Artificial Intelligence," December 2023, https://cdn.pfizer.com/pfizercom/AI_Policy_Position_12112023.pdf.
47. Pfizer, "2024 Impact Report," 2025, 27, https://cdn.pfizer.com/pfizercom/Pfizer_2024_Impact_Report_02JUN2025.pdf.
48. "Pfizer Appoints Berta Rodriguez-Hervas as Chief and Analytics Officer," *CDO Magazine*, August 19, 2024, https://www.cdomagazine.tech/leadership-moves/pfizer-appoints-berta-rodriguez-hervas-as-chief-ai-and-analytics-officer.
49. Pfizer, "2024 Impact Report," 27.
50. "Accelerating Innovation: Pfizer's 2025 AI Festival," Pfizer, December 16, 2025, https://www.pfizer.com/news/announcements/accelerating-innovation-pfizers-2025-ai-festival.

Chapter 9: Applied Governance Practices for Building Ethical AI Organizations

1. Rita McGrath, *Seeing Around Corners: How to Spot Inflection Points in Business Before They Happen – The First Hands-On Guide to Strategic Advantage and Market Leadership* (Mariner Books, 2021), 38.
2. Jeffrey Saviano, host, *Better Innovation*, season 5, episode 1, "Rita McGrath: Seeing Around Corners," Apple Podcasts, October 15, 2021, 1 hour 14 min., https://podcasts.apple.com/us/podcast/rita-mcgrath-seeing-around-corners/id1313870002?i=1000538705715.
3. Barton Edgerton et al., "Four Ways Boards Can Support the Effective Use of AI," EY, April 24, 2024, https://www.ey.com/en_us/board-matters/four-ways-boards-can-support-the-effective-use-of-ai.
4. Danielle Rizak and Alyce Lomax, "AI in Focus in 2025: Boards and Shareholders Set Their Sights on AI," ISS-Corporate, 2025, 3, https://www.iss-corporate.com/resources/reports/ai-in-focus-for-2025-for-boards-and-shareholders/.
5. Cynthia Mabry et al., "Revisiting the Board's Oversight Role After In re: Boeing Co.," Harvard Law School Forum on Corporate Governance, June 1, 2022, https://corpgov.law.harvard.edu/2022/06/01/revisiting-the-boards-oversight-role-after-in-re-boeing-co/; Gail Weinstein et al., "2024 *Caremark* Developments: Has the Court's Approach Shifted?" Harvard Law School Forum on Corporate Governance, May 20, 2024, https://corpgov.law.harvard.edu/2024/05/20/2024-caremark-developments-has-the-courts-approach-shifted/.
6. Edgerton et al., "Four Ways Boards Can Support the Effective Use of AI."

7. Jeffrey Saviano, host, *Better Innovation*, season 7, episode 10, "Demystifying AI Ethics with Reid Blackman," Apple Podcasts, July 22, 2024, 1 hour 23 min., https://podcasts.apple.com/us/podcast/demystifying-ai-ethics-with-reid-blackman/id1313870002?i=1000663020952.
8. American Bar Association House of Delegates, "Resolution 112," August 12–13, 2019, https://www.americanbar.org/content/dam/aba/directories/policy/annual-2019/112-annual-2019.pdf.
9. American Bar Association House of Delegates, "Resolution 700," 2022 Midyear Meeting, February 14, 2022, https://www.americanbar.org/content/dam/aba/directories/policy/midyear-2022/700-midyear-2022.pdf.
10. American Bar Association House of Delegates, "Resolution 604," 2023 Midyear Meeting, February 2023, https://www.americanbar.org/content/dam/aba/directories/policy/midyear-2023/604-midyear-2023.pdf.
11. American Bar Association Standing Committee on Ethics and Professional Responsibility, "Formal Opinion 512: Generative Artificial Intelligence Tools," July 29, 2024, https://www.americanbar.org/content/dam/aba/administrative/professional_responsibility/ethics-opinions/aba-formal-opinion-512.pdf.
12. "Model Rules of Professional Conduct - Table of Contents," American Bar Association, accessed March 11, 2026, https://www.americanbar.org/groups/professional_responsibility/publications/model_rules_of_professional_conduct/model_rules_of_professional_conduct_table_of_contents/.
13. American Bar Association Standing Committee on Ethics and Professional Responsibility, "Formal Opinion 512: Generative Artificial Intelligence Tools," July 29, 2024, 5, https://www.americanbar.org/content/dam/aba/administrative/professional_responsibility/ethics-opinions/aba-formal-opinion-512.pdf.
14. American Medical Association, "Augmented Intelligence Development, Deployment, and Use in Health Care," approved by the AMA House of Delegates, November 12, 2024, 16–21, https://www.ama-assn.org/system/files/ama-ai-principles.pdf.
15. Brian Justice, "To Implement Health AI: First Decide Who's Accountable," American Medical Association, July 24, 2025, https://www.ama-assn.org/practice-management/digital-health/implement-health-ai-first-decide-who-s-accountable.
16. "AMA Adopts New Policy Aimed at Ensuring Transparency in AI Tools," American Medical Association, June 11, 2025, https://www.ama-assn.org/press-center/ama-press-releases/ama-adopts-new-policy-aimed-ensuring-transparency-ai-tools.

17. American Institute of Certified Public Accountants, "Guidelines for Responsible Use of Artificial Intelligence (AI) in *Forensic and Valuation Services Engagements*," October 2025, https://www.aicpa-cima.com/resources/download/guidelines-for-responsible-use-of-artificial-intelligence-ai-in-forensic-and.

18. Presidential Commission for the Study of Bioethical Issues, "New Directions: The Ethics of Synthetic Biology and Emerging Technologies," December 2010, 8, https://papers.ssrn.com/sol3/papers.cfm?abstract_id=2445575.

19. Danielle Allen et al., "*Ethics of Decentralized Social Technologies: Lessons from Web3, the Fediverse, and Beyond*," Edmond & Lily Safra Center for Ethics, Harvard University, 2023, https://ash.harvard.edu/wp-content/uploads/2024/03/Ethics-of-Decentralized-Social-Technologies-1.pdf.

20. Brian Patrick Green, "Six Approaches to Making Ethical Decisions in Cases of Uncertainty and Risk," Markkula Center for Applied Ethics, November 14, 2019, https://www.scu.edu/ethics/focus-areas/technology-ethics/resources/six-approaches-to-making-ethical-decisions-in-cases-of-uncertainty-and-risk/.

21. Amy Gutmann, "The Ethics of Synthetic Biology: Guiding Principles for Emerging Technologies," *Hastings Center Report* 41, no. 4 (2011): 19, 22, https://pubmed.ncbi.nlm.nih.gov/21845917/.

22. Max H. Bazerman and Ann E. Tenbrunsel, "Ethical Breakdowns," *Harvard Business Review*, April 2011, https://hbr.org/2011/04/ethical-breakdowns.

23. David B. Yoffe and Mary Kwak, "Playing by the Rules: How Intel Avoids Antitrust Litigation," *Harvard Business Review*, June 2001, 119–122.

24. Foo Y. Chee, "Intel Loses Challenge Against EU Antitrust Ruling but Wins Reduced Fine," Reuters, December 10, 2025, https://www.reuters.com/sustainability/boards-policy-regulation/eu-court-cuts-intels-eu-antitrust-fine-2025-12-10/.

25. Robert C. Bird and Julie Manning Magid, "Operational Risk and the New Caremark Liability for Boards of Directors," *Boston University Law Review* 103 (2023): 1578.

Acknowledgments

The decision to write this book traces back to the moment at Harvard Business School described in its opening pages. Professionals are struggling to identify and appropriately address artificial intelligence (AI) ethics issues. I came to believe that before they could manage those risks, they needed to articulate what they will and will not stand for in their AI systems, their boundaries of tolerance. The purpose of this book is to present a new governance framework, with ethics at the center, designed to close that gap and prepare professionals to confront AI ethics issues head-on.

I wrote this book following my EY retirement in 2025. It reflects my appointment at the Edmond & Lily Safra Center for Ethics at Harvard University and the work of our amazing research team. Danielle Allen, thank you for creating a role for me at Harvard and welcoming me into the GETTING Plurality Network. That community sharpened the questions at the heart of this book. Eric Beerbohm, your leadership at the Safra Center created the space for this work to grow, including hosting that critically important session at HBS. Jonathan Hack, you fostered such a rich experience at Harvard for our team. We thank you for your steadfast belief in our mission. Nien-he Hsieh, your mentorship strengthened this work in ways I continue to discover.

The MIT community played a defining role in the evolution of this book. Sandy Pentland, our collaboration over many years has deeply influenced how I think about advanced technology based systems in enterprises today. Your influence runs through these pages. Dimitris Bertsimas, Rodrigo Verdi, and Michelle Hanlon, thank you for opening the doors of Sloan to me this year. The classroom became a proving ground for these ideas.

I carry deep respect for these Harvard and MIT leaders who entrusted me with the freedom to pursue this work. These environments provided the intellectual freedom and rigor that allowed the ideas to take shape. Your confidence created the platform on which many of these ideas were tested and improved.

The framework was challenged and strengthened in the classroom, in real time. Kristen Paz, Maura Hegarty, and Chandler Smith, my amazing teaching assistants, you transformed these concepts into a living laboratory. That translation shaped this manuscript.

I recognize EY leadership for giving me the latitude to pursue university roles during my time at the firm. Kate Barton, your support made it possible for me to join the communities at MIT and Harvard that shaped this book.

Mike Edwards, Fernando Morera, and Ryan Cooksey, I'm grateful for your friendship and feedback that you provided along this journey.

It was essential that this book be grounded in research, so we formed an exceptional research and support team. That team contributed far beyond research. Vija Kalnina, as founding research director and scientific editor for the *Boundaries of Tolerance* initiative and book, you masterfully led this effort for us. You guided the research, shaped the manuscript with your editorial judgment, and oversaw the full production process. Your leadership elevated every chapter. I am deeply grateful for your extraordinary contribution, thank you.

We had extraordinary research assistants who joined this Harvard-based team. Vincent Okonkwo, your deep exploration of the Caremark line of cases strengthened the legal foundation of this book. Lily Schwalb, you helped transform dozens of AI incidents into teachable moments. Shuying (Christina) Huo, for teaching me what *boundaries of tolerance* means in the bioethics community. Lily Noyes, you uncovered new real-world AI stories that are carved into these pages. Ryan Wettre, your research discipline brought clarity to complex questions. Colton Mikolajczyk, your creative visual depictions brought abstract ideas to life.

To my editors at Wiley – Brian Neill, Sangeetha Suresh, and Kim Wimpsett – your editorial clarity strengthened the arguments at every turn. My agents – Dan Pearson, Frank Weimann, and the great team at Folio Literary Management – from our first meeting, you challenged my assumptions and improved the ideas that became this book.

Many executives across sectors tested these ideas in real environments. Watching you apply Boundaries of Tolerance principles in practice confirmed that this work mattered. That conviction carried me through the writing.

I would not have taken on this project without the steady presence of my family. Lisa, Matt, Caroline, and Natasha, thank you for your patience during a year that often revolved around this manuscript. I could not have completed this work without your encouragement and belief in its purpose.

About the Author

Jeffrey N. Saviano is a senior lecturer and member of the faculty at the MIT Sloan School of Management and recently held a research appointment at Harvard University. He is a recognized leader in artificial intelligence (AI) strategy, governance, and ethics, with a particular focus on the evolving responsibilities of corporate boards and senior executives in the age of intelligent systems.

Saviano retired from EY after more than 30 years with the firm, where he held multiple senior leadership roles and helped shape its global innovation strategy. He educated and advised more than 100 corporate boards and executive teams on AI strategy, governance, and risk oversight.

His work emphasizes the intersection of emerging technology and fiduciary duty. He has focused on how governance models must evolve to address risks introduced by AI systems. Saviano has helped organizations navigate complex questions related to AI deployment, including risk management, accountability, and the ethical use of data-driven systems. This includes advising on governance structures and oversight approaches for systems that increasingly operate with autonomy. His research explores how professionals can move beyond abstract principles to define practical boundaries for responsible innovation.

Saviano is a frequent speaker on AI governance and disruptive technology strategy. He engages regularly with corporate, academic, and policy audiences on the implications of AI for institutional decision-making. His insights have been featured at the Vatican, the United Nations, the World Bank, and other global institutions. His work contributes to global discussions on the role of corporate leadership in shaping responsible AI adoption. Through his teaching, research, and advisory work, he continues to shape how organizations approach the governance of emerging technologies and the role of professionals in defining the ethical boundaries that guide their use. Saviano and his wife, Lisa, reside in Wrentham, Massachusetts, and Naples, Florida.

Index

B